Beyond Comparison: Sex and D

In *Beyond Comparison: Sex and Discrimination* Timothy Macklem addresses foundational issues in the long-running debate in legal, political, and social theory about the nature of gender discrimination. He takes the highly original and controversial view that the heart of discrimination lies not in the unfavourable comparisons with the treatment and opportunities that men enjoy but rather in a denial of resources and opportunities that women need to lead successful and meaningful lives as women. Therefore, to understand what women need we must first understand what it is to be a woman.

By displaying an impressive command of the feminist literature as well as intellectual rigour, this work promises to be a milestone in the debate about gender equality and will interest students and professionals in the areas of legal theory and gender studies.

Timothy Macklem is Lecturer in Law at King's College London.

Cambridge Studies in Philosophy and Law

Some other books in the series:

Stephen R. Munzer: *A Theory of Property*

R. G. Frey and Christopher W. Morris (eds.): *Liability and Responsibility: Essays in Law and Morals*

Robert F. Schopp: *Automatism, Insanity, and the Psychology of Criminal Responsibility*

Steven J. Burton: *Judging in Good Faith*

Jules Coleman: *Risks and Wrongs*

Suzanne Uniacke: *Permissible Killing: The Self-Defense Justification of Homicide*

Jules Coleman and Allan Buchanan (eds.): *In Harm's Way: Essays in Honor of Joel Feinberg*

Warren F. Schwartz (ed.): *Justice in Immigration*

John Fischer and Mark Ravizza: *Responsibility and Control*

R. A. Duff (ed.): *Philosophy and the Criminal Law*

Larry Alexander (ed.): *Constitutionalism*

R. Schopp: *Justification Defenses and Just Convictions*

Anthony Sebok: *Legal Positivism in American Jurisprudence*

William Edmundson: *Three Anarchial Fallacies: An Essay on Political Authority*

Arthur Ripstein: *Equality, Responsibility, and the Law*

Heidi M. Hurd: *Moral Combat*

Steven J. Burton (ed.): *"The Path of the Law" and Its Influence: The Legacy of Oliver Wendell Holmes, Jr.*

Jody S. Kraus and Steven D. Walt (eds.): *The Jurisprudential Foundations of Corporate and Commercial Law*

Christopher Kutz: *Complicity: Ethics and Law for a Collective Age*

Peter Benson (ed.): *The Theory of Contract Law: New Essays*

Philip Soper: *The Ethics of Deference*

Beyond Comparison: Sex and Discrimination

Timothy Macklem

King's College London

PUBLISHED BY THE PRESS SYNDICATE OF THE UNIVERSITY OF CAMBRIDGE
The Pitt Building, Trumpington Street, Cambridge, United Kingdom

CAMBRIDGE UNIVERSITY PRESS
The Edinburgh Building, Cambridge CB2 2RU, UK
40 West 20th Street, New York, NY 10011-4211, USA
477 Williamstown Road, Port Melbourne, VIC 3207, Australia
Ruiz de Alarcón 13, 28014 Madrid, Spain
Dock House, The Waterfront, Cape Town 8001, South Africa

http://www.cambridge.org

First published 2003

Printed in the United States of America

Typeface Times Roman 10/12 pt.   *System* LATEX 2_ε [TB]

A catalog record for this book is available from the British Library.

Library of Congress Cataloging in Publication data available

ISBN 0 521 82682 9 hardback
ISBN 0 521 53415 1 paperback

For Gail Thorson

Contents

Acknowledgments

Like so many before me, I owe a great deal to a great many, in ways that no acknowledgment could ever recompense. What is more, I owe it in ways that I cannot begin to credit properly. I can only offer my fullest thanks to Carol Creighton, Elizabeth Goldberg, Heather Janack, G. V. La Forest, Grant Lamond, David Lillico, David Paciocco, and Larry Taman.

This book has its roots, some direct, others now remote, in a doctoral thesis submitted at the University of Oxford. I am deeply grateful to the Attorney General of Ontario for research leave, to the Commonwealth Scholarship Commission in the United Kingdom and the British Council for fully supporting that research, to Balliol College for a Kulkes Scholarship, and to Columbia University for an External Awards Fellowship. I also thank my examiners, Nicola Lacey and Christopher McCrudden, for their helpful and constructive comments, and above all my supervisor, Joseph Raz, who was and remains uniquely inspiring, exacting, and supportive, both as a mentor and as a friend.

For support and particular guidance in making the book what it is now I thank the series editor, Gerald Postema, the anonymous reviewers for Cambridge University Press, and Stephanie Achard.

Finally, I particularly thank John Gardner for his friendship and support over the years since we were students together, for reading all I have written, and for offering acute criticism and ever sensible advice.

I cannot express what I owe to Gail Thorson, without whom nothing, and to whom this book is dedicated.

1

The Issues

I. Discrimination and Equality

It is a hot summer's day, ice-cream weather, sunbathing-in-the-park weather. A woman walks down the street, bare-breasted. Asked to cover herself, she refuses. As she sees it, indeed as she explains it to the police officer, if a man is entitled to appear in public naked to the waist, as he certainly is, she is entitled to do the same. It would be discriminatory, she insists, for the law to deny this and so treat her behaviour as indecent. Is she right? Does a woman's nakedness mean the same thing as a man's? If not, should it? What is gained by understanding discrimination in this way? What is lost?

The complexity and significance of the problem become clearer when it is looked at from the opposite perspective. Suppose it is true that a woman, like a man, is entitled to appear in public naked to the waist, in hot weather at least (as in fact the courts decided).[1] What makes this so? The answer has large implications for our understanding of both sexual difference and the nature of value. Whatever may have been claimed by the topless pedestrian in question, it cannot be the case that there are meaningful differences between the sexes, yet that women are entitled to do whatever men are entitled to do (and vice versa), without regard to those differences. That would be to suggest that sexual difference is at once, in the same settings and for the same purposes, both meaningful and not meaningful, relevant and irrelevant. If men and women are to enjoy the same entitlements, despite the apparent differences between them, either our understanding of sexual difference or our understanding of value must give way. It is not possible for us, as individuals or as a society, to maintain a commitment both to the idea that people are not to be distinguished and to recognizing the characteristics and values that distinguish them.

If a woman is as free as a man to go topless in hot weather, it must be because, contrary to what has been conventionally assumed, there is no difference

[1] *R. v. Jacob*, 31 O.R. (3d) 350; 142 D.L.R. (4th) 411 (C.A., 1996).

between the sexes that could affect their entitlement to appear in public naked to the waist. There are a number of reasons why this might be so.[2] It might be because, as a general matter, the differences that genuinely distinguish the sexes, whatever they may be, should not be allowed to make a difference to men's and women's options in life, that is, to men's and women's access to the valuable pursuits that make it possible to flourish in life. Neither women nor men should suffer comparative disadvantage in the project of their lives on account of their sex. If that is true, however, then a policy of nondiscrimination is unfortunately bound to follow one of two paths, which require us to treat either our sexual identity[3] or the values that make our lives worth living as entirely plastic and insubstantial. Either we must reshape men and women, to ensure that they are equal in the face of human values, by eliminating any difference between the sexes that is relevant to the assessment of value (the path of androgyny), or we must reshape human values, to ensure that men and women are never distinguished by them (the path of value relativism). If men's success in any field of endeavour is greater than women's (or vice versa), we must either change the distribution of the qualities that lead to success (fantastic as that may seem), diminishing their presence in the more successful sex, increasing it in the less successful, or alter our sense of what constitutes a successful endeavour, by eliminating from consideration those criteria of success that one sex is able to meet more (or less) readily than the other.

The first of these explanations (or courses of action) dissolves our respect for, indeed the very existence of, sexual difference; the second does the same for value to the extent that value is engaged by sexual difference. Neither seems terribly plausible. Quite apart from the fact (as I take it to be) that neither sexual identity nor human value as we know it is entirely plastic and so susceptible to our will (a fact that might, after all, be merely a moral misfortune), it is hard to believe that eliminating sex discrimination requires us to eliminate either sexual difference or all that makes that difference matter. Indeed the suggestion that it does so comes close to a contradiction. It is in principle possible to eliminate

---

[2] For further reasons, see the next two sections.

[3] In what follows, I use the term "sexual identity" to refer to the concept that is sometimes called sex and sometimes called gender. I have tried to avoid speaking of sex or gender, where possible, to avoid suggesting that I am taking a position in the familiar nature/nurture debate, which I regard as misguided, for reasons set out below. Yet because the term "sexual identity" is potentially confusing, it might be helpful at the outset to make three things clear about the way I have used it. First, in using the word "sexual", as part of the term "sexual identity", I am referring to the distinction between the sexes, rather than the idea of sexuality. It is women and men that I have in mind, rather than the many ways in which men and women express themselves sexually. Second, in using the word "identity", as part of the term "sexual identity", I am referring to the set of qualities and characteristics that is definitive of the distinction between women and men, rather than to the qualities that men and women identify with, which might include the qualities of the opposite sex. Finally, in using the term "sexual identity" in relation to a particular sex, I have in mind both the qualities that men and women share and the qualities that distinguish them, unless stated otherwise.

the practice of sex discrimination by eliminating either sexual difference or the capacity to distinguish value in terms of that difference, just as it is possible to eliminate any form of wrongdoing by eliminating the occasion for it, for example, eliminating theft by eliminating property. Clearly, women could not be discriminated against if women did not exist or, more precisely and fairly, if women could not be distinguished as women in any way that mattered. The question is what would justify us in bringing about such a state of affairs, if bring it about we could.

Eliminating a distinction and its significance is only consistent with the recognition of value and the human qualities and achievements that value responds to where, and to the extent that, the distinction in question is *in fact* either not real or not relevant to the consideration of value. This is a possible claim about property, perhaps, but a highly implausible claim about sexual difference as a whole. It is not really credible to suggest that men and women, properly understood, are indistinguishable from one another in any way that is relevant to value. Yet to eliminate a distinction that is admittedly relevant to value simply because it is often, even typically, invoked improperly is to misunderstand the nature of wrongdoing, which consists not in (wrongly) including among human options, such as the option to engage in the sorts of activities that make sexual difference relevant to the evaluation and pursuit of a successful life, options that can be exercised wrongly, but in exercising wrongly options that should be exercised rightly.

Given that sexual difference is not entirely fictional (although some supposed aspects of it certainly are), and that the values that register sexual difference are not entirely bogus, it must be the case that sex discrimination arises not because sexual difference does not exist or does not matter, but because sexual difference does exist and does matter, although not in the ways that we have taken it to. Is it possible, then, to build upon this thought so as to arrive at an account of sex discrimination that respects both sexual identity and human value, while allowing for mistakes in our perception of each?

I begin by giving, in the next two sections of this chapter, an overview of the nature of the problem and what I take to be its proper solution. These two sections are not intended as a précis of the argument in the balance of the book, or even as a necessary premise to that argument. They can be read now or returned to later. Their purpose is to sketch for the reader certain issues that the book pursues in depth. The four subsequent sections similarly seek to expand upon, without fully defending, certain aspects of the solution I propose that may strike a reader as unfamiliar and even puzzling: rejection of the idea that discrimination depends upon comparison, a consequent reinterpretation of the significance of sexual equality, and reliance upon ideas of what it means to lead a successful life and what it means to be a woman. The final section seeks to say something brief about my choice of which arguments for equality and difference to respond to. As a whole, the chapter approaches the question of sex discrimination from the positive perspective of its remedy, rather than from the negative perspective of the disadvantage women now experience. It asks what might make women's lives go well rather than what has made them go badly. It thus offers a different, briefer way of thinking about the ideas developed and explored in the chapters that follow. That said, however, I should warn that because these issues are complex, their compressed treatment in the rest of this chapter is likely to become fully intelligible only in light of the argument of the book as a whole.

II. Discrimination and Difference

I have developed the narrative so far by referring to the pursuit of equality in the face of physical difference, and it might be reasonably objected that the conclusions I have drawn from this example are not applicable to the pursuit of equality in the face of intellectual or emotional differences between the sexes, or are not applicable to the recognition of sexual difference rather than the pursuit of sexual equality.[4] The short answer is that the only distinction between physical and other forms of sexual difference that could be thought to have a bearing on the argument is that physical differences between the sexes may be less amenable to alteration than intellectual or emotional differences. Yet the possibility of alteration is a question that I deliberately bracketed in the previous discussion in order to focus on the prior question of its desirability. It does not matter whether sexual difference can be changed or not, and so does not matter, for example, whether that difference is the product of nurture (and so allegedly amenable to change) or of nature (and so allegedly not amenable to change) if there is no reason, or at least no reason founded on a commitment to ending discrimination, to make that change.[5]

---

[4] I take it that objects that are equal are the same in some respects (the respects in which they are equal), and different in others (the respects in which they are unequal). In what follows, I treat equality as meaning sameness in this sense. In fact, I do not know of any claim to equality that is not a claim to sameness in the relevant respect. Equal pay, for example, means either the same pay or pay that bears the same relation to the value of the work done as does the pay of the comparator. Equality is often said to be compatible with the recognition of difference, and this is plainly true, provided that the difference to be recognized exists in a respect other than that in which equality is sought. For illuminating considerations of the idea of equality, see Peter Westen, *Speaking of Equality* (Princeton, N.J., 1990), and Derek Parfit, "Equality and Priority", in *Ideals of Equality*, ed. Andrew Miller (Oxford, 1998). For a full consideration of the relation between equality and sex discrimination, see sections V and VI below and the next chapter.

[5] In fact, as Joseph Raz once reminded me, the evidence seems to be that we are capable of changing nature, usually for the worse, and relatively incapable of changing society.

I suggested in the text that there might be *no* reason to change the present character of sexual difference. Strictly speaking, there is always reason to make a change to anything that is good, that reason being the good that lies in the outcome of the change, such as the distinctive good that can be achieved through the condition of being a man. The suggestion in the text remains valid, however, for two reasons. First, the reason to belong to a particular sex cuts both ways, for there is as good reason to be a woman as to be a man. In itself, therefore, it is no reason to change the qualities of one sex to those of the other. Second, if the reason to be a man is thought to be

The latter objection to the narrative so far deserves a fuller response, for it raises considerably more difficult issues. An approach to understanding and remedying sex discrimination that focuses on sexual difference rather than sexual equality by definition places no pressure on sexual identity. It takes sexual identity as a given and uses it to place pressure on human value. Presumably, that is part of its appeal, for the approach seems to permit reconciliation of sexual justice with respect for and pride in sexual identity. It insists that we should not include among the values to which our society responds those that are insensitive to what women (or men) have to offer, or that are more sensitive to what men have to offer than to what women have to offer (or vice versa). And yet, in spite of its attempt to show respect for sexual identity, concerns about this approach remain, which, like those expressed in the previous section, stem from its comparative character.

It will be clear from the sketch just offered that there are two possible readings of this difference-based approach to understanding and remedying sex discrimination. The first treats the approach as no more than a distinctively framed form of the sexual egalitarianism considered above, one that places its egalitarian pressure on human values rather than on sexual identity. An egalitarian condition is to be achieved not by eliminating the difference between the sexes but by eliminating the human values that register that difference. This reading, then, like its egalitarian sibling considered above, insists that genuine differences between the sexes should not be allowed to make a difference to men's and women's options in life, that is, to men's and women's access to the valuable pursuits that make it possible to flourish in life. It achieves its ends, however, not by changing men and women, but by denying recognition to all values that are more sensitive to the qualities and achievements of one sex than those of the other.

In doing so, unfortunately, it denies recognition in the pantheon of our values to all the aspects of sexual identity that make it meaningful and rewarding to belong to a particular sex, that is, to be a woman or a man. A world in which one cannot be disvalued on the ground of one's sex is a world in which one cannot be so valued either, in which nothing either bad or good could flow from being a woman or a man. If realizable, such a world would diminish, perhaps to a critical degree, the prospects of the women and men who require access to their sexual identity, and thus to the valuable options that it makes possible, in order to flourish in life. In that sense and to that extent, the approach would be self-defeating. More generally and more profoundly, in asking society to eliminate all values that register sexual difference, the approach assumes not merely that

---

strengthened by the fact that the qualities of men are culturally preeminent in most societies today and so are more easy to realize value from than the qualities of women, it must be remembered that any change, even if possible and desirable, carries the cost of change, here both short-term trauma and long-term rootlessness and alienation. This means that to make such a change, there must be not only reason but strong reason. The arguments in the text deny that there is any such strong reason.

value is amenable to social decision, but that value is answerable to some feature of society for its very condition as value, which in this context means being answerable to the feature of sexual identity. Values would be genuinely valuable only if they failed to register sexual identity. Unlike the project of eliminating sexual difference considered above, the implausibility here is that of regarding human value as being relative to sexual identity. This implausibility is perhaps brought out more directly and fully in the second reading of the difference-based approach to understanding and ending the practice of sex discrimination, which is concerned to register sexual identity rather than fail to register it.

This reading is one that asks society to tailor its understanding of human value to the character of women, to ensure not that women are equal to men, but that women's known qualities are honoured and respected; or in some versions, to ensure that women's heretofore suppressed qualities are recovered and given voice. Whether by endorsing as good women's qualities as they are presently understood, or by endorsing as women's and as good those human qualities that are said to have been neglected or suppressed in our society's present picture of human existence, the approach asks no questions about what it means to be a woman (or a man). Just as in the earlier reading, it takes sexual identity as a given and uses that identity to place pressure upon human value. Women are either just as we have always known them to be (but have failed to value) or are everything that we have refused to imagine (and so have refused to recognize in our account of value). In both cases, value is said to be relative to sexual identity, although different theories offer different ideas of what sexual identity is.

Assume first the more difficult and less common proposition that value is to be related to sexual identity *as a whole*, in order to ensure the valuing of women's qualities *as well as* those of men. As I have suggested, this proposition is a particular form of value relativism, the doctrine that value is a function of some other feature of the world.[6] Relativists have different views of what it is that value is properly related to. Cultural relativists believe that value is a function of particular cultures, and so regard as valuable (for particular cultures) whatever is treated as valuable by those cultures. Subjectivists believe that value is a function of personal attitudes, and so regard as valuable (for particular people) whatever is treated as valuable by those people. The particular relativists that I have in mind believe that value is a function of sexual identity, and so regard as valuable (for men and for women) whatever is a reflection of that identity.[7]

---

[6] Relativists typically believe that value is relative to such features because it is a product of them, so that for relativists value becomes the name of a cultural attitude, or a personal attitude, or the male or female outlook: see the discussion in Section VI. Thus, to believe that value is relative to sexual identity is (typically) to believe that value is the product of whatever attitude or outlook defines men and women as sexual beings. This, however, raises the problem of differences in sexual outlook, with the ramifications for value discussed in the text.

[7] So some feminists claim that women are subject to a special, female form of rationality, not because rationality has dimensions we have historically neglected or dismissed that women are

By treating men and women, and the qualities that define them, as valuable just as they are, without criticism or qualification, these relativists hope never to reach the conclusion that it is better to be one than the other, better to be a man than a woman, or a woman than a man, in any setting, for any purpose.

It is not possible to make a general case against relativism and for the objectivity of value in the space of this chapter.[8] It is possible to point out, however, that even if value relativism were a coherent doctrine (as I believe it is not), value could not plausibly be regarded as relative to sexual identity, given the particular conceptual structure of sexual identity.[9] One of the consequences of relativism, of the claim that value is a function of some feature of the world as it is, is that all valuable things become compatible with one another, for otherwise they could not coexist in features of the world as it is. That being the case, relativism implies that we need never be forced, for reasons of incompatibility, to prefer one value to another, in our beliefs or actions. This may explain in part the appeal of relativism, at least for those who are troubled by conflicts of values. It removes the possibility of any confrontation between incompatible values, for values that coexist in the world are necessarily compatible with one another. It certainly explains the attraction of relativism to those who seek a world in which it never would be preferable to belong to one sex rather than the other. Yet the very compatibility of values that makes relativism attractive sets a limit to the kinds of things to which value can be related.

This gives rise to fundamental difficulties for those who would relate value to sexual identity *as a whole*. On the one hand, to treat value as a function of sexual identity as that identity is understood *and valued* in a particular culture would only end sex discrimination if the culture in question had no practice of sex discrimination. Otherwise the reference would simply have the effect of affirming that culture's particular form of sex discrimination. Since no culture is free from sex discrimination, it would be a recipe for maintaining rather than ending existing forms of sex discrimination to treat value as a function of sexual identity as it is understood *and valued* in any existing culture.

On the other hand, given the conceptual structure of sexual identity, to treat value as a function of sexual identity as it is understood (but not valued) in any particular culture, in an attempt to ensure that the existing qualities of both sexes are regarded as valuable, does nothing to free that culture from the burden of deciding whether it is better, in any given setting, to think or act like a woman or like a man. Sexual identity depends for its existence on a contrast between the qualities that define a woman as a woman and those that define a man as a man.

---

particularly fluent in, but because how women think is how they should think. This is one way, although not in my view the correct way, to understand the central claim of Carol Gilligan's *In a Different Voice* (Cambridge, Mass., 1982).

[8] For a sketch of that case, see note 19 and the discussion there.

[9] This is to set aside for the moment any questions about the *content* of sexual identity as it is presently understood. The argument here applies however sexual identity is understood.

If it is true that women are caring, for example, then it is true that men are not caring, or at least are less so, or less often so; otherwise the sexes could not be distinguished by their capacity for concern. This contrast makes it impossible to give effect to both aspects of sexual identity at once, so as not to prefer in any given setting the thoughts or actions of a man to those of a woman, or vice versa. It is impossible, for example, to be simultaneously concerned and unconcerned in one's thoughts or actions, or to put it another way, to implement the value of each, in the same setting and for the same purpose. One quality, be it concern or lack of concern, and the sex that exhibits or tends to exhibit that quality, must be preferred to the other. This makes it impossible to regard value as relative to sexual identity as a whole, so as never to prefer one sex to the other. The qualities that define and distinguish the sexes must each have their place, a place that is determined by an account of value that is not relative to sexual identity. That being the case, a relativist who seeks to relate value to sexual identity would have to regard value as residing, in any particular setting, in one aspect or the other of that identity (in which case value would no longer be relative to sexual identity, strictly speaking, but to maleness or femaleness, as the case might be) or in neither.[10]

In fact, few, if any, critics of the present social order maintain that value is relative to sexual identity in just the way I have described, though that may be a necessary implication of their arguments. Rather, they emphasize the need to relate value to the qualities of *women*, so as to ensure that those qualities are at last recognized as good, as the qualities of men presumably already are and long have been. This contention, however, to the extent that it differs from the contention that value is relative to sexual identity as a whole, only exposes a more familiar weakness in value relativism, namely, its inability to criticize the particular social order, or particular feature of that social order, to which value is related. If value were relative to the qualities of one sex, here to the qualities of women, so that the qualities of women were recognized as good by definition, then the qualities of men, if not also said to be valuable in the manner considered above, would have to be correspondingly bad. Setting to one side the inherent implausibility of a suggestion that the present practice of sex discrimination could be brought to an end by simply inverting it, so as to change the identity of its victims from women to men, the attempt to treat women's qualities as good by definition rather than by virtue of their objective

---

[10] This is not to say that value cannot embody a contradiction, for clearly it can. Many features of the world are understood in terms of a contrast that makes it impossible to realize both aspects of them at once, yet they are no less valuable for that reason. Femaleness and maleness are both capable of being valued despite the fact that the different values they may give rise to are incompatible. However, while both ways of being are valuable, it is not possible to realize them both at once. In any setting where both forms of value are realizable, a choice must be made as to which value to realize. In some settings and for some purposes, it is better to be a woman; in others, a man. Practice does not guide value, as not only objectivists but any critic of the present social order must agree.

value is no recipe for a valuable life for women, or for true respect for and pride in one's identity as a woman.

To take sexual identity, as we now understand it,[11] as the premise of value is to place that identity beyond the capacity of value to criticize. And yet, as many have pointed out, such criticism is surely crucial to the ending of sex discrimination. It is possible, of course, to believe that the present social practice of sex discrimination is in no way reflected in the present social understanding of sexual identity, but it is not terribly plausible to do so. On the contrary, it seems almost certain that the present practice of sex discrimination is broadly reflected in the present understanding of sexual identity, so that the picture we as a society now have of what it means to be a woman both includes qualities that women do not possess and neglects qualities that women do possess, in each case to women's disadvantage. If that is so, then to take women's present identity as the premise for understanding value, and hence for understanding discrimination, is to honour as women's and as valuable qualities that are not women's and may not be valuable, and correspondingly, to fail to honour qualities that are women's and are valuable, or that are capable of being used valuably. In other words, and in its own terms, to treat value as relative to women's present identity as women is to make it impossible to regard that identity as anything but good. If that is implausible, then it is implausible, even if intelligible, to regard human value as relative to sexual identity.

These are points about the nature of value, but as my last comments make clear, they also place in question the status of the present understanding of sexual identity, of what it means to be a woman or a man. Value relativism aside, whether the qualities that we take to describe and define sexual difference are real or mythical is a crucial question for any account of sex discrimination. Whatever human value is or is taken to be, it can be engaged in only by those who genuinely possess the qualities, and the corresponding achievements, that human value registers and responds to. To put it another way, even value relativists can only know what values they should endorse by knowing, and knowing accurately, the context to which those values are to be related. To relate value to a difference that is wholly or partially mythical would be to succumb to the very error that value relativists themselves seek to remedy, here the (supposed) error of failing to relate value to sexual difference as it actually is, that is, to what it genuinely means to be a woman or a man. If that is so, it is doubly

---

[11] The account could be premised on sexual identity as it really is rather than as we now understand it. This would not be easy, however, for such an account would typically incorporate an account of what is valuable, so as to distinguish what is material from what is immaterial in the potentially vast description of what anything is. An account of what we are that makes no reference to value risks lapsing into incoherence, counting the number of hairs on our heads, or freckles on our forearms. Even if this problem could be overcome, an account of value that took the qualities of women as they really are as the premise of value would still suffer from the implausibility of defining men as bad and from the more general objections to relativism sketched in note 19.

implausible to treat sexual identity, as we now understand it, as the premise for value.

The question remains, then, as it stood at the end of the previous section: whether it is possible to arrive at an account of sex discrimination that respects both sexual identity and human value while allowing for mistakes in our perception of each. The approaches considered so far have all been comparative in character, in that they have attempted to frame sexual identity and human value by reference to equality and difference. Yet it must be possible to understand women other than in terms of the ways in which they are and are not different from men, just as it is possible to understand men without reference to women. At some point comparisons between the sexes must end, and we must simply ask, and then answer, what it means to be a woman or a man. Whatever answer we arrive at must then be related to value. As I have said, it is not only possible but necessary to understand value other than in terms of a comparison between women and men. This suggests that a proper understanding of the disadvantage that flows from sex discrimination, a disadvantage that involves a denial to women, as they really are, of the ingredients necessary to a genuinely valuable life, must proceed other than by a comparison to the lives of men.

III. Discrimination Without Comparison

To return to the story with which I began, an alternative explanation of a woman's entitlement to appear in public naked to the waist (in hot weather at least) is that the conventional understanding of a woman's nakedness, and in particular of the significance of bare breasts on a public street, is profoundly mistaken. Indeed, it is only one instance of the manifold errors that we as a society have made, and continue to make, about what it means to be a woman, errors that have prevented women from leading successful lives. On that explanation, nondiscrimination would be a matter of removing the prevailing misconceptions of *what it means to be a woman*[12] and of the valuable activities to which a woman's life might be directed, in any case where the effect of those misconceptions is to disadvantage women, by impairing their prospect of leading a successful life.

It is a familiar fact, one not confined to this explanation of sex discrimination, that discrimination typically proceeds from a misconception (to put it gently) of what it means to be a woman. Time and again women are said to lack abilities that they in fact possess, or to possess disabilities that they in fact do not. The options available to them are then tailored accordingly, so as to deny women, on one

---

[12] In referring to what it means to be a woman, as I do throughout this section, I mean simply to refer to what it *is* to be a woman, whatever that may be. For a discussion of the many issues surrounding that idea, see section VII, below. I believe that it is impossible to know which values to pursue, or the extent to which one has been denied access to those values, and so has been discriminated against, without an adequate degree of self-understanding, which, in the case of women, means an adequate understanding of what it means to be a woman.

basis or the other, access to those that they in fact possess the ability to flourish in. This denial of access is typically to women's disadvantage, for women tend to be excluded by it from options that are critical to the success of their lives, although it is not inevitably so, as the life stories of the many women who have flourished despite the obstacles placed before them make clear. Sometimes, having been excluded from one valuable option or another, women are able to discover further valuable options in life that correspond to qualities they both possess and are acknowledged to possess, whose correspondence with women's qualities is typically overlooked, or whose value is typically downplayed.

Such enterprising and fortunate women are moral survivors. More often, the denial to women of access to valuable options, as a result of prevailing misconceptions of what it means to be a woman and of the activities to which a woman's life might be directed, prevents them from leading successful lives. According to the alternative explanation of discrimination under consideration here, the precise extent to which misconceptions about women have this effect is the precise extent of sex discrimination in any given society, for sex discrimination is a matter of so misunderstanding women as to deny them access to options that are critical to the success of their lives. Less profound failures of understanding are not to be dismissed, for ignorance unchallenged often begets greater and more dangerous ignorance, but they do not amount to a wrong, and so do not amount to the wrong of sex discrimination, unless they damage some person's, in this case some woman's, prospects in life.

So women are said (inaccurately) to be unaggressive or unscientific, and are consequently excluded from options whose value is a function of aggression or of a scientific approach. Or they are said (accurately, let us assume) to be unusually caring, but are then steered towards, and often confined to, options in life where the value of care is bound up with other nonvaluable aspects of those options, so as to make the options either unworthy in themselves (where serving others, for example, degenerates into servitude) or less than the whole story of a successful life (where being a good parent to one's children, for example, becomes one's only role in life). A nondiscriminatory reappraisal of what it means to be a woman, in terms both of a woman's qualities and of the valuable activities to which a woman's life might be directed, would enable women to gain access to the many valuable options in life that have long been and still remain closed to them, and correspondingly, would enable women to escape the confines of options that either are not valuable or, if valuable, are too limited a basis on which to build a successful life.[13]

---

[13] I speak here of value, and the extent to which discrimination denies access to value, so preventing women's lives from being successful. Some may find the language of justice more familiar and more apt. They may feel that the idea of justice captures not only the instances of discrimination I draw attention to, which involve misconceptions, but other instances of what we recognize as discrimination that do not appear to involve misconceptions. Suppose, to take a familiar example, a society refuses to provide adequate child care for working women. This could be

Nothing in this story of discrimination and nondiscrimination depends upon a comparison of women to men, one that would describe women as equal to men, or as different from them. Nor would anything in the story be assisted by such a comparison. On the contrary, sexual equality and sexual difference are

said to be unjust, on the basis that it denies women a fair share of social resources. It is less obvious that it involves a misconception of working women and what it takes for them (or at least some of them) to lead a successful life. Yet appearances are deceptive.

One possibility is that the refusal to provide adequate child care is indeed based on a misconception. Some people probably do believe that women should stick to raising children, or at least that if women choose to have children, they should then make their family the focus of their lives, not compromise their domestic role with work outside the home. Set that possibility aside. The other, more relevant, possibility is that the refusal to provide adequate child care is seen by those responsible (and their critics) as an issue of justice. Some may believe that existing levels of child care represent working women's fair share of social resources; others believe that it does not. Either way the disagreement between them is on its face a disagreement about justice.

There are two ways to understand such arguments about justice, both captured in the idea that the right is prior to the good. On the one hand, arguments about justice are arguments about the proper role of the state. Antiperfectionists believe that the obligations of the state are confined to the right, namely, that which can be performed and enforced without reference to particular conceptions of the good life. I do not share that belief, but in any event my project brackets the question of its soundness. I am concerned to explore the nature of the problem of sex discrimination, not decide whose job it is to solve which aspects of that problem. As I see it, the obligation to end the practice of sex discrimination falls on all of us, individually and collectively. Those who believe that the role of the state is limited to securing the right will want to temper that claim. But that is no reason for them to disagree with my account of the nature of discrimination, which is practised by people everywhere, not merely by the state, and whose remedy is everyone's responsibility, not merely the state's.

On the other hand, the belief that the right is prior to the good transcends the question of the proper role of the state, and distinguishes obligations that are justified on the basis of the value of having them from those that are justified independently of that value. Yet as I see it, value underpins reasons and duties, so that the answer to the question of our duty not to discriminate depends ultimately upon the badness of discrimination, which in turn is a function of its tendency to impair the success of someone's life, here the life of a woman. In this sense my account is teleological rather than deontological, as those terms are explained by Rawls in *A Theory of Justice* (Oxford, 1973) at 24ff.

If a successful life is what ultimately matters, so that references to justice are best understood as references to certain aspects of our duty to support one another in the pursuit and achievement of a successful life, then any refusal to provide adequate child care to working women, if not simply a matter of bad faith or weakness of will, must be based on a misconception, even if that misconception is no more than an after-the-fact rationalization and so the product of self-deception. No argument of justice could warrant the denial of a successful life to women if, as I believe, arguments of justice are ultimately directed to making each person's life successful. As a society, we owe women resources such as child care because and to the extent that those resources are necessary to a successful life, and so can withhold them only where they are in that sense unnecessary. The account I give thus reaches some, perhaps many, of the same conclusions as more familiar arguments from justice, not because it is derivable from the idea of justice, but because the idea of justice is derived from the understanding of value on which I rely.

For further discussion of the idea of a successful life, see section VI of this chapter; for consideration of the relationship between misconceptions and disadvantage, see Chapter 6, section II, part C; for further exploration of some of the practical implications of the account I give for issues such as child care, see the final chapter. On reasons and values, see Gardner and Macklem, "Reasons", in *The Oxford Handbook of Jurisprudence and Philosophy of Law*, ed. Jules Coleman and Scott Shapiro (Oxford, 2002), 440, at 450ff.

themselves conceptions of what it means to be a woman, which, given their sweeping character, may be as heavily distorted as those they are invoked to replace. It is of course clearly the case that, contrary to what was once widely assumed, women are in very many ways no different from men, and to that extent are, strictly speaking, not distinguishable in terms of their sex. That is to say, an accurate picture of sexual difference, of the qualities that distinguish women and men, would not include the qualities that men and women have in common, in like kind and degree, in terms of which they are equal to one another. It is as clearly the case that in other respects women are different from men, although not necessarily in the same respects that they have been widely taken to be, so that an accurate picture of sexual difference would be one that captured that difference accurately, rather than some other difference, or none at all.

And yet, just as clearly, it is not possible to arrive at an accurate picture of what it means to be a woman, and of the valuable activities to which a woman's life might be directed, by pursuing the idea that women are equal to men, or are different from men, or some combination of the two. Rather, we know that women are equal to men only when we know what women and men are, and then notice that whatever may once have been pretended, there is no difference between them, and similarly, know that women are different from men when we know what each is and see that they are to be distinguished, and how they are to be distinguished. Indeed, it is not possible to identify either equality or difference other than by identifying the genuine qualities of the objects under comparison, whether the purpose is to show that people are equal, or that they are unequal as the first step in an argument that they should not be so, an argument of the kind considered and rejected in the previous sections.

There is also nothing in this story of discrimination and nondiscrimination about the qualities of men, or about any necessary reciprocity in policies of nondiscrimination. It is possible, of course, to misunderstand both women and men, and to misunderstand them both so badly as to deny them both access to options that are critical to the success of their lives. But it is not necessary to misunderstand men in order to misunderstand women, and in fact there is little evidence that we as a society misunderstand men to an extent that would damage men's lives. On the contrary, it is not only possible in principle, but seems to be the case in practice, that a society can understand men well, or at least well enough, and yet understand women little, or at least too little to enable them to lead successful lives. If it is indeed the case that sex discrimination is one-sided in this way, then the remedy must be similarly one-sided, so as to focus on the true problem, namely, the effect on women, and the success of their lives, of prevailing misconceptions of what it means to be a woman and of the valuable activities to which a woman's life might be directed.

It might be objected that this is to contradict what I have earlier contended, namely, that sexual identity is a bivalent distinction, in which the qualities of one sex are correlative to those of the other. If that is the character of sexual identity, then it follows that to know what it means to be a woman is, *ipso facto*, to know what it means to be a man. Does it not also follow that it is not possible to know what it means to be a woman other than by knowing what it means to be a man? And does it not then follow that the misconceptions of what it means to be a woman that underlie sex discrimination are necessarily reciprocal, so that their understanding and their remedy must also be reciprocal?

There is some truth in this line of thought, but it is a truth that is easy to overstate. To grasp its real implications it is necessary to distinguish two different understandings of what it means to be a woman or a man. On the one hand, to speak of men and women is to speak of *people* who can, in some respects and for some purposes, be distinguished in terms of their sex. On the other hand, and more precisely, to speak of men and women is to speak of that distinction itself. To take the most obvious example of the difference between the two usages, on the former way of speaking, women and men are often equal to one another, indeed, are equal to one another in all respects in which they cannot be distinguished from one another. On the latter way of speaking, women and men cannot be equal, for to the extent that they are equal they cannot be distinguished as women and men. In principle the two usages, while distinct, might be coextensive in practice. However, that would be so only if the sexes were entirely different and so never equal, an idea that is as implausible as the idea, considered and rejected earlier, that the sexes are entirely equal and so indistinguishable.

Two related consequences follow from these two understandings of what it means to be a woman or a man. First, only women and men in the first sense are people and thus can succeed or fail in life. Distinctions do not have lives, except when spoken of metaphorically, and so are not subject to disadvantage in life. Given that the inquiry into sex discrimination is an inquiry into the predicament of people who are disadvantaged in life as the result of the way they have been treated on the basis of their sex, it is an inquiry into the predicament of women and men in the first sense (the sense in which they are people who are equal in some respects, different in others), as the result of their treatment as women and men in the second sense (the sense in which the sexes are different by definition). Second, and consequently, it is perfectly possible to understand people correctly as people (and thus as women and men in the first sense) while misunderstanding them as women or men (in the second, more precise sense). This happens whenever we correctly attribute certain qualities to certain people but then incorrectly attribute those qualities to the status of those people as women or men. Whenever that is the case, one sex may be discriminated against and the other not, depending on the damage that flows from the misattribution.

Suppose, for example, that men are correctly understood to possess a certain quality that women are incorrectly thought to lack. Such a misconception is reciprocally mistaken, since maleness is mistakenly thought to include, and femaleness to lack, a quality that does not in fact distinguish the sexes. But it is not reciprocally damaging, and so is not reciprocally discriminatory, because men (in the first sense, as people) have full access to the quality in question, albeit under the wrong description, while women (again in the first sense) have no access at all to that quality, not merely no access to it under their description as women.[14] As I suggested above, then, it follows that it is perfectly possible, and indeed seems to be the case, that a society can understand men well, or at least well enough, and yet understand women little, or at least too little to enable them to lead successful lives. If sex discrimination is one-sided in this way, the remedy must be similarly one-sided, not reciprocal.

This is not to suggest that it is in any sense an easy matter to establish the meaning of sexual identity or the nature of value, or to decide whether a mistake about either amounts to discrimination. On the contrary, it is extremely difficult, as can be readily appreciated by attempting to consider, from this point of view, the question of whether it would be discriminatory for the law to treat as indecent the fact that a woman has appeared in public naked to the waist. To answer that question one would have to know something about the meaning of a woman's nakedness, enough to know, perhaps, the extent to which bare breasts are sexually freighted, whether as the result of their physical nature or of cultural convention, and further, one would have to know the value (if any) of public decency, and the extent to which (if at all) decency is undermined by heavily sexually freighted conduct in public. Having determined (let us suppose) that bare breasts are not sexually freighted, or that public decency is either not valuable or not undermined by the exposure of bare breasts, one would then have to determine whether the inability to appear in public naked to the waist, as the result of a prevailing misconception of what it means to be a woman and of the valuable activities to which a woman's life might be directed, genuinely disadvantages women. This would involve determining whether appearing in public naked to the waist is not merely a valuable option, but one that is critical to the success of at least some women's lives.[15] It would not be enough to establish,

---

[14] I set to one side here the special and relatively rare cases in which it is possible to have access to a quality only by acting under that description, as it may, for example, be possible to be gay only by acting under the description of oneself as gay. It is a mistake to think that, if the damage to women's lives produced by sex discrimination is the consequence of women's having been forced to act under a false description of what it means to be a woman, then the success of women's lives must be dependent upon their acting under a true description of what it means to be a woman. If women and men are to have successful lives, they must draw upon an accurate understanding of themselves as the people they are, but in doing so they need not act under the description of themselves as women and men, or indeed, and special cases aside, under any description at all.

[15] These conditions are widely thought to be met with regard to breast-feeding in public. Such exposure of a bare breast is not sexually freighted and so should not offend public decency, assuming that public decency is offended by heavily sexually freighted conduct in public. A sense of public decency that was offended by breast-feeding in public, on the ground that bare breasts are heavily sexually freighted, would be discriminatory, for such a sense of decency

as the court did in fact, the content of the community standard of tolerance, for it is entirely possible that the community standard of tolerance is discriminatory, although it happened not to be so in this case (or so we may assume).

IV. Comparison and Noncomparison

As I have said, all these are difficult questions. And yet the alternatives, if less difficult, are less persuasive, for the reasons sketched in the first two sections. One of the great attractions of an egalitarian approach to sex discrimination, for example, is that it is straightforward and easy to apply. Women are entitled to do whatever men are entitled to do. It is not necessary to know anything about women, or about what is good for women, or about the nature of a successful life and when it may be undermined, in order to pursue the equality of the sexes. Straightforward though the egalitarian approach may be, however, it has the unfortunate consequences outlined above. To commit ourselves to it would be to commit ourselves to the destruction either of sexual difference or of all that makes that difference matter.

However, to say that the questions raised by this alternative approach to sex discrimination are difficult, while true, is also somewhat misleading, for it is to neglect the fact that in many respects they are extremely familiar questions. It has long been a central function of antidiscrimination initiatives, and of the feminist movements that have inspired and sustained them, to challenge the prevailing picture of what women are and what they ought to do with their lives. Admittedly, their analysis has almost invariably been couched in terms of equality (and less commonly difference), and so has almost invariably been comparative in character. But the impetus for those initiatives, with which the analysis sits uncomfortably, has been noncomparative, for it has been to challenge, and seek to dispel, a certain conception of what it means to be a woman, in order to bring to an end the disadvantage that conception causes to women. It is this need to ensure that women are able to lead successful lives that determines whether ending discrimination is to be pursued through a strategy of equality or a strategy of difference, and so explains the apparent opportunism of sometimes pursuing one, sometimes the other strategy. What the apparent opportunism reveals is that it is not in fact equality or difference themselves, but an underlying, unarticulated sense of what it means for a woman to lead a successful life, that establishes the particular conception of a woman's life that is to be pursued, which is then compared with the prevailing conception of a man's life and so determined to be equal or different.

not only involves a misconception of what it means to be a woman, but that misconception is damaging to women, for the ability to breast-feed a child in public is critical to all those women whose success in life depends upon the ability to reconcile parenthood and employment (or any other life) outside the home.

Still, to analyze sex discrimination in noncomparative terms seems not merely unfamiliar but puzzling. Doesn't discrimination always proceed by way of a comparison? And isn't that more than a coincidence of ends and means? Isn't comparison central to the idea of discrimination? Even when we move from the idea of discrimination as wrongful and think of it in nonpejorative terms, do we not discriminate when we compare one painting, or one movie, or one form of cuisine, for example, to another and declare it better, whatever the undiscriminating might think? The point goes beyond the earlier rejection of equality and difference. Even if *those* comparisons are misguided ways of understanding discrimination, isn't discrimination dependent upon *some* kind of comparison?

The short answer to these questions is that no form of discrimination is dependent upon a comparison, although each can always be described in comparative terms. Valuable forms of discrimination are those that enable the discriminating among us (or the discerning, as they are sometimes called) to perceive the valuable qualities in certain options before them, such as goods, activities, or even people. Such forms of discrimination involve the accurate perception of the value latent in those options, which may be too obscure, or too *recherché*, for the undiscriminating to recognize. Perception of that value does not require the discriminating to compare the worthy with the unworthy. On the contrary, it is possible to know everything there is to know about the value of an option by focusing entirely on its qualities. Comparison may provide the occasion for the exercise of such discernment, but it is no part of it. Comparison merely makes it possible to relate the valuable qualities already discerned in one option to the valuable qualities in some other option, so as to bring out the contrast between them. Value is the premise of such a contrast, not its product.

The same is true in reverse, when the issue is not valuable, but nonvaluable, forms of discrimination. Nonvaluable forms of discrimination are those that enable the discriminatory among us to neglect or suppress the valuable qualities in certain options by presenting in their place an inaccurate, misconceived picture of those options and of the value (and lack of value) latent in them. The discriminatory (or the prejudiced, as they are sometimes called) reject high art as elitist, or foreign films as pretentious, or vegetarian cuisine as rabbit food, and so fail to recognize the value in those goods and their related activities, typically perhaps because it appears to threaten the rather different values to which they have committed their lives. In neglecting or suppressing the value in these options the discriminatory need never compare the paintings, or the films, or the cuisine that they disdain with those that they admire. Here, too, comparison may provide the occasion for lack of discernment, but it forms no part of it.

Nonvaluable forms of discrimination are not merely nonvaluable but wrongful if their effect is to deprive people of the ability to lead successful lives. To neglect the value in a particular good or activity, in the manner described in the previous paragraph, is by definition nonvaluable, but it is not wrongful unless the neglect undermines some person's ability to lead a successful life, for wrongfulness can be understood only in relation to human possibilities. Goods and activities are not people, do not have lives to lead, and so cannot be wronged. It is true that neglect may lead to a loss of value in the world, for it may cause high art, or foreign films, or vegetarian cuisine to wither or even disappear in a particular culture. Any such loss of value is unquestionably to be regretted, but it is not in itself wrongful. It becomes wrongful when the effect of the loss is to damage some person's life. If the success of some person's life depends upon access to a valuable option that discrimination (or prejudice) has rendered unavailable, then that discrimination is not merely nonvaluable but wrongful.

The same is more clearly true where discrimination is applied to people directly, rather than indirectly through the valuable options upon which those people's lives may depend for their success. If the discriminatory among us (sometimes few of us, sometimes many, sometimes nearly all) do not merely overlook the value in options that are critical to the success of at least some women's lives, but maintain an image of women themselves, say, as unaggressive or unscientific (to return to two misconceptions referred to earlier), and then rely on that image as the basis for assigning goods and opportunities to women, their discriminatory outlook and consequent discriminatory actions are not only nonvaluable but wrongful, to the extent that they undermine some women's ability to pursue a successful life, as they almost certainly will.

The conclusion must be that if wrongful discrimination is nonvaluable discrimination that has a critical impact on some person's life (as is proposed), and if nonvaluable discrimination is noncomparative in character (as I have suggested it is), then wrongful discrimination is also noncomparative in character. Even were it the case, however, that any form of discrimination, valuable or nonvaluable, must proceed by way of comparison, it would not follow that sex discrimination is comparative. Sex discrimination is wrongful, and its wrongfulness is not comparative, but depends, as I have said, on the impact of discrimination, and the misconception it embodies, on the success of some person's life, in this case the life of a woman. In other words, if wrongfulness is noncomparative, then sex discrimination must also be noncomparative, for it is the wrongfulness of sex discrimination that concerns us.

The wrong done to women in denying them successful lives is free-standing, not derivative; it is absolute, not relative. Women should be able to lead successful lives, not because men do, but because every person should. They would be no less entitled to lead successful lives, no less entitled to protest at the misconceptions that deny them such lives, if men's lives were as unsuccessful and as limited by misconceptions as theirs, so that no discrimination (in the comparative sense) was involved. The wrong done to women in such a case would be the very wrong now done to them, merely extended to men as well. The fact that the wrong of sex discrimination is one that is (and always has been) applied selectively, to women, makes it tempting to think it is the selectivity that makes it wrong, that it is wrong to deny women the good of a successful life because that good is one that men enjoy. In fact, it is wrong to deny women the good of a successful life whatever may happen to men.

V. Equality, Difference, and the Ending of Roles

It must be emphasized that it does not follow from the fact that comparative approaches to discrimination mistake the nature of discrimination that they are mistaken in their objects. I have already suggested that the impetus for such approaches has been to challenge a certain conception of what it means to be a woman. That challenge, as I have acknowledged, while not rooted in a comparison, can always be expressed in comparative terms. It follows that to pursue a policy of equality, for example, is to remedy sex discrimination whenever the prevailing misconception of what it means to be a woman describes women as different from men (explicitly or implicitly, directly or indirectly), when in fact they are not. If and to the extent that women really are the same as men, the pursuit of equality will also be the pursuit of a correct conception of what it means to be a woman. What this reveals is that while it is true that a policy of nondiscrimination is not a matter of equality or difference, it is also true that such a policy may be well served by certain local and limited strategies of equality and difference, provided that it does not mistake such means for its ends.[16]

Strategic considerations aside, the other reason for comparative approaches to discrimination, and of equality in particular, is historical and to some extent speculative. We live in an age of autonomy, in which people are by and large the authors of their own lives. This does not mean, of course, that people are independent of one another, that they can conduct their lives without the involvement and support of others. On the contrary, nearly all the valuable options that we can pursue in life are entrenched in social forms that are created and maintained by social practices, upon which we must draw, and to which we must contribute, in order to lead successful lives. It does mean, however, that the farmer's child is free to pursue some life other than farming, if that suits him or her, that the carpenter's child is free not to be a carpenter, the tailor's

---

[16] It may make sense to legislate for equality, not because discrimination is a matter of inequality, but because equality may be a good way of ending a species of discrimination that is not a matter of inequality. For example, we may decide to prohibit sexual distinctions in certain settings, and insist that men and women be treated alike, just because the distinction between men and women is so often abused. We need only be careful that the equality that is thereby achieved does not prevent recognition of genuine sexual differences that women need access to in order to lead successful lives. Or at least, if it does so, that this is a price worth paying for the ending of discrimination in the lives of other women.

child not to be a tailor, and so on. Or at least we believe that they should be free in this sense, and seek to make them so, by developing our social forms and practices in ways that embody such freedom of choice. As a consequence, our sense of roles in life is weak, and our sense that certain people are and should be committed to certain roles, by virtue of their birth, social station, or other feature of their lives, is virtually nonexistent.

This was not always so, of course. Until quite recently, people for the most part lived the lives that they were expected to live rather than the lives they chose. A life was expected to be led through a socially defined role, determined not by choice but by the circumstances of one's birth and sex, among other factors. The extent to which this was in fact true, as a historical matter, need not concern us here, for the point is to draw a contrast between a life based on roles and a life of autonomy, and what each demands of women and men. That contrast should not be exaggerated, for as I have already indicated, autonomous lives are dependent upon social forms and practices. Nevertheless, it is a real contrast, for socially defined roles are less diverse, less flexible, and above all less susceptible to choice, in both their adoption and their execution, than the social forms and practices of an autonomous life.

Unfamiliar, indeed alien, as roles may be to most people today, given that most of them are now lost in the past, they can have real value, a value that is missing from autonomous lives. Roles are created and developed over time, entrenched in social forms and practices, passed down from generation to generation. Their connection to value is (or is supposed to be) tested in these processes, so that their occupants can be assured that what they are expected to do is valuable, to a degree that is not possible in the improvised structure of an autonomous life, where one's choices are all too often undermined by a lack of knowledge or understanding of the options among which one is choosing. What is more, where a role turns out not to be valuable, or not to suit a certain person, the damage done to that person's life can be seen as the fault of the role, not of the damaged person, as it must be, in large part at least, in an improvised life. This means that roles can release people from some of the destructive consequences of blame. Even the fact that roles are typically assigned to people according to the circumstances of their birth and sex, to the extent that that is true, frees people from the angst produced by the knowledge that they may do anything, coupled with the fear that they may lack the capacity to do anything very well, or that they do not know themselves and the world well enough to choose what genuinely suits them from among what is genuinely worth doing.

We are more familiar with the serious drawbacks of roles. They are very often unsuited to the people who are expected to fill them. Sometimes they are unsuited to anyone. Sometimes (and what is close to the same thing) they are not valuable. Even where they are valuable and suit the people who are expected to fill them, they are usually too limited to be the whole story of a successful life, as they are very often expected to be. More profoundly, the matching of particular roles to particular people tends to be justified by the attribution of the appropriate role-related characteristics to the people who are expected to fill the roles in question. So farmers' children are (or at least once were) thought to possess the qualities that make them fit to be farmers and, conversely, unfit to be anything else; carpenters' children are (or were) thought to be fit simply to be carpenters; tailors' children to be tailors; and so on. The point is not that the roles to which people are (or were) thereby assigned are bad, but that the assignment is based not on fitness for the role but on a self-fulfilling attribution of the characteristics appropriate to the role to the person who has already been assigned to it on other grounds.

Such attributions are usually false, although sometimes people are able to adapt, acquiring the qualities that have been attributed to them in order to justify the roles they have already been assigned to. Where the role in question is valuable, the adaptation possible, and the cost of adaptation not too high, this may be a worthy enterprise. Where the role is not valuable, however, the enterprise of adapting one's qualities to suit it becomes an enterprise of justifying, to oneself and others, the nonvaluable role to which one has been wrongfully assigned.[17] Where adaptation is impossible, or its cost too high, the attempt to adapt, and to succeed by adapting, is doomed to failure, and the role, even if valuable, becomes a guarantee of an unsuccessful life to the person who has been assigned to it.

It is a familiar fact that women's lives have long been, and to some extent still are, led through socially defined roles, to which women are committed not by any choice of their own but by the circumstance of their sex. As is also well known, those roles have been almost exclusively domestic or quasi-domestic in character. Above all else, women are expected, just because they are women, to take on the role of wife and mother. As conventionally understood, that role is doubly circumscribed. On the one hand it constrains the fulfilling possibilities of marriage and parenthood, by entrenching a restricted understanding of what it means to be a wife and mother. This, even where it does not demean women overtly (as it often does), fails to recognize the many other valuable, albeit unconventional ways of fulfilling those functions. On the other hand, and to some extent consequently, the conventional role of wife and mother prevents women from pursuing any other occupation, unless that occupation confirms women's fitness to be wives and mothers as conventionally understood. To the extent, then, that women have been permitted to work outside the home, it has been in roles that are understood to call for the same domestic skills that good wives and mothers are thought to possess. Women are permitted to be nurses, teachers, and social workers, for example, because and to the extent that the image that we as a society hold of nurses, teachers, and social workers corresponds to the image that we hold of wives and mothers.

---

[17] I say wrongful because the role is nonvaluable and definitive of a life.

As in the case of roles generally, assignment of women to the roles that they are expected to fill is justified by attribution to women of the appropriate role-related characteristics. So women are thought to possess the qualities that fit them for domesticity and quasi-domesticity (as we understand those), and to lack the qualities that would fit them for anything else, just as farmers' children were once thought to possess the qualities that made them fit to be farmers and, conversely, unfit to be anything else. Again, as in the case of roles generally, this attribution to women of the characteristics that would fit them for the roles that have already been assigned to them is usually false. Sometimes women have been able to adapt themselves so as to acquire the characteristics they are assumed to possess already, and consequently have been able to lead successful lives as both parents and nurses, for example. All too often, however, women have been unable to adapt successfully, or have adapted successfully to a role that either is not valuable in itself or, if valuable, is too limited to be the whole story of a successful life. Where that has occurred, women have found themselves coopted into the enterprise of perpetuating a conception of themselves that is not only false but destructive of the lives of the very people who are expected to perpetuate it. In this way, women have found themselves joined with men in preparing other women to be, or to try to be, the kind of people that they themselves are falsely assumed to be.

By their nature, then, roles are enforced through the attribution of difference. The assignment of a person (or class of persons) to a particular role is justified by attributing to that person the qualities that distinguish her or him from those who are assigned to different roles. Where the attribution is false, so that the people (or classes of people) whom it describes as different from one another are not in fact different in terms of their fitness for a particular role or occupation in life, the assertion of difference is contradicted by the fact of equality. It is for this reason that equality has historically been coupled with autonomy as the great emancipator of people from traditional roles and the limitations those roles have imposed on their lives. The story of liberation has been in large part the story of equality, just because the roles from which people have been liberated have been sustained by false assertions of difference.

To the extent that women still occupy conventional roles, and that their place in them is maintained by an assertion of their difference, it is perfectly understandable that their release from those roles has been pursued through a strategy of equality. Yet what women have actually been liberated from is not inequality or difference, but a conception of themselves that has confined them to roles that, for the reasons sketched above, cannot be the vehicle for a successful life, at least in their hands. Correspondingly, what women have pursued through a strategy of equality is not equality itself, but a recognition of their qualities, as women and as people, that is sufficiently accurate to grant them access to a range of options broad enough to enable them to lead successful lives. In other words, a strategy of equality is vindicated not by some alleged principle of equality, but by the fact of it. The strategy is successful only to the extent that a true understanding of what it means to be a woman reveals women to possess qualities that, on comparison, are no different from those of men, and that, furthermore, women need access to in order to lead successful lives. Conversely, a strategy of equality fails women to the extent that a true understanding of what it means to be a woman reveals women to possess qualities that genuinely distinguish them from men, and that women need access to in order to lead successful lives.

I have already suggested that it is a mistake to think that if the damage to women's lives produced by sex discrimination is the consequence of women's having been forced to act under a false description of what it means to be a woman, then the success of women's lives must depend on their acting under a true description. It is a related and just as serious mistake to think that if women have been falsely described in terms of difference, they can be truthfully described in terms of equality. Assertions of difference may have been women's enemy, but it does not follow that assertions of equality are their friend. If women are to have successful lives they must draw on an accurate understanding of themselves as the people they are, which means identifying and pursuing, on the one hand, what is valuable in life, and on the other hand, what in that value suits the people they are. In other words, they must know both what it means to lead a successful life and what it means (and does not mean) to be a woman, questions that I consider in the next two sections.

VI. What It Means to Lead a Successful Life

In the preceding discussion I have often referred to the idea of a successful life. By a successful life I do not mean a conventionally successful life, marked by wealth, celebrity, or the like. I simply mean a good life, a worthwhile life, a life worth living. I take such a life to be composed of valuable projects and activities that are endorsed as one's personal goals. Lives are unsuccessful if they are restricted to activities that are not valuable, or if valuable are too limited to be the whole story of a life, as women's lives too often have been. Lives are correspondingly successful if they are composed of an adequate range of valuable activities. It is not possible to appreciate the idea of a successful life, therefore, other than by appreciating the nature of value.[18] To misunderstand value is to misunderstand what it means to lead a successful life, and in what

---

[18] I do not mean to suggest that I can or should offer a complete account of the nature of value here. In speaking of what it means to lead a successful life, I intend to address only those aspects of a person's success in life, and the questions of value that underlie and sustain them, that could possibly be brought into play by the distinction between men and women, for what concerns me here are those aspects that are denied by discrimination. I do not consider, therefore, the many other important questions about the nature of value that the idea of a successful life gives rise to, although certain answers to those questions are undoubtedly implicit in what I say.

ways that is denied to women. As I see it, certain familiar but mistaken accounts of value have yielded familiar but mistaken accounts of feminism.

Objective accounts describe value in a way that places pressure on the character and qualities of human beings. We lead good lives not merely by realizing ourselves, so as to give effect to our qualities in our actions, but by ensuring that our qualities and actions conform to what goodness requires. This is most obviously true of the aspect of value that governs our relations with other people, which we call morality. By its very nature, morality is demanding. Less obviously, everything that is of value is demanding. We realize the value in any activity by living up to the standards of that activity, so that we become successful cooks by preparing good food, successful musicians by creating good music, successful doctors by practising good medicine. To the extent that one cook, musician, or doctor is better than another, therefore, his or her life is more successful in that respect. Whether that life is as a consequence more successful overall depends upon the implications of success (and failure) in that respect on the success of the life as a whole, about which views differ.

Certain well-known objective accounts of value are monistic, or one-dimensional, in character. Monistic accounts of value treat the various sources of value in life as no more than means to the realization of some single, more profound value, such as happiness, perhaps, or dignity, or honour, or redemption, a value to which any successful human life must ultimately be dedicated and to which all other values can be reduced. Such accounts of value have a distinctive consequence for the evaluation of any given life, one that has a particular bearing on the question of sex discrimination. Since those accounts treat value as differing only in degree, not kind, the pressure they place on the character and qualities of human beings is necessarily egalitarian. No person deliberately seeks a lesser life, one that is less happy, less dignified, or less honourable than another. That being the case, there is a pressure to pursue whatever activity in life yields the greatest amount of value. If a person's qualities prevent him or her from pursuing that activity, then those qualities are flawed, and should be changed so as to make that person's life as successful as possible. To fail to do so is to condemn that person to an inferior life. In the monistic picture, valuable lives cannot be merely different from one another; ultimately, they can only be better and worse.

What is striking about such accounts of value, and what gives them particular and familiar resonance for those interested in the question of sex discrimination, is their corollary. It is not simply the case that value, as a monist understands it, generates a demand for equality, so as to commit human beings to the pursuit of the same activities as one another, and to the extent required for that pursuit, to the development of the same qualities as one another. It is the corollary: that the pursuit of equality is dependent on the truth of value monism, for it is not possible to regard the different activities that people pursue, the different human qualities that serve those activities, and the different lives that are constituted by those activities, as superior, inferior, or equal to one another other than by treating them as serving a single, ultimate value in terms of which they can be ranked as better than, worse than, or equal to one another.

This explains why campaigners for sexual equality, at least in their more radical incarnations, call for the reformulation of sexual identity along egalitarian lines, so as to make women and men indistinguishable in any way that matters. Sexual equality in this sense could be thought to be necessary only by those who believe that any sexual difference that is relevant to value entails the inferiority of one sex to the other. This further explains why many campaigners for sexual equality treat the lives of men as the standard against which the lives of women are to be judged, and to which the lives of women should aspire. For if men's lives are more successful than women's, as they are wherever sex discrimination exists, and if success and failure in life is a matter of better and worse, then the kinds of activities that men pursue, and the kinds of qualities that men possess, must be better than the corresponding lives and qualities of women. In turn, this explains why the qualities that distinguish the sexes are often so emphatically said to be the product of nurture rather than nature. For it is only a need to change one's qualities that could make it matter that such change is possible, as it is said to be possible of whatever nurture has produced.

A distaste for conclusions such as these has led some, unfortunately, to reject not value monism (as they should), but the very idea of objective value itself, and to embrace relativism instead. Relativist accounts of value, as commonly understood, are those that regard value not as a property of whatever is valued (in this setting, a human activity or the human quality that produces that activity), but as a reflection of the attitudes of those who find it valuable. In short, according to such value relativists, things are valuable only to the extent that people take them to be so. Different relativist accounts have different views as to which general attitudes should be regarded as the foundation of value. While they all agree that value is nothing more than the product (or projection) of a collective outlook, they disagree as to which collective outlook it is the product of. Some believe that value is relative to the secular culture that one inhabits, others that it is relative to religious culture, still others (referred to above) that it is relative to one's sex.

What matters here is that relativist accounts of value place pressure not on the character and qualities of human beings (except to the extent that they fail to conform to the collective outlook that defines value), nor on the prevailing cultural conception of value (which, being the source of value, cannot be mistaken), but on the very idea of value itself. For that reason they are hardly recognizable as accounts of value at all, for they present value as being utterly undemanding, a mere reflection of prevailing preferences, which are answerable to no standard other than the fact of their existence as the focus of some belief or commitment, the very fact that defines them as a preference. According to relativists, we lead good lives to the extent that we reflect whatever relativists believe value is properly related to, and so lead good lives to the extent that we reflect, for example, our religion, or our culture, or our sex, and the understandings of value that those give rise to. It is not merely that relativists regard good Catholics as good because they conform to Catholic doctrine, good Americans as good because they conform (say) to the American dream, good men and women as good because they conform to prevailing notions of masculinity and femininity. To do that would be only to treat the idea of goodness as equivalent to fidelity, as it is in part. It would, quite rightly, leave open the further question of whether (and to what extent) it is good to be faithful in these ways, whether it is a good thing to be a good Catholic, a good American, or a good man or woman in this sense. Relativism forecloses such questions, for to be a good American, for example, is the only sense in which it is possible for a (cultural) relativist to understand the idea of being good.

This relativistic understanding of value has a distinctive consequence for the evaluation of any given life, and a particular bearing on the question of sex discrimination. According to relativist accounts, a successful life must be lived according to one's own standards, be they the standards of one's own culture, one's own religion, one's own sex, or whatever else value is said to be properly related to. There is no other criterion of value available. Relativists believe, therefore, that to live according to the standards of others is the essence of what it means to be oppressed, for to do so is to live under a regime in which one is bound to treat as valuable, and hence as one's own, what is not valuable precisely because it is not one's own. Cultural imperialism becomes the paradigmatic case of oppression because the culture that is imposed, being not one's own, is for that reason not good.

This explains the focus of many accounts of sex discrimination on the question of oppression. I do not mean to suggest that a belief in oppression entails a belief in relativism in the way that a belief in equality entails a belief in value monism. That would plainly be untrue. Tyrants oppress their subjects, not because they fail to take a relativist view of the values applicable to those subjects' lives, but because they use their power to deny their subjects virtually all the ingredients of a successful life, as those ingredients are objectively understood. Some of those who believe that women are oppressed believe that men are tyrants in this sense, and so see discrimination as oppressive without subscribing to relativism. That view is rare, however. The more familiar view is that women are oppressed because and to the extent that they are not evaluated according to their own standards, which are a reflection of their condition as women. This view is indeed relativist, and so is vulnerable to the criticisms made in the second section, above, of the attempt to relate value to sexual identity, as well as to the many more general objections that can be made to value relativism.[19]

---

[19] From the perspective of those concerned with sex discrimination, these objections include the fact that for relativists it is not possible for a culture, or whatever value is properly related to,

Unlike value monists, relativists rightly recognize the significance of character and culture in shaping a successful life, but wrongly conclude that this significance follows from the supposed fact that character and culture are the source of value, rather than being (as they actually are) a possible reason to pursue one genuinely valuable activity rather than another, namely, an activity that suits women rather than some other. It is one thing to recognize that concern for others (for example) is valuable, and then notice that it is a value to which women may have distinctive or disproportionate access, with all that entails for women's success in life, and quite another thing to regard concern for others as valuable just because and to the extent that it is a quality to which women have distinctive or disproportionate access.

If there is reason to believe that human value is neither one-dimensional nor relative, as the weaknesses in these accounts of what it means to lead a successful life and the extent to which such a life can be undermined by sex discrimination suggest there is, then an obvious possibility is that value is both plural and objective. By plural I mean an understanding of value that regards many, perhaps most, sources of value in life as irreducible to any one more profound source, in the monistic manner. By objective I mean an understanding that regards value as a property of the object that is valued (in this setting, a human activity or the human quality that produces that activity), rather than a reflection of the attitudes of those who find the object valuable, in the relativist manner. Being both objective and plural, this account of value has a distinctive consequence for the evaluation of any given life, one that has a significant bearing on the question of sex discrimination. In common with other objective accounts, it describes value in a way that places pressure on the character and qualities of human beings, insisting that we lead good lives, not merely by realizing ourselves, but also by ensuring that our qualities and actions conform to what goodness requires. At the same time, however, and to some extent in common with relativist accounts of value, it acknowledges the critical, albeit limited, role that a person's character and culture may play in determining what is good for them.

If values are plural, so that they differ in kind as well as in degree, it will often be the case that we are confronted with a choice between two options, neither of which can be judged to be better than the other because each must be evaluated according to a different standard, the standard of its kind. This means that we must often decide which option to pursue when there is reason to pursue

---

to be mistaken about what is valuable (as would be the case on any objective account), because the basis of value is not answerable to value judgment itself. Further, any change in the basis of value (from culture to sexual identity, for example), must be predicated not on the wrongfulness of sex discrimination (for relativist values cannot be wrong in themselves) but on the existence of independent grounds to believe that the existing basis of value is mistaken (so that value is properly related to sexual identity rather than culture, for example). Finally, such a change can end sex discrimination only if whatever value is newly related to (on grounds unconnected with the wrongfulness of sex discrimination) is not sexually discriminatory (as existing sexual identity almost certainly is).

both and no reason to prefer one to the other. As I have already emphasized, the difficulty that this gives rise to cannot be avoided by treating our character as the premise for choice among options in life, in the relativist manner. We cannot confine our search for value in life to that which is suggested by the facts of our character or culture. We are all familiar with people and cultures, or aspects of culture, that are narrow-minded, doctrinaire, intolerant, or bigoted. Choices derived from such characters and cultures are to be avoided, not pursued.

There is more to the story, however. While it is true that character and culture cannot be regarded as premises for choice among options, since they cannot be relied on to distinguish valuable from nonvaluable options, it is also true that they have a genuine, albeit subordinate role to play in resolving the problem of choosing among valuable options of different kinds. To appreciate that role fully it is necessary to distinguish between moral and nonmoral qualities of character, or in other words, between virtues and bare capacities.

Moral qualities of character, such as truthfulness or courage, mendacity or cowardice, are subjects, not premises, of moral deliberation, for the reasons just given. One does not become virtuous by developing the qualities of character that one happens to possess, whatever they may be; one becomes virtuous by ensuring that one possesses, or comes to possess, qualities of character that constitute virtues. Yet even in this setting, once we have eliminated from consideration those options that would diminish, or at least that would fail to augment, our moral character, it remains a question which options and which virtues we should pursue, and character and culture may offer reasons to choose one way rather than another. No person can display all virtues, not only because the virtues are too numerous to embody in a single life, but because they are (or may be) incompatible with one another. We must choose between virtues, therefore, and character and culture sometimes provide reasons to choose one virtue over another (by making that virtue accessible, for example), and sometimes determine the implications of separate reasons to choose one virtue over another (by making the chooser either conformist or nonconformist with his or her culture, for example, consistent or inconsistent with his or her character), implications that give rise to further reasons affecting and shaping the choice between options and virtues.

Nonmoral qualities of character, on the other hand, qualities such as strength or suppleness, intelligence or emotion, are not good or bad in themselves but may be used, with equal facility, for either good or bad ends. Strength can be used to injure others or to sustain them, intelligence can be used to foster others or to destroy them. Qualities such as these are neither virtues nor vices, but vehicles for both.[20] What is more, the valuable options that

---

[20] It follows that there is no reason to be proud of characters and types of character that are based upon qualities such as these, though there is reason to respect such qualities and what they make possible.

these qualities make accessible, and the good ends to which they may be put, are both manifold and incommensurable, so that the lives of the strong may or may not be more valuable than the lives of the supple, and similarly for the lives of the intelligent and the emotional. That being the case, nonmoral qualities of character, unlike their moral counterparts, may legitimately function as premises for choice, and indeed in some cases must do so.

Once we have eliminated from consideration all nonvaluable options, the question of which valuable options to pursue remains. Valuable options, like virtues, are too numerous to embody in a single life; they, like virtues, are often incompatible with one another, and certain valuable options are readily accessible to certain people with certain characters, or in certain cultures, while being either accessible with difficulty or entirely inaccessible to other people with other characters, or in other cultures.

So, to take a mundane but clear example, by and large one can flourish as a baseball player only in America or Japan, just as one can flourish as a cricket player only in Britain and parts of the Commonwealth, for sports such as these are profoundly linked to the societies that gave birth to them or subsequently adopted them. What is true of such sports is true, in varying degree, of most aspects of artistic, cultural, intellectual, and social life, particular forms of which flourish in certain cultures while being marginal or absent in others. In general, cultural forms are supportive of, and so helpful to, the pursuit of some valuable activities and critical to the pursuit of others.

Much the same is true of character, however that character may have been arrived at. So the fact that a person is athletic and impatient may be a reason for that person to take up sport rather than needlework, assuming that both are valuable activities, for there is reason to do what one is good at and can flourish in, rather than the opposite. Similarly, the fact that one is caring is a reason to pursue a caring profession, the fact that one is supple a reason to be a dancer, the fact that one is fluent in language a reason to be a writer or broadcaster, teacher or politician, and so on. These reasons are not conclusive, of course, for they do not in any sense require that a person be an athlete rather than a needleworker, or a dancer or writer rather than something else. It may well be that one's character has other valuable implications, that it suggests other valuable possibilities. It may even be that there are reasons to defy the obvious implications of one's qualities and characteristics, in the short term at least. Nevertheless, the reason to do what one is good at establishes certain important implications of choice, for the reason to pursue a particular activity is very largely defeated if that activity is one that one cannot do well, or at least adequately.

The role of character and culture in shaping a choice among options may be summarized, then, as follows. Character and culture are constraints on action, fostering activities that lie within their margins and discouraging activities that lie beyond them. Given that they constrain action, they may constrain good actions, and for that reason cannot be taken as premises for choice. While a valuable life does not depend upon access to all valuable options, it does depend upon access to a range of valuable options wide enough to prevent recourse to those that would diminish the value of a life and the virtue of a character. To the extent that character and culture either direct us to bad options or unacceptably limit our access to good ones, then, they must be reformed, not respected.[21]

Paradoxically, however, what constrains may also enable, by making some things possible and by providing the perspective from which other things are imaginable. That being the case, character and culture have a legitimate role to play in determining the *viability* of a goal, given our limited capacity to change either our character or our culture, and in determining the *intelligibility* of a goal, given that any change we may make in our character or culture must necessarily proceed from the character and culture that we now have to some other that is better. Most importantly, they have a role in determining the *rationality* of a goal given, first, that certain goods are possible or imaginable only within the setting of certain characters and cultures; second, that there is no reason to exchange a character or culture that is capable of one set of goods for a character or culture that is capable of another, incommensurable set of goods; and third, that being or becoming anything, whether by changing or by remaining the same, requires reasons that are capable of showing that what it is possible to be is also desirable to be.[22]

How are we to choose and lead good lives then, in the face of a host of valuable yet incommensurable options, and what role do character and culture play in enabling us to do so? The answer, it seems to me, is that we must enter into a kind of exchange between what we are and what is good, beginning with what we are and know ourselves to be, as individual characters and as members of certain cultures. Knowledge of what we are is a necessary starting point for any inquiry into the kinds of matters that we might rationally, intelligibly, and viably seek value in (and hence the kinds of lives that we might lead), and the kinds of virtues that we might similarly develop (and hence the kinds of people that we might become). A valuable life is not something to be planned from the sidelines, but

---

[21] Furthermore, any reliance on character as a guide to action is dependent upon the capacity to distinguish between genuine and presumed characteristics, between what it really means to be a person of a certain kind and prevailing conceptions of what that means, for while character itself may sometimes bar access to a valuable life, conceptions of character often do so, because their usefulness, which is the reason for their existence, tends to be a function of their reductiveness. See the discussion below and Timothy Macklem, "Defining Discrimination", 11 *King's College Law Journal* 224.

[22] As this description may suggest, these three implications of character and culture are interdependent and mutually informing. Limits of character or culture are worthy of respect only where they are rationally supportable; rational goals are viable and so practical only where they take account of such limits of character and culture (whether by conforming to them or challenging them); intelligible goals are those that synthesize the requirements of reason, character, and culture.

something to be explored and considered, imagined and created, from within. At the same time, just because it is to be explored and considered, imagined and created, a valuable life is not something to be led within set boundaries of character or culture, but must be capable of transcending those boundaries where necessary, so as to accommodate new goods and new implications for existing goods.

The objectivity of value pluralism, then, means that some human qualities and characteristics are to be reformed rather than respected. Its pluralism, however, means that other human qualities and characteristics are not merely the resources upon which we must draw in order to lead successful lives, but the resources that enable us to choose what suits us from among what is good. It seems to me that there are two main implications of these features of value pluralism for the victims of sex discrimination. First, it might be the case that the qualities that now define women as women are morally flawed, and so are to be reformed, or at least suppressed, rather than respected. I take this not to be true. I assume that there are no sex-based moral qualities of character, despite what many have pretended. Women are not passive or weak-willed, spiteful or deceitful, scheming or manipulative, and the like, or at least and more precisely, are no more so than men. Such qualities simply do not form part of sexual identity. The tendency to think they do, where it does not proceed from bigotry, is the product of an overly deterministic view of the implications of human qualities and characteristics.[23]

Some believe that the possession of certain human qualities commits one to the pursuit of certain specific human activities. In particular, it is contended that qualities that have been acquired in circumstances of adversity, by slaves, or serfs, or more generally, by victims of discrimination, commit all those who possess them to slavery, serfdom, or the condition of those who are discriminated against. So, it is suggested, if women are more caring than men (as may or may not be the case), it is only because a history of sex discrimination has ensured that women have devoted themselves to the care of others, usually men and children, and has correspondingly ensured, in the manner described above, that women have acquired the qualities that fit them for that task. Crucially, it is then suggested that to ask women to acknowledge and respond to their special capacity for concern is to ask them to commit themselves to qualities that in turn commit them to caring for others, and so is to ask them to commit themselves to being discriminated against. After all, it is said, it might well be the case that, after centuries of serfdom, serfs came to possess the qualities and characteristics of good serfs. Yet to ask them to acknowledge and respond to those qualities and characteristics would be to ask them to commit themselves to the continuation of their serfdom. No serf would be so foolish, and nor should women be.

---

[23] In fact there may be certain moral distinctions between the sexes. I have suppressed this possibility as marginal and distracting. See chapter 6, note 9.

To the extent that their character reflects a legacy of discrimination, that character should be reformed, not respected.[24]

This argument would be sound if the qualities and characteristics that define women as women were moral qualities, if the history of sex discrimination had ensured that women really are morally inferior to men. I have denied this is the case, although clearly it is no more than an assumption on my part that I can merely invite others to share. Even were it true of some of women's characteristics (as I deny), however, it certainly is not true of all of them, and in particular is not true of the capacity for concern, to take but one example. The qualities and characteristics that distinguish men and women, including, let us suppose, the capacity for concern, are predominantly, and in my view exclusively, nonmoral qualities, capable of being used for bad or good. It is possible to display concern in ways that are demeaning, as the ways in which women have historically cared for men shows, but it is just as possible to display concern in ways that are valuable. After all, it is the capacity for concern that enables human beings to move beyond self-absorption so as to involve themselves in the fate of other human beings, to the benefit of all. If it is really true that men lack the capacity for concern, or enjoy it only in attenuated form, then that is very unfortunate for men.

What is true of the capacity for concern is true of nonmoral qualities generally. Qualities acquired in adversity, like other nonmoral qualities, have endless implications, many of which are bad but many of which are good. This explains why it is difficult, even for tyrants, to compel a bad life, and how it is that so many women (and other victims of discrimination) have been able to escape the negative implications of the qualities they have been assigned including, let us suppose, the capacity for concern. The truth is that except by the use of brute force, it is not possible to compel a bad life (by which I mean an unsuccessful life) other than by endowing people, by whatever means, with immoral qualities of character (as I believe has not happened to women), or by developing and promoting a misconception of those people. A misconception of what it means to be a woman either attributes qualities to women that are false of them or promotes the negative implications of the nonmoral qualities of character that women genuinely possess, so as to ensure that women are not only endowed with a heightened capacity for concern, for example, but are led to use that capacity for demeaning rather than for valuable purposes.

The second implication of value pluralism, then, is that women will escape sex discrimination when they escape those prevailing misconceptions of what it means to be a woman that make their lives unsuccessful, and discover instead what it really means to be a woman, in the broadest sense of that term, so as

---

[24] The best-known argument on these lines is that offered by Catharine MacKinnon in *Feminism Unmodified: Discourses on Life and Law* (Cambridge, Mass., 1987). See particularly the chapter entitled "Difference and Dominance: On Sex Discrimination", at 39.

to enable them to identify the valuable options in life that their qualities and characteristics make *viable*, *intelligible*, and *rational*, in the manner described above.

VII. What It Means to Be a Woman

In the course of this discussion I have frequently referred to the idea of what it means to be a woman.[25] I do not intend anything special to turn on the idea of meaning; I simply have in mind what it *is* to be a woman. The word "mean" is used merely to convey the idea of an explanation in all its fullness, in the same sense that one speaks, compassionately, of what it means to be unemployed, to be old, to lose one's child, or perhaps enviously, of what it means to be healthy, happy, or rich. I have suggested it is not possible for a woman to lead a successful life other than by knowing what it means to be a woman, *in the broad rather than the narrow sense of that term*. In my view, women need to go beyond the discriminatory conception of themselves currently prevalent in society, to discover their true qualities and characteristics, some of which will turn out to be shared with men, so as to be, strictly speaking, no part of their identity as women, as well as the qualities and characteristics that are distinctive to them. Only then can they know which of the valuable options in life suit them and so are worthy of their pursuit. Only then can they know whether the denial to them of access to a particular option, as the result of a misconception of what it means to be a woman, has deprived them of something that, given the kind of people that they are, they need access to in order to lead a successful life.

Yet some regard such a quest as utterly meaningless, at least when pursued by women. It may be, it is said, that men do not know who and what women are, but women themselves surely do. Others regard the quest as essentialist,[26] believing that the search for an understanding of what it means to be a woman implies that women are, or at least ought to be, no different from one another, when in fact they are distinguished in any number of ways, by race, class, nationality, religion, sexual orientation, and so on. They believe a proper understanding of women's present predicament and of their future well-being must be particular and contextual. Still others believe a version of this idea, that being a woman means different things to different people, so that the quest for an understanding of what it means to be a woman is likely to give rise to as many answers as there are women, perhaps as many as there are people.

---

[25] I speak throughout of what it means to be a woman where I might have spoken of what it means to be women, and so have emphasized the diversity of women's experiences. I have used the singular rather than the plural only for the sake of convenience. As I have tried to make clear in this section, I do not for a moment believe that the experience of being a woman is the same for every woman.

[26] I use the term "essentialist" as it is used by people who hold the view described here. In doing so I take no position on whether that use of the term is correct.

Some of these concerns can be readily allayed. It is not true that women necessarily know who and what they are, for we are all vulnerable to error and deception, at our own hands and at the hands of others. It is not easy to know our own qualities, beyond the most obvious. On the contrary, personal qualities are something we discover through a long process of experimentation and self-examination, in which we draw not only upon our own perceptions but upon the perceptions of others. To discover one's qualities through such a process is, for women, to discover what it means to be a woman in the broad, nondistinctive sense. To discover what it means to be a woman in the narrow, distinctive sense, as may be necessary in combating sex discrimination, one must go further, so as to discover, in company with others, something much more difficult: namely, which of the qualities that one knows oneself to possess are distinctive of one's condition as a woman. To know that, it is also necessary to discover what it correspondingly means to be a man.

Such knowledge is far from obvious, and the quest for it is certainly not meaningless. It is all too possible to be mistaken or deceived in such matters. In the case of sexual identity, in particular, misconceptions are not only possible but probable, for in respects such as this we know ourselves in part through the image of sexual (or other) identity presented to us by the society in which we live and of which we are a part, the image given to us by our parents and our peers, an image upon which we are bound to draw and to which we are correspondingly bound to contribute.[27] This explains the importance to campaigners against discrimination, whether sexual, racial, or some other, of image-breaking role models. In the absence of such models, people are inevitably guided in the development of their own self-understanding by the images of themselves, as women and as minority group members, offered to them by their society, images that are all too often distorted, indeed, that are distorted just as often as they are prima facie discriminatory.

Nor is it true that to speak of what it means to be a woman is essentialist, in the sense of implying that all women are alike. It is true, pace Wittgenstein, that women must have some quality or characteristic in common or it would not be possible to know them as women at all, whether in speaking of women generally or in speaking of them particularly and contextually, as black women, working-class women, Israeli women, Muslim women, or lesbians. That quality or characteristic need not be of any great significance, however, except as the foundation for other, more important distinctions between women and men, and it need not play the same role in every woman's life. Exactly what that quality or characteristic is, what significance it is capable of having for women, and

---

[27] As I have already indicated, the fact that we are forced to draw upon and contribute to such misconceptions in any setting where discrimination exists does not mean we must similarly draw upon and contribute to an accurate conception of ourselves as women and men in order to end that discrimination and so lead successful lives.

what role it plays in the lives of different women, are all part of the question of what it means to be a woman.

More important perhaps, a true understanding of what it means to be a woman does not stop there, for it embraces not only the qualities that all women possess but the qualities that only women possess, as well as the qualities that women have a greater tendency to possess than men. It is an error to think that concepts preclude recognition of variety within the concepts. Were that the case, it would be impossible to use any concept, including particular and contextual concepts of what it means to be a woman, without being essentialist. If the concept of a woman is used narrowly and dogmatically, so as to exclude recognition of the many different ways in which it is possible to be a woman, that is the fault of those who so use the concept. It is no fault of the concept itself, as is clear from the fact that it is impossible to speak of essentialism in this manner, so as to criticize such narrow and dogmatic usages, other than by using the concept of a woman in a nonessentialist manner, so as to draw attention to the many different kinds of women that such a mistaken use of the concept is said to exclude.

On the other hand, to say that being a woman means different things to different people, so that the quest for an understanding of what it means to be a woman is likely to give rise to as many answers as there are women, is true but conflates two very different ideas, which it is crucial to distinguish in order to understand sex discrimination.[28] Being a woman can mean different things to different people precisely because the condition of being a woman is multifaceted in the way I have just described, so that different women emphasize different aspects of that condition in the course of constructing and pursuing their different lives. In so emphasizing the different aspects of their condition, women pursue what it means to be a woman in the broad, nondistinctive sense, the sense in which they are both like and unlike men. The search for a successful life cannot be confined to what is suggested by one's character as a woman in the narrow, distinctive sense, for to so confine it would be to discriminate against oneself, while to permit it to be so confined would be to permit oneself to be discriminated against. It would be to deny recognition to all those aspects of one's qualities and character in respect of which one is nondistinctive, namely, the respects in which women are no different from men, respects to which any woman needs access in order to lead a successful life.

So what it means to be a woman in the broad sense is, on the one hand, to be capable, despite what many have claimed, of being a miner or a metalworker, a doctor or a lawyer, a physicist or a mathematician, and the many other things in regard to which the capacities of women cannot be distinguished from those of men. On the other hand, what it means to be a woman in the broad sense

---

[28] I set aside here the possibility that such a statement is to be understood as the expression of a subjectivist or relativist outlook.

is also, in part, to be unlike men, and so to be capable of exercising those capacities that are distinctive to women in the sense I have described. So what it means to be a woman in the broad sense is also to be capable of bearing children, to be capable of thinking in the special ways that women are said to have made peculiarly their own, to be capable of showing what is said to be a woman's distinctive brand of concern. As I have emphasized, not all women possess these qualities and capacities, and not all women who possess them wish to exploit them, just as not all human beings possess (or wish to exploit) all the qualities that are distinctive to human beings. Some women both possess and pursue these qualities and other women do not. In both these ways, then, broad and narrow, nondistinctive and distinctive, being a woman means different things to different women, so that different women emphasize different aspects of their condition as women in the course of constructing and pursuing their different lives, some emphasizing metalwork, others motherhood, others both metalwork and motherhood.

Yet being a woman can also mean different things to different people because different people have different *conceptions* of what it means to be a woman, conceptions that overlap but do not always coincide with reality. Where a conception of what it means to be a woman is false, the gap between image and reality may be immaterial, inspiring, or damaging to those women who are affected by it. Where a misconception of what it means to be a woman is damaging to a woman's capacity to lead a successful life, it is discriminatory, for the reasons outlined above.

Misconceptions are immaterial if they have no bearing on the success of a person's life. Men think many foolish things about women, but they do not always harm women in doing so. Some misconceptions of women are simply trivial, so that their perpetuation is an annoyance rather than an injury. If men think that all women love clothes, or conversation, or admiring babies, they are mistaken, but the mistake is unlikely to have a bearing on the success of any woman's life, special cases aside.[29] Other misconceptions have real potential to damage women but fail to do so in particular cases, because they happen to be irrelevant to the lives of those against whom they are directed. If a man thinks women are unqualified for scientific positions, he is mistaken in a way that has real potential to damage women, but his mistake will be irrelevant as long as it

---

[29] These misconceptions will strike many people as offensive, and for good reason, for they are often used to trivialize women and so to stigmatize them. It is tempting to take the next step, and conclude that such misconceptions are in themselves discriminatory, just because they are trivializing and stigmatizing. Yet in fact their discriminatory character is a function not of their falsity alone but of their potential to damage women, by denying them the understanding and respect they need to lead successful lives, personally or professionally. One is bound to notice that while women correspondingly think foolish things about men, such misconceptions are less trivializing and less stigmatizing, and so less discriminatory, precisely because they are very much less likely to have the effect of denying men the understanding and respect necessary to a successful life.

has no bearing on the success of any woman's life, which is just as long as he has no influence over access to scientific positions.[30]

Misconceptions are inspiring if they encourage people to become what they otherwise could not have become. In some settings a limited degree of self-deception, and even of deception by others, can lead a person to believe that she has qualities that she does not in fact have, yet has the capacity to acquire, qualities that she would not be able to acquire without the assistance of the deception. This is a familiar phenomenon. What is popularly known as the American dream convinces people that they have qualities and capacities that they in fact lack but may acquire through proper belief in the dream. Role models in sports, entertainment, politics, and the professions convince many who share the sex, race, ethnic origin, or other salient feature of the role model that they too can flourish in those fields, and so inspire people to acquire the qualities and capacities necessary to flourish in them. Sometimes the people in question can do this; sometimes they cannot. For just that reason, reliance on such misconceptions is dangerous, despite their inspirational potential. Role models rightly make clear that sex, race, and the like are no barrier to flourishing in the fields that the role models have made their own. They are misleading, however, if they are taken to suggest that all that is needed to flourish in those fields is to dispel the misconceptions of sex and race that have long stood as barriers to women, racial minorities, and the like. This might or might not be the case for particular people, and where it is not the case, the misconception is very likely to be damaging to that person's life.

Where the gap between reality and a particular conception of what it means to be a woman is neither inspirational nor immaterial, it is damaging and discriminatory. There are limits, therefore, to the extent to which it can legitimately mean different things to different people. A conception of what it means to be a woman can legitimately depart from reality, in any significant way, only if that departure assists rather than impairs the ability of those affected by it to succeed in life.

How difficult is it to know what it means to be a woman, and to distinguish that from the many misconceptions that women have suffered under? Less difficult than it might seem. Every person, in order to lead a successful life, must develop a degree of self-knowledge. We need to know what we are in order to know

---

[30] It is always a question of when this is the case. If, for example, a father discourages his daughter from pursuing the study of science when she has both the ability and the inclination to do so, he will cause her real harm if it turns out that access to a scientific career is critical to the success of her life, as it may be if it is the best or the only vehicle for her talents. However, as many women have shown, it is entirely possible that the daughter's abilities are broad enough, and her inclinations flexible enough, to permit her to make a success of her life in a field that her father is prepared to recognize that women are qualified to explore. It is true that this will require her to broaden her horizons in a way she would not have had to but for her father's attitude, but that may well be good for her. Of course, the daughter may simply decide to defy her father's attitude, whether or not it constitutes an act of discrimination against her.

what we might be good at, and we need to know what we might be good at in order to know how we might flourish. We sometimes make mistakes in this, as I have already noted, but by and large we come to know ourselves well enough to know whether we are philosophical or practical, artistic or scientific, passionate or even-tempered, romantic or down to earth, and so on. In this way we develop a sense of what sort of friends and interests we might have and what careers we might pursue. Such self-knowledge, when generalized across people and sharpened through contrast, yields an understanding of what it means to be a person of a certain kind, to be an American, a Brazilian, or an Egyptian; a Catholic, a Muslim, or a Buddhist; an artist, a scholar, or an entrepreneur; a homosexual or a heterosexual; black, white, or other; a woman or a man. Sometimes, as I have indicated, it is necessary to draw on such collective self-understanding in order to lead a successful life; more often it is not. So, whether broadly or narrowly understood, there is nothing obscure or inaccessible about what it means to be a woman; it is the stuff of everyday living.

Sometimes, however, often in the case of women and other victims of discrimination, our self-knowledge contradicts the picture that others typically have of us, a picture that our self-understanding has revealed to be a misconception. To put it in the conventional, comparative idiom, we know ourselves to be the same as other people in respects in which we are thought to be different, or to be different from other people in respects in which we are thought to be the same. Insistence upon what we know ourselves to be, and a corresponding rejection of what others have taken us to be, thus underpins and sustains claims to recognition of equality and difference, in ways that are entirely familiar. Women have historically sought equality with men because and to the extent that they knew themselves to be no different from men, because they knew, or at least strongly suspected, they possessed abilities they were said to lack, and lacked disabilities they were said to have, so as to be capable of being bankers, philosophers, carpenters, plumbers, and a host of other unexpected things, contrary to what had long been pretended.

Underneath every sound claim to equality, then, lies an assertion of factual equality. Women have not sought equality, in banking, philosophy, or anywhere else, in a manner that is indifferent to factual equality, on the basis, let us suppose, that whether or not created equal they must be treated as if they were equal. On the contrary, women's claims to equality have been founded on the belief that women are not *in fact* in any sense inferior to men in any of the respects in which equality has been sought. What this shows is that an understanding of what it means to be a woman is implicit in every claim to equality, and conversely of difference. It is true that the claims are almost always expressed in comparative terms, perhaps because they are almost always addressed to men, who, it might be thought, are most likely to appreciate such claims to the extent that they can relate them to themselves. Yet the claims are made possible only by an understanding of what it means to be a woman, and by an awareness of the importance of a general recognition and acceptance of that fact to women's ability to lead successful lives. So what it means to be a woman is not only the stuff of everyday living, but the basis of our approach to sex discrimination.

Accessible, even familiar, as the question of what it means to be a woman may be, however, there are real limits, both personal and professional, to how far I can address the substance of that question in this book. This may disappoint some readers and frustrate others, given the significance of the idea to what I have to say, though for my own part I see it as an impetus to further, more practical, and perhaps more concrete inquiries, that will in turn reflect back on, and permit a reexamination of, what I have said here. As I see it, the limits to what I am able to say about what it means to be a woman are no more than a necessary recognition of the limits to any person's grasp of what all recognize to be a complex, collective, and multi-disciplinary problem. I know something about myself, and thus something about being a man, and correlatively, about being a woman. My knowledge is sufficient for the purposes of living my life (or at least so I hope), just as the knowledge of others, men and women, is generally sufficient for the purposes of living their lives. Yet my knowledge is by its nature no more than a local, limited perspective on an idea that can be fully described only by reference to a collective, cumulative understanding on the part of women and men generally. The development of such an understanding is a challenge that feminism has long grappled with, and with a good deal of success. We know much better than we once did what women are capable of, what their needs are, what their ambitions look like. However, further development of this understanding, in other than philosophical terms, is not a project to which I have any special contribution to make. My task here is constrained not only by the limits to my personal knowledge but by the nature of my professional capacities. I can plausibly develop and build upon the understanding yielded by my self-knowledge where I have the professional capacity to do so, and no further. For that reason my project is philosophical, not sociological. As I have said, it is designed to lay the groundwork for further enquiry by others, of whatever kind.

VIII. Radical Inquiries

In the discussion so far I have approached the question of sex discrimination from the perspective of its remedy, asking whether equality, or the recognition of difference, or a sufficient degree of understanding, is what is required for women to lead successful lives. Most accounts of sex discrimination, however, including that embodied in the law, approach the question from the opposite perspective. Their immediate concern is not so much with women's well-being as with the loss of that well-being, not with the achievement of a success-ful life (which might depend on many things) but with the identification and removal of a certain species of disadvantage that stands as a barrier to that success. In what follows I revert to the conventional approach, so as to ask, for example, whether inequality or the failure to value women's difference are adequate accounts of the disadvantage that women face in the form of sex discrimination.

In considering this question I have focused on the work of Catharine MacKinnon and Drucilla Cornell. I have done so for two reasons. First, both MacKinnon and Cornell adopt radical approaches to the question of women's disadvantage, radical not so much in the sense of urging extravagant conclusions as in the sense of going to the root of the problem. I know of no purer, more uncompromised commitment to the equality of women than that exhibited by MacKinnon, no purer, more uncompromised commitment to the recognition of difference than that exhibited by Cornell. Both writers pursue the ideas to which they have committed themselves to their ultimate conclusion. The consequence of this is that any defect in their accounts is a defect in the very ideas to which they have committed themselves, namely, the ideas of equality and difference, not a defect in the quality of their commitment to those ideas. This means that, in its most undiluted form at least, the work of MacKinnon and Cornell offers an ideal setting for the examination of comparative approaches to the understanding of sex discrimination.[31] If an examination of MacKinnon's work, for example, makes it clear (as I believe it does) that the pursuit of equality is in itself antithetical to the well-being of women, then equality can form no part of the recipe for ending women's disadvantage, for a commitment to equality cannot be rescued by being tempered or supplemented if the nature of its defect is not its radicalism or its incompleteness but its egalitarian character. Not every radical approach to equality would make this clear, but no less radical one could do so.

My second reason for focusing on the work of MacKinnon and Cornell is that both are self-avowed feminists and so see the problem of sex discrimination as something more than the visitation of a general wrong upon women. Both are prepared to contemplate the idea that the practice of sex discrimination is deeply entwined with the prevailing understanding of what it means to be a woman. If that is true, then sex discrimination can be understood only through the work of writers such as them, whose analyses of discrimination are rooted in the present circumstances of women. Even if that were not true, however, the work of such writers would remain as good a place as any to begin an inquiry into the meaning of sex discrimination.

---

[31] For this reason, I have not attempted to give a representative account of either writer's work; my concern is primarily with issues of equality and difference, and only secondarily and consequently with the substance of what MacKinnon and Cornell have had to say. Cornell, in particular, has in recent work somewhat tempered the radicalism of her early writing. To the extent that she has done so, however, she has removed the justification for my consideration of her work, and for that reason I have deliberately chosen not to follow her in this regard.

That said, it is only fair to acknowledge that radical views are often couched in radical style, for many writers believe that fresh conclusions require fresh ways of thinking. This is certainly true of Drucilla Cornell, whose earliest and most radical work draws on postmodern Continental scholarship in an attempt to explore the full implications of the pursuit of difference. In my view it is not possible to assess fairly her account, and the radical promise of difference it offers, other than by coming to terms, to some extent at least, with the method of scholarship she employs. For that reason, as the reader will notice, the chapter on difference represents something of a stylistic departure from the rest of the book. How challenging this is depends upon how familiar the reader is with postmodernist analysis; how inspiring it seems depends upon the reader's sense of the rewards of such analysis. Challenging though it may be, building bridges between fundamentally different ways of thinking about feminism is necessary both to feminism and to scholarship.

2

Equality

In four books published between 1979 and 1994,[1] Catharine MacKinnon, drawing on the record of women's experience of sexual harassment, pornography, and rape, has developed and articulated a trenchant critique of the understanding of sex discrimination prevalent in American law and social practice. In its place she offers a feminism that is entirely unmodified, unqualified by a situation in any larger, more abstract politics of liberalism or socialism.[2] MacKinnon's feminism takes its factual inspiration from the experience of women as told by women, and its analytic method from Marxism. On these bases she constructs a theory of sex discrimination as the unequal distribution of power between men and women, the comprehensive social process by means of which sexuality and gender are defined and constructed so as to maintain the hegemony of men.[3]

MacKinnon's uncompromising approach and powerful rhetoric have succeeded in establishing hers as the most prominent and perhaps most influential feminist voice in American law. Her writing and her advocacy have played a significant part in winning judicial endorsement, not only in the United States but in Canada as well, of the idea that sexual harassment constitutes sex discrimination.[4] More broadly, her general thesis that discrimination is a matter of the subordination and disadvantage[5] of one social group to another has been judicially endorsed as the correct interpretation of the

---

[1] Catharine MacKinnon, *Sexual Harassment of Working Women: A Case of Sex Discrimination* (New Haven, Conn., 1979), *Feminism Unmodified: Discourses on Life and Law* (Cambridge, Mass., 1987), *Toward a Feminist Theory of the State* (Cambridge, Mass., 1989), *Only Words* (London, 1994).

[2] MacKinnon, *Feminism Unmodified*, 6.

[3] *Id.* at 48–50.

[4] *Meritor Savings Bank v. Vinson*, 106 S. Ct. 2399 (1986); *Janzen v. Platy Enterprises*, [1989] 1 S.C.R. 1219.

[5] As MacKinnon herself acknowledges, this thesis draws upon the concept of group disadvantage outlined by Owen Fiss in "Groups and the Equal Protection Clause", 5 *Phil. & Pub. Aff.* 107 (1976): see *Sexual Harassment of Working Women*, *supra* n. 1, at 4, n. 9.

constitutional guarantee of equality contained in Canada's *Charter of Rights and Freedoms*.[6]

Yet when pursued beyond the starkest examples of the degradation of women through sexual harassment, rape, and pornography, MacKinnon's analysis actually offers disappointingly weak support for her intuitive conclusions concerning sex equality. The vocabulary and terms of her critique, the very features that give it its rhetorical fierceness and edge, show themselves to be inadequate bases upon which to articulate a positive agenda for the achievement of women's well-being.[7] The ideal of equality that underlies that critique[8] is not explored or challenged by MacKinnon with anything like the rigour that she brings to the examination of her facts, the physical experience of lives lived in the shadow of male dominance. Ultimately, this analytic failure undermines not only MacKinnon's capacity to move beyond critique but her critique itself, premised as it is upon the inability of present antidiscrimination law to secure the equality that she seeks to describe.

I. Introduction

According to MacKinnon, genuine feminist thought, feminism unmodified by cowardice or compromise, is based upon two insights. First, it recognizes that our concept of sex, our fundamental understanding of maleness and femaleness, is not in any sense natural but is socially constructed.[9] It is thus impossible to speak of women's present position in society as a deviation from what is natural, from what women ought to be entitled to, given their nature. Attempts to analyze discrimination in that way, to determine the respects in which women are by nature the same as or different from men and to treat them accordingly, MacKinnon dubs the difference approach. She contends that the reference point of this approach, its idea of what is natural, is implicitly determined by the existence of men. The difference approach thus neglects the extent to which

---

[6] *Law Society of British Columbia v. Andrews*, [1989] 1 S.C.R. 143. But see *Miron v. Trudel*, [1995] 2 S.C.R. 418; *Egan v. Canada*, [1995] 2 S.C.R. 513; *Thibaudeau v. Canada*, [1995] 2 S.C.R. 627, in which the Court retreated to the very notions of stereotype and relevance rebutted by MacKinnon, a position it endorsed in *Law v. Canada* [1999] 3 S.C.R. 497.

[7] Drucilla Cornell has criticized MacKinnon's work on this basis, arguing that its understanding of women's condition actually serves to perpetuate the forms of oppression that it seeks to undermine. See Drucilla Cornell, "Sexual Difference, the Feminine, and Equivalency: A Critique of MacKinnon's *Toward a Feminist Theory of the State*", 100 *Yale Law Journal* 2247 (1991); *Beyond Accommodation: Ethical Feminism, Deconstruction and the Law* (New York, 1991).

[8] MacKinnon has consistently characterized the prevailing interpretation of discrimination in American law as the difference approach, while characterizing her own thesis initially as the inequality approach and later as the dominance approach: *cf. Sexual Harassment of Working Women*, supra n. 1, at 116, and *Feminism Unmodified*, supra n. 1, at 40. It is clear, however, that the basis for her rejection of dominance is a commitment to equality: see *Feminism Unmodified* at 8, 43.

[9] See *Sexual Harassment of Working Women*, supra n. 1, at 127; *Feminism Unmodified*, supra n. 1, at 25, 41, 54, 173.

the very idea of what is natural in sex has been socially constructed so as to privilege men and disadvantage women.

The second insight of feminism unmodified, then, is that the particular pattern of sexual definition in our society is one of the domination of men and the subordination of women. Society might have constructed sex in equal terms, but in fact it did not do so. The difference approach to sex discrimination thus presents a false picture of symmetry in its suggestion that the differences between men and women are merely reciprocal when in fact they constitute a sexual hierarchy. MacKinnon argues that the dominance of men in our society is not the consequence of sexual difference, but rather that what we know as sexual difference is the result and the reflection of male dominance:

Differences between the sexes do descriptively exist; being a doormat is definitely different from being a man.... One is not socially permitted to be a woman and neither doormat nor man.[10]

To call men and women merely different from one another, then, obscures the fact that the heart of that difference, and the reason for its existence, is the dominance of men.

MacKinnon's exposition of her thesis tends to fuse rather than distinguish these two insights, so that she often equates the social construction of sex with male dominance, and the recognition of sexual difference with biological determinism. In part, this may simply be a matter of rhetorical emphasis, designed to draw an audience's attention to the most critical and contested elements of her thesis, since she clearly contemplates the social reconstruction of sex in egalitarian form. But whatever the reasons, MacKinnon's argument focuses on a global distinction between what she calls the difference and the dominance approaches to the understanding of sex discrimination, rather than on the underlying contrasts of the biological as opposed to the social construction of sex, and of sexual difference as opposed to sexual dominance. It is important to the analysis and understanding of her work, however, and particularly of its broader implications for the well-being of women, to pay attention to these component distinctions in order to appreciate their consequences for the problem of reconstructing sex in a nonhierarchical form.

II. Difference and Dominance

A. The Difference Approach

According to MacKinnon, the approach to equality "that has dominated politics, law and social perception"[11] in the United States regards sex discrimination as

---

[10] *Feminism Unmodified, supra* n. 1, at 8.
[11] *Id.* at 32.

the use of "gender difference in social decision making without justification in what is taken to be gender biology".[12] On this view, if women are treated differently from men for reasons that have no basis in women's nature, that treatment is irrational or arbitrary. The proponents of this view, which MacKinnon calls the difference approach, regard the irrational and arbitrary treatment of people as unequal and discriminatory. They believe that to impose on some a burden from which others are relieved, or to deny to some a benefit that others enjoy, is unequal and discriminatory if no rational basis exists in the character of those people that could justify that distinction. If, for example, a woman is denied the opportunity to perform a task on the ground that as a woman she lacks certain skills, skills that she in fact possesses, she is treated arbitrarily and hence discriminated against on the basis of her sex.

In MacKinnon's words, this is an approach that "tries to map [the] reality" of sexual difference, rather than to change it:[13] "Its underlying story is: on the first day, difference was; on the second day, a division was created upon it; on the third day, irrational instances of dominance arose".[14]

i. THE SAMENESS BRANCH. On MacKinnon's analysis, the difference approach has two branches. The first and predominant branch, which she calls the sameness branch, evaluates women according to their correspondence with the qualities possessed by men. It establishes a single standard of reference for the assessment of discrimination, a standard that is in practice created and maintained by men in their own image, and then asks whether women are capable of meeting that standard. Those women who can meet the standard gain *equal access* to the benefits that men already enjoy.[15]

MacKinnon concedes that this branch of sex discrimination theory has enabled a significant number of women to avoid being disadvantaged on the basis of sex. She argues, however, that it has done so only because and to the extent that those women have ceased to be identifiable as women. On her analysis, the sameness branch simply assesses the degree to which men have been successful in their attempt to construct society and sex in a form that reflects the subordination of women. If subordination has become so much a part of women's social identity that it is regarded as naturally female by men and women alike, disparate treatment of women on that basis is justified. Only if men have failed in their attempt, so that women retain the capacities that society has been designed to deprive them of and consequently function not only like men but as men, yet are treated differently from men, is discrimination found.[16]

---

[12] *Sexual Harassment of Working Women, supra* n. 1, at 110.
[13] *Feminism Unmodified, supra* n. 1, at 44.
[14] *Id.* at 34.
[15] *Id.* at 33–34.
[16] MacKinnon assumes that men and women are naturally equal in their capacities.

The sameness branch of the difference approach thus benefits those rare women who have been so unaffected by their history and culture as to be functionally male, those, that is, whom the social construction of sex has in effect overlooked. For the vast majority of women, who suffer from systemic disadvantage rather than from arbitrary treatment, that is, who suffer from disadvantage that is incorporated in their existence as women, it has nothing to offer:

[It] has in mind people who have not been changed by racism or sexism, who are in the same position as corresponding whites and men, but have irrationally and arbitrarily been treated differently. . . . To the extent to which such groups really are not equal,[17] their status is found legally justified. . . . The approach protects primarily women who for all purposes are socially men, blacks who for all purposes are socially white, leaving untouched those whose lives will never be the same as the more privileged precisely because of race or sex.[18]

MacKinnon implicitly presumes that for the most part the social world functions rationally, and accordingly she regards this approach to the question of sex discrimination as looking for discrimination in the few mistakes made by the system of sexual construction,[19] while overlooking entirely the discrimination that is inherent in the way that sex is constructed. Consequently, she sees it as an approach whose design and structure render it incapable of identifying the very problem of inequality that it purports to address.[20] On the contrary, she claims, it implicitly endorses those inequalities that are so deep-rooted as to have become part of the social structure of sex. Of this approach's standard of reference MacKinnon writes:

It is a racist, sexist standard. If you can prove that you have what are socially white and male qualifications – money, education, credibility – and that you are basically white and male in every cultural way but were oddly mistaken for, say, a Third World woman and so were turned down for some benefit, at that moment the white man may see that you have not been treated equally.[21]

---

[17] MacKinnon refers here to her understanding of equality, rather than to the understanding relied upon by the theory she is criticizing. In fact, however, the difference theory sees equality as the nonarbitrary treatment of people, and so would regard people who have not been treated arbitrarily as equals in terms of that treatment, whatever the differences in their social and economic positions.

[18] *Sexual Harassment of Working Women, supra* n. 1, at 126.

[19] *Feminism Unmodified, supra* n. 1, at 168.

[20] *Id.* at 8: " . . . a discourse of gender difference serves as ideology to neutralize, rationalize and cover disparities of power, even as it appears to criticize them". See also *Sexual Harassment of Working Women, supra* n. 1, at 119: "Antidiscrimination theory, in its antidifferentiation guise, can never confront the issues on which it turns: what social distinctions are based on sex for what reasons, and hence with what permissible consequences?" Here again, as in the text accompanying note 17, MacKinnon assumes that it is the avowed purpose of antidiscrimination policy to address inequality as she sees it, rather than to address arbitrariness or irrationality. That is, she takes prohibitions on arbitrariness to be strategies for the removal of women's disadvantage, not different understandings of inequality itself.

[21] *Feminism Unmodified, supra* n. 1, at 65.

As far as MacKinnon is concerned, this approach to sex discrimination amounts to "an embrace of the model of the oppressor".[22] "[I]f this is feminism, it deserves to die."[23]

For MacKinnon, then, the primary weakness of the sameness branch of the difference approach to sex discrimination is its treatment of the present content of sex as natural or biological rather than socially constructed. This failure to probe the deep structure of society and the foundations of sex there renders the approach incapable of criticizing those differences in the treatment of women that have come to be entrenched in the very existence of women, so as to make women inherently incapable of meeting the standard expected of them, by the very definition of their sex.

Of course, an approach that sees sex as natural might nevertheless conclude that the dominance of one sex over the other is artificial. Difference, in MacKinnon's view, need not imply any form of dominance; it is society that makes differences dominant by assigning value to them.[24] Yet the sameness branch of the difference approach silently takes maleness as the standard against which to measure women, and thus grants to the male sex the unjustified status of a norm. In doing so it hides the fact of male dominance and female subordination behind a mask of mutual difference.

ii. THE DIFFERENCE BRANCH. The second branch of the difference approach to sex discrimination MacKinnon calls the difference branch. Like the sameness branch, it sees men and women in terms of what it regards as their natural differences. Unlike the sameness branch, however, the difference branch evaluates women in terms of their divergence from the qualities possessed by men, rather than their conformity to them. It thus establishes a double standard of reference for the assessment of men and women, and in special circumstances (such as pregnancy) uses a female referent as a basis upon which to compensate women for their inability to meet the male standard. It is on that basis, MacKinnon suggests, that affirmative action programmes and other forms of accommodation have typically been justified.[25]

Under this branch of the difference approach women gain *equal value* for selected aspects of their femaleness, as opposed to the equal access to the

---

[22] *Id.* at 123.

[23] *Id.* at 5, quoting Andrea Dworkin.

[24] *Sexual Harassment of Working Women, supra* n. 1, at 140: "Functional difference cannot by itself justify systematic social inferiority. There is nothing in a difference that dictates inferiority; there is only the society that makes the content of those differences into inferiorities." MacKinnon thus contends that not only the content of sex but the value attached to any application of that content is socially constructed. She believes that societies do not mistake the value of activities engaged in by women, for there is no truth to the value of those activities to mistake. Rather, societies subordinate women by according greater value to the activities they assign to men than to those they assign to women. But see note 64 and accompanying text.

[25] *Feminism Unmodified, supra* n. 1, at 33.

benefits of maleness that they gain through the sameness branch. According to MacKinnon, the difference branch

... views women as men view women: in need of special protection, help, or indulgence. To make out a case, complainants have to meet the male standard for women: femininity.[26]

On its own terms, then, the difference branch looks like special pleading, a case of women attempting to have it both ways.[27] Under the sameness branch women are entitled to the same benefits as men if they can show that they possess the same qualifications as men. Under the difference branch, however, they are granted the same benefits as men despite having different qualifications, treatment that the sameness branch would appear to condemn as discriminatory. For that reason the benefits provided by the difference branch are vulnerable to objection on the basis that they constitute reverse discrimination. MacKinnon suggests that at a minimum the approach is generally regarded as "patronizing but necessary to avoid absurdity".[28] She sees it as asking the following question: " ... should we treat some as the equals of others, even when they may not be entitled to it because they are not up to standard?"[29]

Despite its appearance of special pleading, however, the difference branch might be justified without embarrassment as a principled exception to the broader concept of sex equality embodied in the sameness branch. MacKinnon's criticisms of it, therefore, need to be and in fact are more fundamental than the suggestion that it seems patronizing. In her view, contrary to its appearance and reputation, the essential flaw of the difference branch is that it upholds rather than contravenes the principles underlying the sameness branch, and hence shares their failings. She argues that the difference branch, as much as the sameness branch, implicitly relies on maleness for its standard of reference, though in this case assessing women in terms of their inability rather than their ability to comply with it:

... for purposes of sex discrimination law, to be a woman means either to be like a man or to be like a lady. We have to meet either the male standard for males [the sameness branch] or the male standard for females [the difference branch].[30]

Accordingly, MacKinnon is deeply critical of those feminist theorists, such as Carol Gilligan, who in her view build upon the difference branch by seeking to describe and value the character and capacities of women as they are presently formed and understood. For MacKinnon, the characteristics that we know as

[26] *Id.* at 71.
[27] *Id.* at 33, 39, 71.
[28] *Id.* at 33.
[29] *Id.* at 43.
[30] *Id.* at 71.

female are nothing other than the manifestations in sexual identity of the conditions of oppression under which women's lives have been led. Women who seek to endorse and value their qualities as women in fact endorse the concept of femaleness that has been constructed by men, and hence confirm and sustain their own subordination. Of Gilligan's thesis that women speak in "a different voice", MacKinnon observes:

> . . . she achieves for moral reasoning what the special protection rule achieves in law: the affirmative rather than the negative valuation of that which has accurately distinguished women from men, by making it seem as though those attributes, with their consequences, really are somehow ours, rather than what male supremacy has attributed to us for its own use. For women to affirm difference, when difference means dominance, as it does with gender, means to affirm the qualities and characteristics of powerlessness.[31]

MacKinnon argues that while the voice that women speak in is undoubtedly distinctively female, it is paradoxically and more fundamentally the voice of men, the voice that men have invented for women to speak in, the voice given to those who occupy the subordinate roles that men have invented for women to perform. For MacKinnon, the attempt to regard this voice as women's own and to value and appreciate it as such is merely "a sentimentalization of our oppression as women":[32]

> I do not think that the way women reason morally is morality "in a different voice". I think it is morality in a higher register, in the feminine voice. Women value care because men have valued us according to the care we give them. . . . Women think in relational terms because our existence is defined in relation to men.[33]

Furthermore, MacKinnon argues, not only does the difference branch fail to see that what it describes as women's voice is in fact the voice created for women by men, but it fails to see that this voice is not so much different as subordinated. Women's voice is the voice of the dominated, as much in what it is compelled to leave unsaid as in what it is driven to say:

> . . . when you are powerless, you don't just speak differently. A lot, you don't speak. . . . You aren't just deprived of a language with which to articulate your distinctiveness, although you are; you are deprived of a life out of which articulation might come. Not being heard is not just a function of lack of recognition, not just that no one knows how to listen to you, although it is that; it is also silence of the deep kind, the silence of being prevented from having anything to say.[34]

Like the sameness branch, then, the difference branch treats as natural sexual differences that MacKinnon believes are socially constructed. Accordingly, it

---

[31] *Id.* at 38–39.
[32] *Id.* at 123.
[33] *Id.* at 39.
[34] *Id.*

mistakenly regards as inherent in women's nature, and then seeks to value or
to accommodate, characteristics that have actually been assigned to women by
the power structures of society. Those characteristics, MacKinnon maintains,
are the hallmarks of powerlessness, and are no more naturally female than they
are naturally black or naturally aboriginal. Their female character, she argues,
is the consequence, not the cause of their location in women.

Like the sameness branch too, therefore, the difference branch conceals sexual hierarchy behind a mask of sexual difference. The women's voice that it
calls different is in fact subordinate; the difference that it notices is not the reciprocal difference of men from women and women from men but the difference
of women from the norm established by men.

Overall, then, the failure of the difference approach in both its branches is
the failure to probe the nature and origins of the differences between men and
women, a failure to make those differences themselves the subject of political
criticism. Instead of challenging sexual difference, the approach focuses on the
consequences that can legitimately be attributed to it. In MacKinnon's view,
however, the fundamental inequality of men and women can be understood only
through an analysis that reveals the artificiality of the dominance of men over
women, and its reflection in the construction of the sexes as we know them.

B. The Dominance Approach

For MacKinnon, the inequality of men and women, properly understood as
the dominance of men over women,[35] is the source of the difference between
the sexes rather than one of the possible consequences of that difference.[36]
Discrimination against women is not a matter of treating women arbitrarily or
irrationally, but of treating them as less.[37] It is to be looked for not merely in
individual decisions that disfavour women but in the fabric of society as a whole
and the manner in which it constructs the concepts of maleness and femaleness,
for it is through the definition of sex that the subordination of women is primarily
established and enforced.[38] The pursuit of equality is thus a matter of probing
the social construction of sex, and demanding an end to hierarchy there.

In MacKinnon's words, this is an approach that "tries to challenge and
change" the reality of sexual difference, rather than merely to map it:[39]

Here, on the first day that matters, dominance was achieved, probably by force. By
the second day, division along the same lines had to be relatively firmly in place. On

---

[35] To repeat, in *Sexual Harassment of Working Women, supra* n. 1, MacKinnon calls this approach
the inequality approach; in *Feminism Unmodified, supra* n. 1, she calls it the dominance approach.
"In this approach, an equality question is a question of the distribution of power" (*id.* at 40).

[36] *Feminism Unmodified, supra* n. 1, at 51.

[37] *Id.* at 43.

[38] *Id.* at 51.

[39] *Id.* at 44; see also *id.* at 40.

the third day, if not sooner, differences were demarcated, together with social systems to exaggerate them in perception and in fact, *because* the systematically differential delivery of benefits and deprivations required making no mistake about who was who.[40]

i. THE SOCIAL CONSTRUCTION OF GENDER. For MacKinnon, as I have emphasized, gender is a social rather than a biological condition. As she puts it, "[g]ender has no basis in anything other than the social reality its hegemony constructs".[41] People's existence as men or as women is established by their birth, but their existence as male or as female is established by society. "Masks become personas become people, especially when they are enforced."[42] Being a man, therefore, is not a necessary, nor always a sufficient condition for the enjoyment of male power: some men lack access to that power; some women can aspire to it:[43]

[T]he fundamental assumption of the inequality approach . . . is that the social meaning given to the gender difference has little or no biological foundation, nor is biology itself even particularly relevant. The issue is not that some differences are social while others are biological, but which of the social disadvantages of sex courts will prohibit.[44]

In the case of our society, the governing basis for the construction of sexual identity is and always has been the dominance of men and the subordination of women. What we perceive as the male sex, therefore, is the record of the dominance of men, and what we perceive as the female is the record of the subordination of women. In short, maleness describes the qualities associated with the exercise of power; femaleness describes the qualities associated with the condition of powerlessness. Those women who gain a degree of power become male to that extent; those men who lose it correspondingly become

---

[40] *Id.* at 40.

[41] *Id.* at 173. MacKinnon's argument here might be criticized for its reliance on the existence of a natural dominance that her theory denies. If on the first day that matters men achieved dominance by force (see note 40 and accompanying text), they then enjoyed some degree of natural dominance: those who can achieve dominance by force by definition possess the capacity to dominate. Yet she denies that any dominant quality is natural to one sex and not the other: see her discussion of physical strength, *id.* at 120. In my view, however, there is no conflict between these two positions. MacKinnon acknowledges the existence of a limited number of biological distinctions between men and women, centred on their different reproductive capacities. Those distinctions could have enabled men to exercise at least temporary power over women, and so institute a hierarchy within which all subsequent sexual differences have been drawn. The fact that a biological feature enabled hierarchy to be established is not a refutation of her thesis. It does not show that sexual hierarchy is natural, or is sustained by biology.

[42] *Id.* at 119. ". . . social conditions shape thought as well as life. Gender either is or is not such a social condition. I'm claiming that it is" (*id.* at 54).

[43] *Id.* at 52.

[44] *Sexual Harassment of Working Women, supra* n. 1, at 121.

female. In this way hierarchy constructs sexual difference as we know it.[45]
Addressing her audience, MacKinnon observes:

Me, for instance, standing up here talking to you – socially this is an exercise of male
power. It's hierarchical, it's dominant, it's authoritative. You're listening, I'm talking;
I'm active, you're passive. I'm expressing myself; you're taking notes.[46]

As inequality of power constructs sex so it constructs sexuality. Sexuality,
MacKinnon argues, is simply the eroticization of the patterns of dominance
and submission found in sex, so that questions of desire can never be isolated
from questions of power.[47] It follows that the erotic is inextricably connected
with the violent, that the violation of women by men that is dramatized in
pornography and enforced through rape constitutes sexuality as most men and
women understand it.[48] All sexual relations are in this sense sadomasochistic:[49]

I think that sexual desire in women, at least in this culture, is socially constructed as
that by which we come to want our own self-annihilation. That is, our subordination
is eroticized in and as female; in fact, we get off on it to a degree, if nowhere near as
much as men do. . . . I'm saying femininity as we know it is how we come to want male
dominance, which most emphatically is not in our interest.[50]

As sex informs sexuality so it informs the construction of those other features
of the social fabric within which men's and women's lives are led. In this way
the patterns of dominance identified as the male sex become norms for society,
endorsed and believed in by both men and women:

Man's position of power does not only assure his relative superiority over the woman,
but it assures that his standards become generalized as generically human standards that
are to govern the behavior of men and women alike.[51]

---

[45] " . . . men are not socially supreme and women subordinate by nature; the fact that socially
they are, constructs the sex difference as we know it." "The question of equality . . . is at root a
question of hierarchy, which – as power succeeds in constructing social perception and social
reality – derivatively becomes a categorical distinction, a difference" (*Feminism Unmodified*,
supra n. 1, at 51, 40).

[46] *Id.* at 52.

[47] *Id.* at 50, 171–74.

[48] *Id.* at 161–62: " . . . sexuality is commonly violent without being any the less sexual. To deny this
sets up the situation so that when women are aroused by sexual violation, meaning we experience
it *as* our sexuality, the feminist analysis is seen to be contradicted. But it is not contradicted,
it is *proved*. The male supremacist definition of female sexuality as lust for self-annihilation
has won. . . . To reject forced sex in the name of women's point of view requires an account
of women's experience of being violated by the same acts both sexes have learned as natural
and fulfilling and erotic, since no critique, no alternatives, and few transgressions have been
permitted." On this analysis, it is indeed the case, and ought not to be, that sexual display by
women is a display of submissiveness.

[49] *Id.* at 161.

[50] *Id.* at 54.

[51] *Sexual Harassment of Working Women*, *supra* n. 1, at 3, quoting Georg Simmel, *Philosophische
Kultur* (Leipzig, 1911).

It will be recalled that the difference approach, in its sameness branch, defines sex discrimination as the refusal to recognize women's capacity to meet that norm. Nevertheless, when women genuinely lack that capacity, so that a refusal to recognize it in them is apparently nondiscriminatory, the difference branch will in some situations authorize programmes to compensate them for their inadequacy. Such programmes are often described as affirmative action for women; men implicitly have no need of them. However, MacKinnon argues in a famous passage, the reason why women appear to need such programmes while men do not is that an affirmative action programme for men is already built into the structure of society, and concealed there as a neutral norm:[52]

In reality . . . virtually every quality that distinguishes men from women is already affirmatively compensated in this society. Men's physiology defines most sports, their needs define auto and health insurance coverage, their socially defined workplace biographies define workplace expectations and successful career patterns, their perspectives and concerns define quality in scholarship, their experiences and obsessions define merit, their objectification of life defines art, their military service defines citizenship, their presence defines family, their inability to get along with each other – their wars and rulerships – defines history, their image defines god, and their genitals define sex. For each of their differences from women, what amounts to an affirmative action plan is in effect, otherwise known as the structure and values of American society.[53]

It must be emphasized that MacKinnon's inquiry into the nature and origins of sex is not intended to be a criticism of the fact that sex has been socially constructed. In her view, there is no basis other than social decision upon which to construct sex, since biology has little or nothing to contribute to the roles played by men and women in society. What she is critical of, and seeks to expose, is, first, the goal of male dominance that has governed the construction of sex as it now exists; second, the presentation of that social and political goal as a natural or biological fact; and third, its subsequent endorsement as the social norm against which the capacities of men and women, and their inequalities, are to be assessed.

ii. ENDING HIERARCHY. For MacKinnon, equality means the equal distribution of power. Sexual inequality, therefore, "is at root a question of hierarchy",[54] a matter of "systematic dominance, of male supremacy".[55] In other words, "gender is an inequality first",[56] and a difference second, not a difference first and an inequality second. In MacKinnon's view, sexual identity as it has been formed in our society is to be condemned simply for the fact that it enshrines

---

[52] *Feminism Unmodified, supra* n. 1, at 65, 71.
[53] *Id.* at 36.
[54] *Id.* at 40.
[55] *Id.* at 42.
[56] *Id.*

a power relation, and thus sustains the ability of one group of people to obtain and consolidate power over another. The sexual difference that hierarchy has produced

describe[s] the systematic relegation of an entire group of people to a condition of inferiority and attribute[s] it to their nature. If this differential were biological, maybe biological intervention would have to be considered.[57]

What MacKinnon finds objectionable in the present structure of sexual re-lations, therefore, is not that men hold power rather than women, or that men hold power exclusively rather than jointly with women, but that power, in the sense of dominance, is held at all. She makes clear that she rejects any theory of equality whose ambition is no greater than to admit women to a share in the spoils of dominance:[58] "To us [feminists] it is a male notion that power means that someone must dominate. We seek a transformation in the terms and conditions of power itself."[59]

Nevertheless, it is not entirely clear what MacKinnon understands power to mean here, that is, under what circumstances she believes that a group of people can be said to be dominant in society. It is not that her argument suffers from any shortage of examples of dominance and subordination; on the contrary, it is sustained throughout by images of women's social predicament. What is unclear is what principle MacKinnon sees as uniting these examples and explaining them as subordination.

MacKinnon argues that the mere existence of differences between people does not in itself require the existence of a hierarchy among them.[60] She fur-ther maintains that any kind of dominance or hierarchy is illegitimate in an egalitarian society.[61] Yet she fails to articulate a coherent thesis of the rela-tionship between difference and dominance. Dominance begets differences, she makes clear.[62] Differences need not beget dominance, she maintains.[63] Yet some differences must beget dominance or dominance would not need to beget difference in order to sustain itself.[64] The question is, which of the present and potential differences between the sexes have this effect, that is, which of them

[57] *Id.* at 41.
[58] *Id.* at 4, 31.
[59] *Id.* at 23.
[60] *Sexual Harassment of Working Women, supra* n. 1, at 140. See also note 24.
[61] *Feminism Unmodified, supra* n. 1, at 43.
[62] *Id.* at 51.
[63] See note 24 and accompanying text.
[64] The differences that are assigned to men and to women in order to ensure the dominance of men must do something more than distinguish those who are to be benefited from those who are to be burdened, in the way that the biology of reproduction distinguishes the sexes and skin colour the races. Otherwise, the assignment of difference would be unnecessary, since it would add nothing to the distinction that biology has already drawn. The differences in question must be such as to generate a hierarchy by their nature, at least in the society in which they are called into being.

enshrine male dominance and which do not, and what principle describes the distinction? There seem to be three possibilities present in MacKinnon's work.

At the most concrete level, male dominance is presented by MacKinnon as the sexual subjugation of women. Much of her work is concerned with, and draws its power from, women's account of their sexual harassment, battery, rape, prostitution, and child sexual abuse, and the representation of all these in pornography.[65] It might plausibly be inferred that these practices constitute male dominance, which could be ended, therefore, by their successful prohibition.

Yet it is clear that MacKinnon sees these violations of women, crucial though they are to the understanding of subordination, as merely the most outrageous and demeaning examples of male dominance, not as its definition. The subordination of women is also present in their poverty, in what MacKinnon calls their "material desperation".[66] The ending of dominance, she argues, requires not only the physical protection of women but the achievement of such goals as full access to abortion,[67] the sharing of child care responsibilities,[68] and the guarantee of equal pay, including wages for housework.[69] The meaning of dominance cannot be confined, therefore, to sexual subjugation in the physical sense, although MacKinnon would certainly call the subjugation it involves sexual.[70]

At a broader, but still sex-based level, male dominance is frequently presented by MacKinnon as a matter of degradation, the consignment of the female sex to a status of acute and entrenched inferiority, a status akin to that of blacks in the United States. As support for this view of women's subordination, she draws a number of parallels between the condition of women and that of blacks,[71] although she makes it clear that she regards the condition of women

---

[65] *Id.* at 41, 171.

[66] *Id.* at 41.

[67] *Id.* at 99.

[68] *Id.* at 37.

[69] *Id.* at 24, 28, 41.

[70] This follows from her thesis that sexuality is shaped by the patterns of dominance and subordination in which it is set. If men are in any sense dominant, that dominance will be eroticized as sexuality.

[71] See, for example, *id.* at 167. Feminists have often been vigorously criticized for their invocation of a distinction between the condition of women and blacks as disadvantaged groups, a distinction that is said to imply that women are not black and that blacks are not women. The effect of this distinction, it is argued, is to render black women invisible to both feminist and race theory: see, for example, bell hooks, *Ain't I a Woman: Black Women and Feminism* (Boston, 1981). Similar points have been made from the lesbian perspective. This line of criticism seems inapt with regard to Catharine MacKinnon, however, whose understanding of disadvantage transcends the borders of sex, race, and class: see notes 78–91 and accompanying text. In other words, paradoxically, despite her clear and powerful personal commitment to the feminist cause, MacKinnon's theory is primarily concerned with disadvantage and only consequently concerned with women. Indeed, it is fundamental to her argument that women are knowable only in terms of the condition of powerlessness that they share with blacks and the poor. Her theory is not so much inattentive to the condition of black women, therefore, as inattentive to and undistracted by any and all shadings in the character of powerlessness: see her criticism of Carol Gilligan.

as more degraded than that even of blacks, since anything that black men suffer black women suffer more. "If bottom is bottom, look across time and space, and women are who you will find there":[72]

To argue that sex oppression is a pale sister of racial oppression, so that even to compare them mocks the degradation of blacks and minimizes the violence of racism, strongly underestimates the degradation and systematic brutality, physical as well as emotional, that women sustain every day at the hands of men.[73]

MacKinnon maintains that sexual subordination is comparable to racial subordination because both involve "the stigmatization and exploitation and denigration of a group of people on the basis of a condition of birth".[74] When whiteness and maleness define the meaning of humanity for a society, by establishing the standards of human behaviour there, to be black or to be a woman is literally to be less than human.[75]

On the basis of this kind of argument, MacKinnon might plausibly be interpreted as contending that dominance means conferring the status of a norm upon the set of characteristics that describes white males as different from women and blacks, a status achieved by means of the social construction of sex and of race.[76] Ending dominance, on that analysis, would be a matter of ending the present degradation of women and blacks by reconstructing the meaning of sex and race so as to ensure that in the future social norms are no longer defined exclusively in terms of white male characteristics: "Once no amount of difference justifies treating women as subhuman, eliminating that is what equality law is for."[77]

This reading of dominance and subordination seems to come much closer to the heart of what MacKinnon understands hierarchy to mean. To appreciate her position fully, however, it is necessary to go one step further, and not to be misled by her use of terms such as degradation, oppression, brutality, and subhuman treatment, or by her references to the status of a group of people who once were enslaved and who have never fully escaped the consequences of that fact. MacKinnon emphasizes throughout her work that dominance and subordination, as she understands them, are present in any social practice that

---

[72] *Id.*

[73] *Sexual Harassment of Working Women, supra* n. 1, at 129. See also *id.*: the history of sexual distinctions in society is "no less vicious, wasteful, or unwarranted, than the history of racial distinction".

[74] *Feminism Unmodified, supra* n. 1, at 167.

[75] It is difficult to reconcile this argument and other examples of the devaluation of women with MacKinnon's thesis that the male and female sexes are entirely defined by their roles of dominance and subordination. See notes 93 to 104 and accompanying text.

[76] See, for example, *id.* at 65: "The white man's meaning of equality . . . has not valued any cultural or sexual distinctiveness except his own."

[77] *Id.* at 43.

treats a group of people as inferior in any respect.[78] That is true whether or not the practice is based on functional differences,[79] whether or not the differences, if functional, are conditions of birth,[80] and whether or not the treatment reaches the level of brutality.[81] In short, dominance is present in any difference that implies the inferiority of those defined by it. As MacKinnon puts it in the context of sexual dominance:

If sex inequalities are approached as matters of imposed status, which are in need of change if a legal mandate of equality means anything at all, *the question whether women should be treated unequally means simply whether women should be treated as less.*[82]

On MacKinnon's analysis, therefore, the ending of dominance and hierarchy is a matter of recognizing that

... discrimination consists in the systematic disadvantagement of social groups. This approach to inequality is marked by the understanding that *sex discrimination is a system that defines women as inferior from men*, as well as ignores their similarities.[83]

Understood in this way, however, dominance and hierarchy have implications well beyond the issues of sex and race and their treatment in antidiscrimination law. Indeed, MacKinnon makes it clear that in her view unequal power relations are as present in the social practices that distribute wealth as they are in the social practices that define sex and race.[84] Just as the social construction of sex defines women in terms that ensure their inferior status, so the social construction and valuation of other human characteristics define the poor, most of them female but many male, in terms that ensure their poverty.[85] If the basic reality of the subordination of women to men is that "[w]omen are seen as not worth much",[86]

---

[78] See, for example, her assertion that a speaker addressing an audience is engaging in an exercise of male power, at note 46 and accompanying text.

[79] *Sexual Harassment of Working Women, supra* n. 1, at 140.

[80] *Id.* at 117, 121.

[81] *Id.* at 105: "Under an inequality approach, detrimental differentiations based on sex are discriminatory. ..."

[82] *Feminism Unmodified, supra* n. 1, at 43. My emphasis. See also *Toward a Feminist Theory of the State, supra* n. 1, at 248: speaking of what sex equality law would look like under the dominance approach, MacKinnon writes: "Statistical proofs of disparity would be conclusive."

[83] *Sexual Harassment of Working Women, supra* n. 1, at 116. My emphasis.

[84] *Feminism Unmodified, supra* n. 1, at 61: "My second urgent question [for explanation and for organizing] has to do with class and with race. I would like to see some consideration of the connections between the theory of sexuality I have outlined and the forms of property possession and ownership *and* the erotization [*sic*] of racial degradation and money. A third urgent issue is the relation between everything I've said and all forms of inequality. Am I describing only one form within a larger system, or is this *the* system, or is this too abstract a question?"

[85] *Id.* at 4, n. 9: Speaking critically of Owen Fiss's theory of group disadvantage, MacKinnon writes: "Treatment of the poor, a group that is, after all, totally socially created, is grudging to the point of exclusion."

[86] *Feminism Unmodified, supra* n. 1, at 171.

then clearly the poor are subordinated in MacKinnon's sense, since by definition they are seen as not worth much.

Subordination may thus be established through economic as well as through sexual and racial practices. All of these practices may be used to the same end, and in fact all are; each sustains the ability of one group of people to obtain and consolidate power over another. Accordingly, MacKinnon specifically rejects any interpretation of group disadvantage that addresses sexual subordination but fails to address the condition of the poor.[87] She insists that blacks and women should be entitled to relief from disadvantage not only on the basis of their race and sex, but also on the basis of any other social practices that make them poor:[88]

We need to systematically understand in order to criticize and change, rather than repro-duce, the connection between the [general] fact that the few have ruled and used the many in their own interest and for their own pleasure as well as profit and the [gender-specific] fact that those few have been men.[89]

And further:

. . . gender in this country appears partly to comprise the meaning of, as well as bisect, race and class, even as race and class specificities make up, as well as cross-cut, gender. A general theory of social inequality is prefigured, if inchoately, in these connections.[90]

This comprehensive understanding of dominance and subordination, then, ap-pears to be what MacKinnon has in mind when she says: "To us [feminists] it is a male notion that power means someone must dominate. We seek a trans-formation in the terms and conditions of power itself."[91]

III. Implications

One might disagree with MacKinnon's contention that sex is a social rather than a biological construct, or with her assumption that what has been socially constructed can be socially reconstructed through an act of collective will. One might also disagree that equality requires us to abolish all social hierarchies, and therefore to eliminate any dominance of one sex by the other in any respect. It is possible that one could construct a response to her work on either or both of these grounds.

---

[87] *Sexual Harassment of Working Women, supra* n. 1, at 4, n. 9.
[88] *Id.*: In rejecting Owen Fiss's approach to group disadvantage, she writes: "Since poverty is not seen to be completely all-pervasive, cultural, disabling, maintained by false consciousness, and as difficult to change as the meaning of being black, it seems unlikely that women would fare well under this interpretation."
[89] *Id.* at 61–62.
[90] *Feminism Unmodified, supra* n. 1, at 2–3.
[91] *Id.* at 23.

It seems to me, however, that neither of these grounds is the most fruitful basis on which to assess the merits of her argument. I find it more enlightening to explore the consequences of her argument on her own terms. In particular, the implications of her two main theses – first, that the differences between people are entirely socially created, and second, that those differences amount to inequality whenever they define one group of people as inferior to another in any respect – need to be pursued to their conclusions. This is something that MacKinnon herself does not do. Indeed, it is a notable feature of her exposition that her discussion of the ideal of equality, and the changes required to achieve it, is much briefer and less assured than her description of the physical circumstances of sexual inequality. Her ear for what women have to say seems acute, and her understanding of the nature of their predicament, of the ways in which they have been dominated, devalued, and silenced, appears to be rich and attentive. Yet she says little of what it would ultimately take for women to be empowered and valued, of what it would mean for women's voice to be heard in full.

This is not to suggest that MacKinnon is under any obligation to define a solution to the problem she describes. It is to say, however, that her analysis must be compatible with such a solution. In the absence of any extended consideration by her of the problem of reconstructing sex and other social differences in a nonhierarchical form, there is reason to be concerned about the consequences of her argument in favour of sex equality. It seems to me that the only way to meet that concern is to pursue those consequences sympathetically, in terms of MacKinnon's own analysis.

I do not intend at this stage, therefore, to question the substance of her theses, and will proceed rather on the basis of her own assumptions, namely, that sex is in fact a social construct, that in our society it has been constructed in such a way as to establish and entrench the dominance of men over women, and that the only legitimate basis on which it can be reconstructed is the ending of that dominance.

A. The Social Construction of Sexual Identity

If sexual identity as we know it has been entirely socially constructed, if it has no basis in either nature or biology, then there can be no basis for its reconstruction other than social decision.[92] On this view, their different reproductive systems aside, men and women are by nature blank slates, indistinguishable in their

---

[92] I do not mean to suggest that there is no constraint of any kind upon such social decision, for in that case there would be nothing to complain of in sex as we know it. I point out only that there is no constraint upon such social decision in the facts of nature. Clearly, any social reconstruction of sex will be legitimate only if it is based upon a morally enlightened attitude to the relations between human beings, which for MacKinnon is a commitment to the avoidance of hierarchy. On that issue, see the next subsection.

capacity to be created and defined by the society in which they live. Neither sex has a presocial, natural character that can be referred to in order to establish its true identity or reveal its equality with the other. On the other hand, the character that has been inscribed by society over the course of human history upon the blank slate provided by nature, namely, the content of sex as we know it, while true, is illegitimate, and so must be replaced. In short, there is no true meaning to sex other than the meaning that MacKinnon seeks to reject. This view of the origins of sex has a number of significant implications.

First, if women have no natural existence as women, it cannot be the case that *their* voice has been silenced. Women may indeed have been assigned the role of silence. They may have been prevented from speaking at all,[93] or they may have been prevented from using language as others do and as they might wish to.[94] They may have been assigned silent roles, that is, in a society in which voice is an aspect of dominance. But they cannot have been silenced *as women*, for in MacKinnon's theory there is no inherently female voice to silence. There cannot have been any suppression of a natural or genuine female identity, because no such identity exists.[95] Accordingly, women's nature cannot be awakened or revealed; it can only be invented.

What is striking about MacKinnon's treatment of this aspect of her argument is that the only programme of invention she offers for the reconstruction of sex is the avoidance of hierarchy. That programme, however, is not in any sense distinctively female. On the contrary, MacKinnon emphasizes that subordination within a hierarchy, as she understands it, is experienced by blacks, the poor, and women alike. She specifically rejects any interpretation of subordination that would focus on sex- or race-based disadvantage to the exclusion of that experienced by the poor. On her account, disadvantage is not based on the content of sex or race; the content of sex and race is based on disadvantage.[96] Women who pursue her programme for equality, therefore, may escape subordination, but in doing so they can neither discover nor invent themselves as women.

The corollary to this view of the origins of sexual identity, as MacKinnon herself points out, is that nothing of what now defines women can be said to be intrinsically theirs. Our society has assigned certain qualities to women, and those qualities have thereby become women's qualities for us: both men and women claim to recognize them as such. In truth, however, those apparently female qualities have been established by the social decision of men. What we see as women's features, therefore, are no more than the features of men's

---

[93] See *id.* at 45: "Take your foot off our necks, then we will hear in what tongue women speak."

[94] I include here the idea that they may have been prevented from having anything to say, from having a life out of which articulation might come, so as to suffer what MacKinnon calls silence of the deep kind: see *id.* at 39.

[95] In the absence of legitimate social action establishing it, which has yet to take place. See following paragraph and note 104.

[96] See notes 88–89 and accompanying text.

purpose, and where that purpose has been to create and maintain a hierarchy, they are simply the features of subordination. If subordination wears a different guise in women than it does in blacks or in the poor, that too is the result of the social decision of men. Women have no distinctive or inherent claim even to a subordinate identity.

It is for this reason that MacKinnon rejects Carol Gilligan's attempt to discern and describe qualities that could be said to constitute women's different voice. Given male dominance, the voice and the qualities that Gilligan sees as women's are in fact men's. They are the characteristics of the oppressors, not of the oppressed. It is merely a sentimentalization of oppression, MacKinnon charges, to attempt to value them as women's.[97]

Furthermore, the more successful and thus comprehensive the construction of sex, the more difficult it is for women to define themselves in opposition to it, as MacKinnon again points out. If the construction of sex is effectively governed by an all-embracing purpose, it may be impossible for women to develop a perspective from which to criticize it. Women in that position are the victims of a consciousness that might be called false if there were any that could be called truer:

What I've learned from women's experience with sexuality is that exploitation and degradation produce grateful complicity in exchange for survival. They produce self-loathing to the point of extinction of self, and it is respect for self that makes resistance conceivable. The issue is not why women acquiesce but why we ever do anything but.[98]

The second dimension of the thesis that sex is socially constructed is that men also lack any natural identity as men. It cannot be the case, then, that authority has been conferred upon the male voice and male identity. On the contrary, men have assigned themselves roles that are the correlatives of those they have assigned to women: they speak where women are silent, and they are understood where women are not.[99] But in so doing they do not speak in the male voice, but in the voice of dominance; they are not understood as men, but as those with the power to establish the terms and conditions of understanding. Those terms and conditions are not male in any sense other than that of their having been established by those they define as men.[100] The character of men

---

[97] *Id.* at 123. Drucilla Cornell, however, maintains that MacKinnon also understands women as men wish them to be understood, in terms of their oppression. MacKinnon, Cornell alleges, endorses that reality, although she refuses to value it. See *Beyond Accommodation, supra* n. 7, at 124.

[98] *Feminism Unmodified, supra* n. 1, at 61.

[99] See *id.* at 37 ("... men's differences from women are equal to women's differences from men"); 42 ("... men are as different from women as women are from men, but socially the sexes are not equally powerful"); 51 ("Feminists have noticed that women and men are equally different but not equally powerful").

[100] *Cf. id.* at 173: "Gender has no basis in anything other than the social reality its hegemony constructs. Gender is what gender means. The process that gives sexuality its male supremacist

as a sex, the male identity as we know it, is no more, therefore, than a reflection of the dominance enjoyed by men.[101]

It cannot be true, then, as MacKinnon at times appears to suggest, that the male identity has formed the social world.[102] Rather, the experience of social dominance has formed male identity.[103] Seekers of equality can find nothing male in men, therefore, except the fact of dominance. Consequently, they cannot end the hegemony of men except by abolishing hegemony itself, or relocating it in women. It may be for this reason that MacKinnon calls for the ending of all forms of dominance and hierarchy, rather than for the ending of male dominance.

None of this is intended to suggest that in order to be inherent and genuine, sexual characteristics must be founded in biology. It is simply intended to clarify and to develop the implications of MacKinnon's claim that sex is entirely socially constructed. The primary consequence of that claim is that the only basis for the reconstruction of sex is social decision. It follows that critics of existing sexual roles cannot appeal to the natural as a basis for their criticism. It is indeed possible and perhaps necessary to speak of women's subordination and oppression in order to describe the role that women now play in society. It is not possible, however, to associate that subordination with the suppression of genuinely female qualities.[104]

meaning is the same process through which gender equality becomes socially real." MacKinnon criticizes the difference approach for endorsing a male referent, but her critique reveals that what is called a male referent is not male at all, but dominance located in men. What the difference approach endorses are the criteria of dominance.

[101] Or if men have assigned themselves features for reasons other than the dominance of women, they have subsequently assigned dominant value to those features. In that way, difference is made dominant. See *Sexual Harassment of Working Women, supra* n. 1, at 140.

[102] See *Feminism Unmodified, supra* n. 1, at 36. There may indeed be an affirmative action plan in effect for men, "... otherwise known as the structure and values of American society", but it cannot be a plan that affirmatively compensates men for their differences from women, apart from those few differences conceded to be biological. MacKinnon asserts that "[m]en's physiology defines most sports..." and in a supporting note cites a ban on breast protection in boxing. That physiological difference, being part of the reproductive system, is clearly biological, but MacKinnon is careful elsewhere to challenge the biological basis of physical capacities such as strength: see *id.* at 120. On other sexual distinctiveness, see *id.* at 65.

[103] See, for example, MacKinnon's discussion of athletics, *id.* at 121.

[104] As indicated at note 95, this follows from the contention that genuinely female qualities do not exist in the absence of legitimate social action establishing them. If what is genuinely female cannot be found either in nature or in the product of illegitimate social actions based upon dominance, it can be established only through legitimate social action that has yet to take place. On one view, therefore, what is genuinely female has not been suppressed because it has not yet been created and defined.

On another view, however, it could be argued that what is genuinely female has been suppressed in the prospective or imaginative sense. From that perspective, women have been denied the opportunity to become what legitimate social action would have permitted them to become. However, MacKinnon defines legitimate social action as that which avoids dominance, understood broadly and not in terms of sex. While the absence of legitimate social action has denied women *legitimate* qualities, therefore, that is, qualities not based upon subordination,

Nor, on this thesis, can critics of existing sexual roles maintain that women are entitled to share the qualities that define men as a sex. Those qualities are no more than the qualities of dominance produced by the system of sexual subordination. As such, they could be shared by a minority of women but they could not coherently be shared by all. MacKinnon herself makes this clear in rejecting the difference approach to discrimination on the basis that it would do no more than admit a few women to a share in the spoils of dominance.[105]

Nor is it possible, on this thesis, to suggest that some selection of the qualities that at present define women as a sex should be valued in the same way that men's qualities are valued. What we know as women's qualities are the qualities of subordination, and hence to value them is to value subordination. What MacKinnon seeks are the qualities of sexual equality, and those are as yet unknown.

Ultimately, if it is true that sex is merely the product of social decision, it is necessary to establish the proper basis for social decision. For MacKinnon the exclusive, or at least the governing, basis for the social reconstruction of sex is the avoidance of hierarchy.[106]

B. Ending Hierarchy

If ending hierarchy is the goal that is to animate the reconstruction of sex, then the differences that are henceforth to define men and women must be established in such a way that they neither express nor foster dominance, nor lend themselves to conversion into dominance. This will have to be true not merely of the differences between men and women, but of the differences that are to distinguish any one group of people from another, whether on racial, cultural, physical, intellectual, or other grounds, since MacKinnon's condemnation of dominance extends to all forms of difference that define one group of people as subordinate to another, whatever the context.

i. LIVES AND THEIR ASSESSMENT. In discussing our present understanding of the different physical abilities possessed by men and women, MacKinnon observes:

It is not that men are trained to be strong and women are just not trained. Men are trained to be strong and women are trained to be weak. It's not *not* learned; it's very specifically learned.[107]

---

it cannot have denied them legitimately *female* qualities, since MacKinnon's idea of what is legitimate is not sex-specific. See note 95 and accompanying text.

[105] *Id.* at 4, 31.

[106] Presumably, MacKinnon would acknowledge that the reconstruction of sex may be animated by goals other than the ending of dominance, but she would insist that those goals be compatible with the ending of dominance, that is, that they not enable one sex to dominate the other in any way. As indicated in section III above, I intend not to question MacKinnon's assumption that the only legitimate basis on which sex can be reconstructed is the ending of dominance and hierarchy but to pursue its implications.

[107] *Id.* at 120.

On this analysis, physical ability as we know it is constructed by society in such a way, first, as to make one group of people strong and another weak. Next, strength and weakness are assigned to men and women, respectively, and presented as a natural consequence of sex. Finally, what is established and presented by these means as the natural male capacity for strength is endorsed as the social norm against which the physical abilities of both men and women, and their inequalities, are to be assessed. It is this three-stage process, which may in fact have taken place either sequentially or simultaneously, that MacKinnon describes as the construction of sex in hierarchical form.

Reconstruction of physical ability in this setting might take a number of forms. It might take the form, for example, of ensuring that men and women are, on average, as strong as one another, or as supple, or as fleet of foot. In that case, neither sex would be able to dominate the other physically, not because men and women would be different but equal, but because they would be indistinguishable in that respect. This solution thus abolishes hierarchy by ensuring that men and women are identical in the face of a common standard, strength, for example. This is the path of identity, or as it can be called in the context of the sexes, androgyny. It has nothing to do with sexual difference, which in this situation would exist only in some dimension other than that of physical ability.

Alternatively, reconstruction of physical ability might take the form of refusing social recognition to qualities such as strength, on the ground that they foster dominance, as a result of either their history or their nature.[108] This too would render the sexes indistinguishable in terms of the qualities in question; in that sense, it would have the same effect as the first option. Moreover, it would still leave men and women open to comparison in terms of some other, as yet unstated, criterion of physical ability, according to which they could be found unequal. If we are to prevent hierarchy, then, whatever physical abilities are to be assigned to men and women must render them equal in the face of whatever standards are employed to assess those abilities. This, however, is the path of sexual difference, in its sameness branch. It foresees the comparison of different people according to the same as yet unstated criterion, whatever it may be, and seeks to prevent hierarchy by designing people in such a way that they perform equally according to that standard.

Finally, reconstruction of physical ability might take the form of ensuring that while the sexes have different physical capacities, such as strength and weakness, our appreciation of athletic endeavour does not involve comparing the capacities associated with one sex and those associated with the other. This might be achieved by conceiving athletics in terms other than those of a competition in which one quality or characteristic, and by extension the group

---

[108] See id. at 121.

of persons that possesses it, is rendered dominant.[109] Ending competition in athletics would permit the sexes to be different without either being dominant. This solution seeks to abolish hierarchy by establishing separate identities for men and women and assessing them, if at all, according to different standards. This is the path of sexual difference in its difference branch.

These illustrations suggest the pervasiveness of the form of analysis that is embodied in what MacKinnon calls the difference approach to sexual equality. That analysis, it will be recalled, seeks to establish sexual equality through an assessment of the different capacities of men and women, according to either a common standard or different standards. What MacKinnon has attempted, in her criticism of the approach, is not so much to escape from this form of analysis as to escape from the discriminatory assumptions under which she contends it is now carried out, assumptions that are embodied in the social construction of sex. The elimination of any deliberate sexual biases present in the difference approach, however, does not necessarily lead to the elimination of dominance from its results. If MacKinnon achieves her ends, dominance may no longer govern the comparisons employed to establish the equality of the sexes, but it may still be present in their effect.

In claiming that sex is entirely socially constructed, MacKinnon has set aside the idea that what we know as male or female is in any way determined by nature or biology. In claiming further that sex has been constructed by society in terms of the dominance of men and the subordination of women, she has sought to reveal and forestall any reference to the male standard as a norm. In rewriting in this way the second and third stages of the process of sex formation described above,[110] she has attempted to nullify the power of sexual conventions and the privileged status that they confer upon men, and consequently has attempted to give the greatest possible remedial scope to the claims of sexual equality.

But the revelation that the male standard relied upon by the difference approach is neither natural nor normal does not resolve the tensions that MacKinnon has accurately identified in the two branches of the difference approach, those of sameness and of difference. The abolition of dominance does not remove the difficulties involved in achieving equality through the recognition of difference. On the contrary, it appears to highlight them.

---

[109] See *id.* at 121: "From a feminist perspective, athletics to men is a form of combat. It is a sphere in which one asserts oneself against an object, a person *or a standard*. It is a form of coming against and subduing someone who is on the other side, vanquishing enemies. It's competitive. From women's point of view, some rather major elements of the experience appear to be left out, both for men and for women. These include . . . kinesthesis, pleasure in motion, cooperation . . . , physical self-respect, self-possession, and fun." Emphasis added. MacKinnon appears to see these interpretations of athletics as inherent in the attitude of the participants, not in the activity itself. She records her own extended participation in "martial arts as a physical, spiritual, and political activity": *id.* at 117.

[110] See notes 107–8 and accompanying text.

To return to the model of sexual construction set out above, if men and women are reconstructed so that they possess the same capacities, so as to be as strong or as supple as one another, for example, then clearly the three-stage process that MacKinnon describes as the social construction of sex in hierarchical form will be bypassed altogether. But there will be no hierarchy of the sexes only because and to the extent that there is no difference between them. What is achieved by this means is not sexual equality but androgyny.

I do not intend to pursue the possibility that men and women could be reconstructed in this way so as to be the same as one another, either generally or for all public purposes. Such a remedy is not merely implausible; it is the course of sexual identity rather than sexual equality. It is certainly not what MacKinnon has in mind in seeking the well-being of women in the name of feminism unmodified.

Nor do I intend to pursue the possibility that, however reconstructed, men and women might avoid the problem of sexual hierarchy by inhabiting entirely separate worlds. Dominance is a problem born of a world in common and its resolution lies there. Even if separate worlds were conceivable as a practical matter, so that it were possible to contemplate a response to sexual and other forms of social hierarchy through segregation of the dominant and the subordinate, those worlds would at some point have to interact, at which point the issue of hierarchy would reemerge, albeit in the shape of a conflict between worlds rather than between sexes.

On the other hand, if men and women are reconstructed so that they possess different capacities, so that one sex is supple and the other swift, for example, and if furthermore there is no assumption that this arrangement is natural or that the capacity possessed by men is the norm, the three-stage process will have been reconceived in such a way that it does not embody dominance by design. But whether one sex will dominate the other in this situation will depend upon the approach taken to the lives in question and their assessment. A genuine realization of sexual difference, and the revised evaluation of women that that would entail, would ultimately make sexual hierarchy inconceivable. However, the reconstruction of men and women in such a way as to eliminate any inferiority of one sex to the other would have the perverse consequence of making that realization of sexual difference impossible.

ii. STANDARDS OF ASSESSMENT. The standards in terms of which human beings are assessed and compared may be one-dimensional. We may seek to discover who can cover a given distance in the shortest time, or who can lift the greatest weight, or who can obtain the most correct answers on a multiple choice examination. More complex assessments may sometimes be converted into these terms, as when letter grades are given for a performance, or an interview, or a piece of written work. Through the use of standards such as these we seek to quantify the character of human beings. The terms of assessment we use are concrete, specific, univocal, capable of registering the differences between people in one respect only. In other words, they define the existence of a human capacity while denying the complexity of its character.

When different people are assessed in terms of such a standard, a hierarchy is established, whose character is defined by the ground of assessment. Some people will be found to be swifter, or stronger, or quicker-witted, and hierarchies of speed, strength, and intellectual capacity will be recognized accordingly. Indeed, the purpose of assessing and comparing people in these terms is usually to establish such a hierarchy. This is not to suggest that we tend to value hierarchies for their own sake; we are more likely to value them instrumentally, as a means of allocating opportunities or resources, or because we value a particular activity and so value the performance of those who are shown to carry it out most successfully.

Assessments of this one-dimensional kind are capable of defining people as equals, but only when those people exhibit capacities that are identical in terms of the standard in question. People will be found to be equally swift, for example, if they can cover a given distance in the same time, equally strong if they can lift the same weight, equally bright if they receive the same test score. In other words, people are determined to be equal under standards of comparison such as these when their capacities are found to be indistinguishable in the relevant respect.

Men and women are frequently found to be equal in this sense, but their equality in this respect is established at the expense of their sex.[111] That is to say, equality of the sexes exists here if and when men and women are found to be indistinguishable in terms of the capacity in question. If men and women are either revealed or reconstructed so as to be as swift as one another, as the standard defines swiftness, they will no longer be gendered in that respect. The more comprehensive the respects like this in which they are equal, the more comprehensive will be their identity.

Occasionally, not only sexual equality but universal equality can be established in this way. In some respects all human beings will be found to be the same, whether they have been created so by nature or by society. A standard of this kind may be employed as a means of recognizing or establishing that commonality. More often, however, a standard that may reveal men and women, on average, to be as swift as one another reveals certain men and women to be swifter than others. The equality that is asserted in one dimension, that of sex, is thereby denied in another, the dimension the standard defines.

---

[111] This is not to say that a finding of equality in some respect *erases* sexual difference in that respect, but that a finding of equality in some respect is a finding that there is no difference between the sexes in that respect. However, a reconstruction of sexual identity in terms of equality, such as MacKinnon contemplates, would indeed erase the existence of sex.

From the perspective of one-dimensional standards, then, recognition entails inequality, and equality entails nonrecognition. Swiftness is here defined by the differences that the standard of swiftness establishes between people. To the extent that the standard establishes the swiftness of men, or of blacks, it establishes hierarchies of sex, race, and speed. If the standard can find no difference between men and women, or between blacks and whites, in terms of swiftness as it understands it, then sex and race do not exist in that dimension. If, further, the standard can find no difference between any two people, then it can no longer distinguish the swift from the slow; and if that standard is exhaustive of our understanding of speed, then the dimension of speed itself will cease to exist for us.

At one level, then, a call for equality in this context is a call for identity of capacity. If men and women are reconstructed so as to have identical capacities, they will be equal in this sense, but not as men and women, because sex will no longer exist in this setting. In the context of standards of this kind, sexual equality as MacKinnon defines it, namely, the circumstances in which the sexes are different but not inferior to one another in any respect, is indeed a contradiction in terms – as she puts it, something of an oxymoron.[112]

At another level, a call for equality in this context can be interpreted as a call for identity between the treatment of people and their performance according to the standard in question. So understood, equality requires that people who perform equally according to the standard be treated equally, and that people who perform differently according to the standard be treated in proportion to their difference. On this view, therefore, inequality arises not only when people the standard determines to be similar are treated differently, but when people the standard determines to be different are treated similarly. It follows that this understanding of equality condemns the failure to recognize and enforce, rather than the failure to suppress, any sexual hierarchy defined by the standard in question. This is the equality of the difference approach in its sameness branch, not the equality that MacKinnon calls for.

---

[112] *Id.* at 33. MacKinnon has attempted to eliminate hierarchy by rewriting the three-stage process of sex construction so that it does not embody dominance in its design. She has attempted to ensure that we do not assign what we see as virtues to men and treat as virtues those qualities that we claim to have discovered in men. But even when dominance has been abolished as a governing principle in the design of sex, the social standards in terms of which men and women conduct their lives, understood in a one-dimensional sense, will still have the effect of defining one sex as inferior to the other in the dimensions they describe. If men and women are to perform equally, they must possess the same capacities. This is not to say that women must meet male standards, as MacKinnon alleges they are expected to do under the difference approach. That would be the case only if dominance remained part of the design of sex. Rather, it is to say that the sexes will perform equally only when the relevant standard is insensitive to sex, so they can no longer be distinguished as men and women. One might attempt to establish the equality of the sexes by comparing their performance in all dimensions. To do so, however, it would be necessary to employ a complex standard of the kind considered below, one that takes into account a range of incommensurable achievements.

Human beings can be evaluated in quite different terms from these, however. The standards according to which people are assessed and compared can be complex and sensitive, rather than one-dimensional and authoritative. Indeed, it is frequently the case that we seek to understand and appreciate, not simply to measure and rank, the qualities and capacities that people possess. When we recognize physical grace or expressiveness, when we appreciate wit or charm or good humour or kindness, when we value intelligence, compassion, or understanding, we tend to employ complex standards of assessment in order to do so. The significance of those standards, then, is that they enable us to comprehend the character and capacities of other human beings in their own terms.[113]

We may seek to pursue this method of comprehending human beings further by making comparisons among different people and the different qualities they have to offer. Comparisons of this kind, however, are conducted in the same qualitative terms as the assessments on which they are based. Accordingly, we may compare different kinds of physical expressiveness so as to recognize them all, different qualities of character so as to appreciate them all, different capacities of mind so as to value them all. When we compare the register of a woman's voice to that of a man's, for example, we do so not to rank them but to recognize something about sex and something about the human voice. In making comparisons like these we continue to employ complex standards because our purpose is to develop an awareness of the complexity and range of human possibilities.

One-dimensional standards of evaluation notice variety in that dimension, but they neither appreciate nor foster, for example, the qualities of those whom they define as slow, or weak, or stupid; their purpose is to appreciate the qualities of those whom they define as superior.[114] For that reason, it is plausible to call them male standards when they define as superior those qualities that are found exclusively or predominantly in men.[115] And because such standards do not foster virtues other than those they define, it is plausible to regard them as silencing those dimensions of experience that they fail to recognize.[116]

---

[113] MacKinnon implicitly endorses such standards in her description of a woman's understanding of athletic activity. See note 109.

[114] If and when they are multiplied, one-dimensional standards can give rise to a plurality of virtues. Only a complex standard of evaluation, however, can foster that plurality, or appreciate its consequences. See note 112.

[115] This is not to say that such standards exist in any given society in order to serve the interests of men. They are there because they define activities that are genuinely valuable, the pursuit of which contributes to the success of the lives of certain human beings, women as well as men. Nevertheless, it is plausible to regard them as male in the sense that the other one-dimensional standards I have referred to are standards of swiftness or strength.

[116] This is not to concede that MacKinnon can consistently describe our present standards of evaluation as male, or claim that those standards have silenced the female voice. The premise underlying her comments is that male and female have no meaning except as descriptions of the location of dominance and subordination in men and women. The discussion here is premised on the assumption that men and women are to be reconstructed so as to realize the possibilities of sexual difference, and so will have identities that can be dominant, or that can be silenced.

If we want to appreciate and value the full significance of different lives, therefore, we must employ standards whose complexity and sensitivity mirror the complexity and variety of the qualities we hope to discover or create. It follows that if we hope to reconstruct sex in such a way as to establish what it means to be a man or a woman in all its possible richness and variety, we must employ complex standards of assessment that allow us to appreciate what men and women have to offer. This is not a matter of employing separate standards for men and women. It is a matter of employing a common standard of sufficient complexity to be capable of recognizing and appreciating what each sex is capable of becoming.

Viewed from this perspective, men and women who seek to explore and pursue the meaning and consequences of their existence, including their existence as men and women, have different and ultimately incommensurable fates. This is no more than what it means for them to be different people, to belong to different sexes, and to pursue the full implications of those facts. Insofar as men and women differ from one another, therefore, the complex standards of appraisal and comparison that we employ in order to appreciate the meaning of sex yield assessments that are couched in terms of sex. They describe lives that are not superior or inferior, but different, and the tenor of their assessments reflects that difference. When men and women are assessed in terms of standards of this complexity, neither hierarchy nor equality, as MacKinnon defines them, is possible. All that can be revealed is the fact of sexual difference, understood on its own terms and in its full implications. To adopt any other, more limited, standard for the evaluation of men and women would be to deny them the possibilities and the significance of their sex.[117]

It might be thought, nevertheless, that the different fates of the two sexes could themselves be weighed in such a way as to be found equal or unequal. It might be thought that men and women could be reconstructed so that the sum of the benefits and burdens felt distinctively by men matches the sum of those felt distinctively by women; then the lives of the two sexes would be evenly balanced in the scales of equality.

This, however, is to assume that such scales exist or could be defined; to assume, in other words, that there is a common currency in terms of which men's and women's distinctive lives could ultimately be assessed and compared.[118] On the contrary, the implication of assessing sexually distinctive lives in their

---

[117] I have presented my comments in terms of sex, but they apply to any quality or set of qualities that is not only true of human beings but critical to the success of certain human lives. I am not assuming here that sex has any particular content, therefore, let alone that it completely defines the existence of men and women. Complex standards reveal the complexity of human existence in general as well as the complexity of sex, and thus reveal the extent to which the success or failure of a given human life may depend upon the exploitation of a wide range of qualities, be they sexually neutral, sexually distinctive, or both.

[118] It is also to assume that individual lives could be assessed in this way, which a complex approach to their evaluation would deny.

own terms is that the scales on which they are assessed must be drawn from those lives themselves. The nature and metric of value are thus part of what is at issue, part of the territory that each sex seeks to describe for itself.[119] The definition of sex is a definition not only of the qualities that are to compose our understanding of men and women, but also of the weight to be assigned to those qualities. There is thus no common understanding of value that we can appeal to in order to ascertain the equality or inequality of the sexes.

To the extent, then, that the implications of sexual difference are realized, sexual dominance as MacKinnon defines it – as the inferiority of one sex to the other in any respect – does not arise. Lives understood in this way are neither inferior nor equal to one another. A one-dimensional standard can be used to define and assess individual qualities, but it cannot so define sex. A call for the recognition of sex is a call for assessment in terms of a complex standard, under which neither hierarchy nor equality, as MacKinnon defines them, arise. A resolution to the problem of dominance in sex, therefore, must lie elsewhere.

IV. Conclusion

For Catharine MacKinnon, sex discrimination is simply the unequal distribution of power between men and women, "the systematic relegation of an entire group of people to a condition of inferiority".[120] In her view, the only way to right this wrong is to eliminate women's inferiority by establishing sex equality:

> If sex inequalities are approached as matters of imposed status, which are in need of change if a legal mandate of equality means anything at all, the question whether women should be treated unequally means simply whether women should be treated as less.[121]

On examination, this interpretation of sex discrimination reveals itself to be incapable of either identifying or redressing the problem of sex in our society. For women who care about their existence as women, MacKinnon's form of analysis is not only inadequate but also self-destructive as a basis from which to pursue well-being. The simple, one-dimensional standards of assessment that enable some people, such as women, to be seen as inferior to others also dictate that inferiority can be ended and equality achieved only through eliminating the difference between those people and their so-called superiors. Under standards such as these, recognition of difference entails inequality and equality entails non-recognition of difference. The inferiority of one sex to another, once perceived in this way, is avoidable only through the elimination of sex itself, the very category

---

[119] This is not to endorse MacKinnon's view that the content of value is relative to sex (see note 24). It is to suggest that each sex can give an account of its distinctive approach to life only in terms of a set of standards that is sensitive to whatever values are genuinely realized by that approach to life.

[120] *Id.* at 41.

[121] *Id.* at 43.

that MacKinnon's argument is intended to reclaim. Any hope of redeeming the position of women, therefore, if it is not to involve the destruction of their existence as women, must rest on some other interpretation of their predicament.

For certain of MacKinnon's critics, however, the weakness of her argument lies not in its commitment to equality but in what they see as its focus on women in general, and its corresponding insensitivity to the differences between women. According to those critics, MacKinnon's analysis could be redeemed by an acknowledgment of the many different settings in which inferiority arises, and a consequent acknowledgment that equality necessarily means very different things to different women. It is important to emphasize here, therefore, that what MacKinnon's analysis actually places at issue, as she herself makes clear, is the nature of the predicament faced by women and other victims of discrimination as a condition of inequality. It is not the subsequent determination of which women or which people can properly be said to be unequal to which others, and in what respects, and consequently can be said to be discriminated against in our society in those respects.

As far as understanding discrimination as a matter of inequality is concerned, MacKinnon's egalitarian critics are, by definition, not in disagreement with her. Yet the equality that they, no less than she, are committed to calling for ends all forms of difference to which it is applied, not just some of them. It follows that as long as the problem that women face, collectively or separately, continues to be seen as the inferiority of one group of people to another, with its remedy their equality, no account of men and women, or of the social goods in dispute between them, will have consequences different from MacKinnon's own. The consequences of equality are a function of the concept, and of the perspective that makes that concept comprehensible. They are not a function of the identity of the groups to be equated, be they men and women in general, or particular men and women, or of the ground of the equation, be it those groups' abilities or their needs.

It is MacKinnon's commitment to equality, therefore, and not her commitment to women as a group, that makes her insensitive to human difference. Indeed, her focus on the condition of women is at odds with her commitment to equality, which treats the condition of women as equivalent to the condition of blacks and, prospectively, to the condition of men. It follows that critics who wish to be sensitive to the manifold differences between human beings, be they differences between men and women or differences between women, and yet wish to show women to be in all respects equal both to one another and to men, are caught in a contradiction.

As indicated above, this follows from the fact that the inferiority of a group to any other can be eliminated only by eliminating the difference between the two, however that difference is defined. The method of assessing people that shows some to be inferior to others, whether it is because they are women, or black women, or lesbians, or otherwise, also dictates that that inferiority can be eliminated only by eliminating the difference on which it turns. We might eliminate difference by reconstructing the social world in terms that do not reflect difference, or by reconstructing the description of people in such a way as to ensure that there is no difference between them to reflect. We might, in other words, eliminate that dimension of our social experience, or we might eliminate that dimension of group identity. Either of these courses has the effect of eliminating our perception of the difference in question, whatever groups that perception of difference defines.

If, on the other hand, this simple, one-dimensional method of assessing people is set aside in favour of a complex approach, one that is sensitive to the differences between people and the different standards of evaluation required to appreciate those differences fully, on their own terms, then the people in question become incommensurable. Their inferiority as people can no longer be asserted, their equality need no longer be sought, and some other explanation of women's predicament and its remedy must be found. Seeing people in complex terms is a prerequisite to fully acknowledging their difference, actual or potential, natural or socially created; yet seeing them in this way makes both their inferiority and their equality inconceivable.

There is another danger in understanding discrimination as a matter of inferiority, the resolution to which must lie in the pursuit of equality. As MacKinnon herself warns, a society that confines itself to redressing the problem of inferiority for any particular group of people by eliminating the difference upon which the inferiority of those people is based, so as to establish their equality with their former superiors, merely displaces that inferiority onto another group of people.[122] To alter the identity of the victims of discrimination, or the character of what they are denied, is to alter the location of discrimination, not its nature or significance. In short, equality for some, or in some respects, relocates rather than reduces inferiority. It might make the patterns of discrimination in our society simpler, perhaps, or more fluid, but in the end it would merely find new victims for old wrongs. As MacKinnon herself puts it, "if this is feminism, it deserves to die."[123]

If, for example, women's inferiority was found to be a product of their physical weakness, relative to men, in a society that valued physical strength, members of that society might seek to reconstruct the existence of men and

---

[122] *Id.* at 23 ("To us it is a male notion that power means that someone must dominate. We seek a transformation in the terms and conditions of power itself"); 4 ("... it is antithetical to what women have learned and gained, by sacrifice chosen and unchosen, through sheer hanging on by bloody fingernails, to have the equality we fought for turned into equal access to the means of exploitation, equal access to force with impunity, equal access to sex with the less powerful, equal access to the privilege of irrelevance"); 31 ("The feminist question is not whether you, as an individual woman, can escape women's place, but whether it is socially necessary that there will always be somebody in the position you, however temporarily, escaped from *and that someone will be a woman*").

[123] *Id.* at 5.

women so as to make the sexes equally strong. Alternatively, they might seek to reconstruct the forms and practices of that society so as to end all reference to strength. But in the former setting some would still be weak and hence inferior, although they would no longer be predominantly women, and in the latter setting some, probably women, would still be inferior, although inferiority would no longer turn on weakness.

If we are concerned about a group of people as victims of inequality, we cannot confine our concern to the members of that group as long as other victims of inequality exist unless, perhaps, we regard the limitation of our concern as a necessary first step in a practical strategy for the removal of all inequality. If, on the other hand, we are concerned only about the inequality of a certain group of people, our concern must be explained in terms of those people, and what it is about them that makes their inferiority, and not that of others, objectionable. It cannot be explained in terms of a commitment to equality, which has, by definition, no preference for any particular group of people.

It is for this reason that MacKinnon pursues a theory of sex that is subordination-based rather than a theory of subordination that is sex-based. Her concern is with inequality generally, and her analysis is designed to apply to all forms of inferiority and to all people who suffer it, whether in the shape of sex, race, or class, and not to women alone.

Yet we cannot conceivably eliminate all inferiority and establish equality in the manner that MacKinnon's analysis calls for. To do so would be to eliminate all difference between human beings insofar as they are evaluated in terms of the simple, one-dimensional standards of assessment that make them commensurable. Even if this were conceivable as a practical matter, the effect would be to make people social equals only by rendering them socially indistinguishable, thereby negating the very respect for human difference on which most accounts of egalitarianism are premised. The achievement of equality for women would eliminate womanhood, a consequence that most, but perhaps not all, would regard as highly unfortunate if not catastrophic. And it could not plausibly be pursued as a way of eliminating hierarchy, except in a partial, incoherent form that would merely redraw rather than redress the patterns of subordination in our society.

The difficulties attendant on Catharine MacKinnon's analysis, therefore, are not a product of the context in which she has chosen to pursue the ideal of equality, that of the disadvantage experienced by women of all kinds, but of the ideal of equality itself. It follows that those difficulties extend to any analysis of difference and dominance that shares that ideal. Recognition of this fact has led writers such as Luce Irigaray to condemn the ideal of equality in language very nearly as trenchant as MacKinnon's own:

Even a vaguely rigorous analysis of claims to equality shows that they are justified at the level of a superficial critique of culture, and utopian as a means to women's liberation.

The exploitation of women is based upon sexual difference, and can only be resolved through sexual difference. Certain tendencies of the day, certain contemporary feminists, are noisily demanding the neutralization of sex. That neutralization, if it were possible, would correspond to the end of the human race. . . . Trying to suppress sexual difference is to invite a genocide more radical than any destruction that has ever existed in History. What is important, on the other hand, is defining the values of belonging to a sex-specific *genre*.

Unless it goes through this stage, feminism may work towards the destruction of women, and, more generally, of all values. Egalitarianism, in fact, sometimes expends a lot of energy on rejecting certain positive values and chasing after nothing. Hence the periodic crises, discouragement and regressions in women's liberation movements, and their fleeting inscription in History.[124]

Notwithstanding the limitations imposed on MacKinnon's argument by its reliance on the ideal of equality, however, at least two features of that argument have undeniably succeeded in redrawing the boundaries of any subsequent analysis of sex discrimination that hopes to be comprehensive. First, MacKinnon's vigorous critique of the authenticity of the sexual divide as we know it has significantly deepened the debate over sexual and other forms of human difference, so as to compel that debate to be conducted at the level at which our very understanding of difference is constructed. She makes it clear that practices of discrimination do not merely define certain social groups as inferior, but actually help to constitute the understanding of those whom they define as inferior.[125] Consequently, in considering the position of women and other victims of discrimination, answers to the question of human difference and its value can no longer be assumed, or set aside as external to the problem of discrimination. MacKinnon's analysis, through its exploration of the social construction of sex in hierarchical form, renders incomplete the attempts of those who seek to establish the ways in which certain presumptively valid forms of difference ought to be respected and valued.[126]

Furthermore, MacKinnon's acute ear for the experience of women as told by women, and her correspondingly rich and attentive description of women's lives, is uncontested even by those who disagree with her theoretical analysis.[127] Any rival account of women's predicament will not reflect an adequate understanding of women's lives if it neglects the empirical reality that MacKinnon describes, although it must, of course, remain free to reject her interpretation

---

[124] Luce Irigaray, "Equal or Different", in *The Irigaray Reader*, ed. Margaret Whitford (Oxford, 1991), 32.

[125] In MacKinnon's view, of course, sex discrimination does not merely help to constitute women's identity; it defines them utterly.

[126] See, for example, Christine Littleton, "Reconstructing Sexual Equality", 75 *California Law Review* 1279 (1987); Iris Young, *Justice and the Politics of Difference* (Princeton, 1990); Martha Minow, *Making All the Difference: Inclusion, Exclusion and American Law* (Ithaca, N.Y., 1990).

[127] See, for example, Drucilla Cornell, *Beyond Accommodation, supra* n. 7, at 116, 154, 166.

of that reality as simply a condition of inferiority if it hopes to redeem the position of women as women. In other words, for those who would go beyond MacKinnon's analysis, it is at once necessary to respect her account of women's experience and to avoid understanding women solely in terms of that experience, thus making any escape from it conditional on suppressing sexual difference.

The challenge confronting those considering the issue of sex discrimination is to develop an analysis of women's lives that fully captures women's experience of disadvantage, and its embodiment in their existence as women, without embalming them in that experience. Women cannot be expected to seek their redemption in ways that marginalize or neglect the truth of the lives they lead, or to attend to that truth in ways that forestall their redemption. In other words, it is essential that the analysis of sex discrimination not itself diminish women, either in terms of the understanding it offers of the suffering they experience as women or in terms of the opportunity it presents for a redemption that they can aspire to as women.

It is this challenge that Drucilla Cornell has taken up, in two books that draw their immediate inspiration from the work of Luce Irigaray and other French feminist thinkers.[128] The first of these in particular, *Beyond Accommodation*, seeks to build on Jacques Lacan's psychoanalytic analysis of the social construction of gender by developing what Cornell sees as the positive implications of Jacques Derrida's deconstruction of Lacan's account of sex as a social and psychic reality. Cornell's feminism is intended, at least in part, to serve as a rebuttal of MacKinnon's analysis of women's condition. However it is a rebuttal that accepts rather than contradicts MacKinnon's empirical description of women's degradation and its implications for the authenticity and value of women's present existence as women.[129]

The challenge that Cornell takes up, which she calls a central dilemma of feminism, is framed by her at the outset of *Beyond Accommodation*:

If there is to be feminism at all, we must rely on a feminine "voice" and a feminine "reality" that can be identified as such and correlated with the lives of actual women; and yet at the same time all accounts of the feminine seem to reset the trap of rigid gender identities, deny the real differences between women (white, heterosexual women are repeatedly reminded of this danger by women of color and by lesbians) and reflect the history of oppression and discrimination rather than an ideal or an ethical positioning to the Other to which we can aspire.[130]

---

[128] Drucilla Cornell, *Beyond Accommodation, supra* n. 7; *The Philosophy of the Limit* (New York, 1992). *Beyond Accommodation* sets out a feminist vision that is founded on the general theory of *The Philosophy of the Limit*. Cornell uses this last phrase to describe her own reading of deconstruction, or postmodernism: *Beyond Accommodation*, at 207 n. 1; *The Philosophy of the Limit*, at 11. Like her, I use whichever term seems clearest in a particular setting.

[129] *Beyond Accommodation* at 119–64; 116, 134, 141, 154, 166.

[130] *Id.* at 3.

To meet this challenge, and so overcome the dilemma she describes, Cornell offers a theory of the feminine that sees sex as a psychic fact, formed by men's and women's different entry into the realm of language. The sexual reality that MacKinnon describes is, in Cornell's view, constructed as a cultural text, a text that can and must be deconstructed in favour of a new feminine reality, a new approach to the writing of the feminine. In redescribing the feminine in this way, as a site for deconstruction, Cornell seeks to give expression to those dimensions of feminine experience that are now repressed into the unconscious by their inexpressibility in language and culture. At the same time she seeks to acknowledge their contingent status when expressed, and their capacity and obligation to yield through further deconstruction to other dimensions of the feminine, dimensions that they themselves would otherwise repress and render inexpressible.

By these means Cornell hopes to affirm the possibility of a new vision of feminine difference, a vision that is essential, she argues, if women's lives are not to be once again subordinated to masculine values. Yet, in the same structural moment,[131] she hopes to ensure the instability of that vision by continuing to invoke the ethic and techniques used to destabilize its predecessor, thereby preventing it or anything else from ever standing in as the unshakeable truth of what it means to be a woman.[132] Hers is a vision of the feminine that is traced in explicitly utopian terms, sufficiently concrete and knowable to embody the repressed language of women's experience, yet sufficiently flexible and indeterminate not to exclude any subsequent feminine language or narrative, written on behalf of women as a whole or as the expression of particular women's experience. It is an approach, Cornell claims, that succeeds in resolving the dilemma of feminism as she has framed it, one that acknowledges the reality of women's present subordination without endorsing its status as truth, one that offers the opportunity of a new feminine reality without enclosing women in its description, one that is at once there for women and not there to limit them. Cornell offers women the possibility of both a new content to the feminine and a new view of its status. As she puts it, hers is a feminism always modified, forever engaged in a process of its own revision and reinvention.[133]

---

[131] Cornell calls this moment of affirmation and disruption structural, to make clear that it does not take place in time. It is a stage that cannot be surpassed: see *Beyond Accommodation, supra* n. 7, at 95, 107.

[132] I have described Cornell's affirmation of the feminine as a *vision* of feminine difference, but it is important to note that she is committed to what she calls the remetaphorization rather than the reconceptualization of the feminine. In brief, she believes that a metaphor acknowledges and embodies its contingent status, while a concept does not. See the next chapter.

[133] Drucilla Cornell, "The Doubly-Prized World: Myth, Allegory and the Feminine", 75 *Cornell Law Review* 644, at 687 (1990).

3

Difference

Underlying Catharine MacKinnon's analysis of women's present predicament is the thesis that the difference between women and men as we know it is entirely socially constructed, that women and men are by nature merely blank slates upon which society has chosen to draw the patterns of sexual difference with which we are familiar, and from which women suffer. There are two assumptions implicit in this thesis: first, that freeing women from their present predicament depends upon changing what women (and men) now are, and second, that what is the product of society is amenable to such change while what is the product of nature is not. For MacKinnon and many, perhaps most other feminists, these two assumptions are relied upon in the service of egalitarian ends. We must change what women now are so as to ensure that their qualities and characteristics (and the lives that those qualities and characteristics make possible) are equal to those of men.

Yet there is no necessary connection between belief in sexual equality and the belief that the present character of sexual identity is a social construct that must be changed if women are ever to flourish, for it is perfectly possible to believe that the present character of sexual identity can and must be changed for reasons other than equality. It is perfectly possible, for example (or at least so it is claimed), to believe that new and different forms of sexual identity must be pursued for the sake of their very novelty and difference, for the sake of the release that such fresh visions of sexual difference would provide from the confines of sexual identity as it has been laid down in the present forms and practices of our society.

It is change of this kind that Drucilla Cornell seeks. Drawing on Continental psychoanalytic traditions, and in particular on Jacques Derrida's deconstruction of Jacques Lacan's refiguring of Freud's analysis of women's lack, Cornell argues that sexual identity as we know it is a fantasy, created for the benefit of men and at the expense of women, the purpose of which is to conceal the existence of the many possible alternatives to our present understanding of the human condition, which if recognized would expose the inherent vulnerability and contingency of our status as human beings. Since this fantasy of sexual identity is a social construct, it is amenable to change. And since it is by its very definition oppressive, not only of all the possibilities it excludes, but of women, who are made to pay the price of that exclusion, through the conversion of the inadequacy and incompleteness that is a feature of the human condition into a feature of being a woman, then it must be changed. According to Cornell, here following Derrida, we must deconstruct sexual difference as it is given to us to ensure that we remain forever open to all the possibilities that our condition as human beings from time to time implies.

The question is whether this vision of human existence, and of the role of women in it, is possible or desirable. If it is neither, and if Cornell is therefore mistaken in her quest for difference for its own sake, then difference provides no more reason than equality to change our present understanding of sexual identity. It would follow that it does not matter whether and to what extent the present character of sexual identity is a social construct, for there is no need, or at least no need that can be described in the comparative terms of equality or difference, to change that identity in order to ensure that women flourish.[1] Analysis of sex discrimination would then have to begin with an understanding of sexual identity as it is, and go on to ask what in society's present conception of sexual difference, and of the ways in which that difference matters, must be changed if women are to flourish.

Cornell's account of the nature of difference and of the obligation to respond to it is rich and complex. Moreover, it draws on Continental writing that may be unfamiliar to readers in the Anglo-American tradition, specifically the psychoanalysis of Jacques Lacan and the postmodernism of Jacques Derrida. As a result, the journey through her work is challenging. Yet it is not possible to appreciate the possibilities that her account of discrimination gives rise to without entering to some extent into the Continental mode of thought that she adopts. In what follows I have done just that, tempering and explaining where necessary.

I. Introduction

Drucilla Cornell's account of gender[2] is built on a refiguring of the two insights that define Catharine MacKinnon's analysis of sex discrimination. Like MacKinnon, Cornell believes that gender as we know it is not natural but

---

[1] I leave aside here the possibility that sexual difference needs to be changed, not to change the nature of the relationship between women and men, but to eliminate any immoral qualities or characteristics that are definitive of one sex or the other. As I indicated in the first chapter, I doubt that there are such qualities and so have discounted the possibility.

[2] In this chapter I follow Cornell in using the term "gender" rather than "sex" when referring to the distinction between men and women. Cornell uses the term "sex" in a way that seeks to transcend that binary distinction, particularly in her more recent work: see *The Imaginary Domain: Abortion, Pornography and Sexual Harassment* (New York, 1995), at 5–7; *At the Heart of Freedom: Feminism, Sex, and Equality* (Princeton, 1998), at 6–8.

socially constructed. Like MacKinnon too, she believes that in our society that construction has taken place in hierarchical form. But Cornell's understanding of the nature and status of the social construction of gender, and the hierarchy that it embodies, is entirely different from MacKinnon's.

For Cornell, as for Jacques Lacan, the influential French psychoanalyst whose reasoning she adopts here, people are formed and their identities established as a consequence of their entry into the realm of language and the text of culture. According to Lacan, whatever else may define them, all people are inscribed in this manner as either male or female.[3] Seen in this way, gender is a social construct written in the psyche, or as Cornell puts it at one point, a sentence written in flesh.[4] It is a sentence that is quite literally a piece of fiction, a narrative embodied in language and ungoverned by any more fundamental truth of gender.[5] Yet it is this fiction that constitutes what we know as gender reality.

The social construction of gender as a narrative fiction implies that there is no prediscursive gender reality to recover.[6] This is not to say, however, that the text of our culture as it is presented to us exhausts the meaning or possibilities of gender.[7] If that were so, gender reality as we know it would be inescapable, a conclusion that Cornell believes Catharine MacKinnon is driven to and that she herself deplores.[8] On the contrary, the fact that gender is given to us as a cultural text precludes neither the existence and significance of a referent for gender beyond that text, nor the existence of a beyond to the entire realm of language and culture, the existence of which is inexpressible but implicit in both text and referent. Far from it; for Cornell, the status of gender as fiction means, first, that the feminine exists only as it is written and rewritten, and, second, that like any other fiction its meaning lies neither in the text itself, as it is given to us, nor in some prior sense or referent that is recovered through the text, but in the undecidable relationship between the two.[9] In Cornell's view it is a philosophical error, which she labels essentialist, either to try to look behind language in the hope of discovering there the truth of what it means to be a woman or to conclude that what it means to be a woman, as that fact is constructed in our culture and presented in language, is the truth of gender and not a fiction.[10]

---

[3] *Beyond Accommodation: Ethical Feminism, Deconstruction, and the Law* (New York, 1991) at 197.

[4] *Id.* at 197, 198. See also Jacqueline Rose, "Introduction-II", in *Feminine Sexuality: Jacques Lacan and the École Freudienne*, ed. Juliet Mitchell and Jacqueline Rose, trans. Jacqueline Rose (New York, 1982), 27–57, at 55.

[5] *Beyond Accommodation, supra* n. 3, at 3, 129.

[6] *Id.* at 104.

[7] Drucilla Cornell, "The Doubly-Prized World: Myth, Allegory and the Feminine", 75 *Cornell Law Review* 644, at 675 (1990).

[8] *Id.* at 686.

[9] *Beyond Accommodation, supra* n. 3, at 2, 26–29.

[10] *Id.* at 26–29, 129–30.

While there may be no prediscursive gender reality that can be invoked as authentic, therefore, the very fact of our entry into the realm of language indicates the existence of a realm beyond language.[11] The fiction that we know as gender implies the Other against which it seeks to consolidate itself, that which it renders inexpressible.[12] This inexpressibility means that the Other, while never entirely excludable, cannot be directly known or appealed to. Nor, by the same token, can the fiction of gender be simply discarded, for men and women cannot be separated from the metaphors in which their lives are constituted.[13] The Other is always accessible, but only interstitially, in the excess of meaning inevitably present in the metaphor of our lives. Any attempt to engage in the rewriting of the text, then, or as Cornell puts it, to engage in its remetaphorization, is an act of recovery of the Other, undertaken in the awareness that the Other cannot be approached directly and that its complete recovery is impossible.

According to Cornell, the present subordination of women is the consequence of the repression of the Other in the realm of language, the realm that Lacan calls the symbolic order. For all human beings, the consolidation of their identity as speaking subjects, through entry into the realm of language, creates an abiding sense of loss. This universal awareness of our relation to what language has made Other, and so separated us from, is reduced by our system of gender to an awareness of and insistence upon the subject's identification of itself in terms of a projected image of what it lacks. Genuine Otherness thus becomes embodied in the realm of language as a fantasy image that sustains the subject's unity and coherence. That fantasy image is then located in women and established as femaleness. By these means the image of Woman is defined as other to an equally fantastic image of the unitary subject, an image located in men and established as maleness.

So mistakenly understood, the Other is not truly different at all, but an aspect of the subject's self-definition and an emblem of his self-sufficiency. In this way, all those possibilities and presences that are Other to the symbolic order are reduced to the negative aspect of the subject's self-definition and then inscribed as Woman.[14] Women are thus culturally defined in our society not as truly different, but merely as other to men, "the non-essence to their essence, the nothing to their substance".[15] Women have no capacity to define themselves as presences or subjects in their own right,[16] but are culturally identified in terms of a lack that defines the identity and presence of men. It is by these means,

---

[11] *Id.* at 28, 103–4.

[12] *The Philosophy of the Limit* (New York, 1992) at 1, 142.

[13] *Beyond Accommodation, supra* n. 3, at 3, 198.

[14] *Id.* at 82.

[15] *Id.* at 146.

[16] In saying that women cannot be subjects in their own right, I mean to say that they cannot be genuinely Other ". . . in a social world in which the feminine Other is inexpressible as subject": *id.* at 150.

Cornell maintains, that the social construction of gender in hierarchical form takes place.

Cornell's second insight, then, is to see hierarchy not as a matter of superiority and inferiority, or only consequently so, but as a matter of presence and lack. In our culture, identity as a human subject is given a false status, one that consolidates the myth of masculine presence and is sustained by the correlative myth of feminine lack. Gender is thus at once the method by which hierarchy is established and its embodiment. For Cornell as for MacKinnon, hierarchy constructs gender as we know it. For Cornell, however, implicit in this very hierarchy, although repressed and inexpressible there, is its Other, an infinite set of possibilities that constantly threatens to disrupt the hierarchy and expose its false status.

Our society's approach to the construction of gender is to be condemned not simply because it is false, but because it violates what Cornell describes as the ethical relation to the Other, replacing acknowledgment of the Other with repression and denial, which in turn are visited upon women and for which women pay the price. The goal of feminism, therefore, is not to see that women are accommodated in what is by definition a masculine culture, but to pursue an ethical vision of a nonviolent relation to the Other, by affirming the feminine as a site for deconstructing the present cultural order and reinscribing that order in nonexclusionary terms.

Like MacKinnon, Cornell tends to fuse the presentation of these two insights, perhaps because they are presented to us as fused in what we know as gender reality, a fiction that is socially constructed in hierarchical form. But, as in MacKinnon's case, it is essential to a full appreciation of Cornell's work to distinguish the elements of her analysis and their separate implications.

II. The Deconstruction of Gender

Masculinity, in the Lacanian analysis, is formed in the shape of a fantasy about the nature of human identity. It is a fantasy that presents identity as unified, coherent, and independent, and is founded on the suppression and exclusion of what that identity renders Other. Femininity is formed as the correlative and sustaining fantasy of woman as the not-all, to use Lacan's term. According to Cornell, we can hope to reveal the true character of human existence only by disrupting these fantasies so as to reveal the presence of the Other that is implicit in all images of existence. This in turn requires that we establish what she describes as a nonviolent relationship to the Other, thereby ending its status as mere otherness, the negative reflection of our image of identity, and its location in women.[17]

---

[17] See *The Philosophy of the Limit, supra* n. 12, *passim.*

In some respects, Lacan's own account of gender might be thought to contain an implicit acknowledgment of the possibility of the kind of disruption that Cornell calls for. On his analysis, the fantasy that we know as sexual difference in the symbolic order, despite its comprehensiveness, depends upon the notion that all experience can be equated with conscious experience, and hence upon the notion that sexuality exists exclusively in the terms in which it is permitted to be expressed in the symbolic order. In fact, he claims, sexuality is constituted by the experiences of both the conscious and the unconscious, and it is in the unconscious that those experiences that are inexpressible within the symbolic order are lodged and played out. Such experiences are no less lived because they are inexpressible. As Lacan explains:

It none the less remains that if she is excluded by the nature of things, it is precisely that in being not all, she has, in relation to what the phallic function designates of *jouissance*, a supplementary *jouissance*. . . .

There is a *jouissance* proper to her, to this "her" which does not exist and which signifies nothing. There is a *jouissance* proper to her and of which she herself may know nothing, except that she experiences it – that much she does know.[18]

Moreover, according to Cornell's reading of Lacan, this experience of *jouissance*, the experience of the feminine Other,[19] is not only lived but intermittently revealed in the interstices of the symbolic order.[20] The character of language is such that it cannot stabilize itself and prevent slippage in its form. That inevitable slippage reveals indirectly, through the excess of meaning present in linguistic figures such as metaphor and metonymy, what language has rendered Other.[21]

To put it succinctly, nothing ever means quite what it is supposed to mean. As a consequence, given that identity exists as a linguistic construct, the loss that necessarily attends the achievement of identity is intermittently revealed through the slippage of language in the shape of *jouissance*. This slippage means that the Other possibilities of the feminine, those aspects of experience that are pushed under and repressed into the unconscious by the symbolic reduction of woman to man's other, can never be entirely excluded despite the fact that they can never be directly known or expressed.

Yet despite this acknowledgment of the existence of *jouissance*, and the recognition of its interstitial presence in the symbolic order, Lacan regards the status of gender as self-replicating and so insoluble.[22] In doing so, Cornell believes, he overlooks the revolutionary implications of his own analysis.[23]

---

[18] "God and the *Jouissance* of Woman", in *Feminine Sexuality, supra* n. 2, at 144, 145. See also *Beyond Accommodation, supra* n. 3, at 40.

[19] *Beyond Accommodation, supra* n. 3, at 211 n. 28.

[20] *Id.* at 40, 79.

[21] *Id.* at 131.

[22] *Id.* at 53, 68, 79–81. See also *The Philosophy of the Limit, supra* n. 12, at 86, 175.

[23] *Beyond Accommodation, supra* n. 3, at 79.

Moreover, she maintains, here following the work of Jacques Derrida, in recognizing the authority of the present structure of sexual difference, Lacan does not merely recognize, so as to describe, the social construction of gender in hierarchical form but actually helps consolidate that hierarchy.[24] Through her representation of Derrida's theory of deconstruction in the shape of a doctrine that she calls the philosophy of the limit, and through the application of that doctrine to Lacan's analysis of human identity and sexual difference, Cornell seeks to deconstruct the present status of gender in the symbolic order, and to show that in its character as a text it has neither the capacity nor the right to stabilize itself in the face of the Other.

A. The Problem of Escape

i. LACAN: NONIDENTITY. For those seeking to reform the world that Lacan describes, so as to realize this hope of bringing to an end the present fantasy of gender, it might appear that one possible response to his account would be to argue that women contain within themselves, or at least are capable of acquiring, the capacity to transcend their present predicament, so as to achieve true identity as human subjects. In its most straightforward sense, however, this response is simply not available to those who are genuinely interested in reforming the world that Lacan describes, and who consequently take Lacan's account of the nature and origins of human identity as their premise. According to his account, men achieve identity as human subjects only in and through the act of dominating women in such a way as to deny them identity.[25] For those who accept Lacan's view, therefore, that to become a human subject and gain identity as we know it one must adopt a position of dominance in a hierarchy of sexual difference, it is clearly not possible to argue that both men and women can become human subjects.

Lacan maintains that implicit in our concept of identity is the idea that the achievement of identity for anyone entails the enforcement of nonidentity upon someone else, or more properly, upon something that might have been someone else but for that act of enforcement. If that is the case, we can prevent nonidentity only by abolishing identity in the only sense that we have ever known it, the sense in which we understand ourselves as distinct from one another, the sense in which we know ourselves as separate human beings. In its place we would have to develop a fresh understanding of the nature of human existence, one that was capable of expressing the sense of contingency and vulnerability that Lacan believes lies at the heart of human existence. This is

---

[24] *Id.* at 80, 129–30.

[25] I refer here to men and women. Cornell, however, refers to masculine and feminine in order to emphasize that these are positions that may be taken up by biological males or biological females, although in most cases the masculine position is occupied by men and the feminine by women.

an ambition that Lacan is understandably pessimistic about realizing, and it is for this reason that he regards the present hierarchy of sexual difference as inescapable. It follows that those who are committed to the view that women can transcend their present predicament must find a way to avoid sharing Lacan's pessimism about the consequences of his own analysis, or reject that analysis altogether.

More to the point, perhaps, at least from a feminist perspective, even if men and women were able to achieve such a fresh understanding of human existence, free of the taint of gender hierarchy, they would thereby become indistinguishable in their existence as human subjects, that is, in the only dimension in which the difference between them has any meaning. It follows that this approach to the ending of dominance would mean, in much the same way as it does for Catharine MacKinnon, the elimination of the feminine as a category, and thus the elimination of sexual difference, for the simple reason that the feminine, as Lacan insists we now know it, is nothing other than a synonym for subordination in the form of suppression of identity. The ending of gender oppression as Lacan sees it would mean the ending of the feminine.

It might well be the case, of course, that following this ending of the feminine some new understanding of sexual difference would arise at some point in the future, in some form and for some purposes we have yet to imagine. Nevertheless, sexual difference, as Lacan claims we now know it, would come to an end, without any guarantee of its legitimate replacement, or indeed any reason to look for, let alone expect, such a replacement. This response to what Lacan contends is the nature of women's predicament, therefore, is one that is based on the elimination rather than the rehabilitation of the concepts of both personal identity and gender. It is a form of feminism that would give rise to a world without women, and to people without identity.

ii. DERRIDA: UNDECIDABLE IDENTITY. Surprisingly perhaps, this is, in simple terms, the solution to the problem of gender advocated by Jacques Derrida, who, in the course of deconstructing Lacan's account of sexual difference in order to demonstrate its capacity for transformation, seeks to deconstruct the . very concept of identity.[26] Derrida believes he can dispel Lacan's pessimism about the prospect of dismantling gender hierarchy only by undermining the status of the concept that, according to Lacan, lies at the heart of that hierarchy, the concept of identity itself.

---

[26] In the following discussion I have adopted rather than sought to question Cornell's interpretation of Derrida's work. Whether Cornell's account of Derrida is in fact accurate, and whether a sounder basis for feminism might be found in a different interpretation of his work, are questions I do not consider, for it is her work that concerns me, not his. However, it is clear that Cornell would have to be fundamentally mistaken in her view of Derrida, which I see no reason to believe, for the latter to be true, because what I take to be the weakness of his account, as she presents it, lies not in its peripheral features but in its core elements.

In Derrida's picture of existence, the nature and status of the human subject is fundamentally indeterminate, or as he puts it, undecidable. For Derrida, as for Lacan, our present concept of personal identity is simply a fantasy, the apparent coherence of which is asserted and maintained only at the price of gender hierarchy. The truth of human existence is that our lives are constituted as images in language and culture, so that we exist as metaphors in and through which meaning is continuously negotiated but never established. We exist, that is, as locations for an ongoing, indeed never-ending, dialogue between text and referent, between subject and Other, and it is only in this dialogue that the nature and meaning of our existence can be looked for. It follows that human existence can never be finally established or embodied in a concrete understanding of identity. On the contrary, any appearance of identity that our lives may present is in the most profound sense merely provisional, being always already engaged in the process of its own deconstruction, so as to yield to the truth of undecidability.

In this picture there is not only no room for identity as a human subject, but neither need nor room for an image of the feminine, because any such image, on Derrida's account, is as fictional as the image of identity, and accordingly as vulnerable to deconstruction. It is for this reason that Derrida invokes in place of gender what he describes as a new choreography of sexual difference, in which that difference would be, as he puts it, danced differently, this time to a polysexual signature. The price for women of this approach is clear, as is the reason why Cornell, in common with a number of others, seeks to distance herself from its consequences.[27] In the world that Derrida describes, the existence of all human beings would become as flimsy, as empty, as the nonidentity that Jacques Lacan argues is the fate of women.

It is true that the condition of nonidentity Derrida has in mind is unlike that which Lacan describes, in that it is not imposed upon one group of people so as to sustain the identity of others. At one level, therefore, the general realization of the Derridean condition of nonidentity would bring to an end the existence of gender hierarchy. Nevertheless, the consequence of doing so would be that no human being would enjoy what we now know as identity, and that women would cease to exist as women, given that the only dimension in which sexual difference exists for us, at least according to Lacan's account, would be eliminated in the elimination of identity. Furthermore, elimination of sexual

---

[27] It should be emphasized here that while Cornell admits that Derrida himself hesitates, as she puts it, before any affirmation of the feminine, she nevertheless argues that the affirmation of the feminine that she calls for is entirely consistent with his philosophy. Rather than distance herself from Derrida's work, therefore, she distances herself from those readings of the work that see Derrida as seeking to erase sexual difference: see *Beyond Accommodation, supra* n. 3, at 98, 102, citing Luce Irigaray, *This Sex Which Is Not One*, trans. Catherine Porter (Ithaca, 1985), 86–105; Jacqueline Rose, *Sexuality in the Field of Vision* (London, 1986), 18–23. See also note 37 and accompanying text.

difference would occur without any prospect of a legitimate replacement, since Derrida seeks to undermine the establishment and consolidation of any and all forms of difference, be they matters of identity or of gender.

iii. CORNELL: FEMININE POSSIBILITY. It is important to pause here to appreciate the exact nature of Cornell's purpose in engaging with the work of Lacan and Derrida. To do so is to appreciate the significance to her of the idea of the feminine as an image of an existence beyond identity as we know it, one that offers possibilities without imposing constraints. In seeking to extend and build on the conclusions arrived at by Lacan and Derrida, Cornell seeks to escape what she sees as the inevitably disabling consequences of any concrete, determinate understanding of what it means to be a woman, disabling for women's capacity both to transcend their present circumstances and to articulate a vision of their future that neither reiterates the terms of their oppression nor establishes conditions of womanhood that are in themselves exclusionary. In Cornell's view, all determinate images of womanhood are inherently oppressive, simply because they are determinate. If drawn from the terms of women's present existence as women, such images continue to oppress women and make escape from oppression conditional on abandoning their gender. If couched in terms of women's as yet unrealized existence as women, they make any escape from oppression an escape into a new form of confinement, one defined by the qualities taken to establish the authenticity of their existence as women.

This is the reason for Cornell's attraction to Jacques Lacan's account of the nature of human existence. In presenting the feminine as a condition of nonidentity, Lacan describes an oppression whose physical features accurately reflect the circumstances of women's experience as Cornell recognizes and understands them, without linking that condition of oppression to any determinate image of what it ought to mean to be a woman. Paradoxically, given that Lacan himself regards the condition he describes as inescapable, Cornell sees his account of oppression as the only one that offers women any hope of escape from their present predicament. This is precisely because Lacan confirms what Cornell regards as the truth of women's exclusion from identity, yet denies that there is any truth to the identity from which they have been excluded, and by implication denies that there is any truth to any other determinate image of existence, such as conventional accounts of the feminine.

Thus it is Cornell's understanding of oppression as the product of a determinate understanding of existence that leads her to take the image of the feminine to be a metaphor for nonidentity, in terms both of what she sees as the present oppression of the feminine, as recorded by Lacan, and of what she sees as the possibility of escape from that oppression, as envisioned by Derrida as she reads him. In both its antecedents and its conclusions, therefore, her argument turns on the understanding of existence as an ultimately undecidable condition, the consequence of which for human beings is the impossibility of their identity as human subjects, and the indeterminacy of the sexual difference between them. It is only through a Derridean vision of the future that Cornell believes it is possible to avoid the problems presented by any determinate account of the feminine, and it is only through a Lacanian account of gender hierarchy that this Derridean future can be understood to address the problem of gender oppression.

Clearly, however, there is a tension involved, if not a contradiction, in any attempt to affirm an image of the feminine using an approach to the understanding of human existence that is apparently committed to the deconstruction of any and all such images. If Cornell is to succeed in her argument, she must balance what she sees as the need to provide the feminine with some determinate basis for calling itself the feminine at all against the need to avoid determining the content of the feminine, so as to establish it as an image that is itself liable to deconstruction. Unless Cornell can strike this balance successfully, and resolve the tensions her account of the feminine generates, it will fall either into the very establishment of existence that she condemns or into the very absence, which Lacan describes as the present fate of the feminine, that she seeks to transcend. If she cannot strike that balance, Lacan's account of the feminine will indeed be inescapable, as he maintains, and consequently will have to be rejected by all those who believe in the possibility of redeeming the position of women as women.

B. The Ethical Relation to the Other

As Lacan sees it, the problem of discrimination against women in our culture, or more accurately, of discrimination against the feminine, is the product of a false understanding of the nature of our existence as human subjects. The unjustified authority that we grant to the masculine is the authority we grant to the subject, and the unjustified disability that we correspondingly impose upon the feminine is the disability we impose upon the Other. In our culture, identity and gender are established in a way that betrays their true meaning; the description we are given of them is false to the character of their existence. That description lends an authority to the masculine subject that it strips from the feminine Other.

Yet if Lacan is correct in believing that our present understanding of identity and gender is fundamentally false, as Cornell takes him to be, he is correct on the basis that our existence as images in language and culture is in fact contingent and vulnerable. If that is the case, the remedy to gender oppression that Cornell seeks can never be finally expressed in terms of gender difference, for the truth of that difference, like the truth of existence from which it derives, is undecidable. It follows that the feminine can never be established as an ideal. It can be approached only indirectly, through a description of the opposing impulses that it seeks to contain without ever determining. Those impulses are, on the one hand, the impulse toward deconstruction and undecidability, expressed as a commitment to openness to the Other, and on the other hand, the impulse toward establishment and decision, expressed as the consolidation of an image of the feminine as the location within which this openness to the Other must find its setting.[28] It is the tension between these impulses, which Cornell describes as the ethical relation, that she seeks to give effect to in her reaffirmed, albeit profoundly disrupted, description of the feminine.

To this end, Cornell addresses the present gender hierarchy by invoking in its place an image of the feminine that she calls the subject of dialogue, an image that is binary by definition and undecidable by nature, so that it can never be grasped as a unified concept. That being so, her description of the feminine cannot be examined and evaluated as if it were a unified concept, but can be approached only through independent examinations of its component practices, namely, the deconstruction of the masculine subject and the affirmation of the feminine Other, and the undeniable but undecidable impact that each is said to have on the understanding of the other.

More important, however, in examining the components of Cornell's image of the feminine, it is essential to remember that on her account of existence each of those components exists only in terms of the other. Neither can be taken as an end in itself; to do so would be to describe the content of the feminine in terms of one of its components to the exclusion of the other. The subject of dialogue must, by reason of its nature as an image, remain undecided between its components, something it can do only by respecting the contribution of each. It can be no more legitimate to present our existence entirely in terms of the recognition of the Other than it is to present our existence, as Cornell believes we now do, entirely in terms of the denial of the Other.

It follows that what Cornell describes as the writing of recovery of the Other cannot be based on acknowledgment of the Other alone. Abolition of the status of the masculine as the exclusive image of the human subject leaves undetermined what forms human existence may take, consistent with recognition of the Other, and what images may be used to present it: many are incompatible, most are controversial, and all entail some form of exclusion of the Other. The issue of sexual difference, therefore, is ultimately one of the proper character of the relationship to the Other, and by extension a matter of establishing which forms of symbolic existence, and consequent exclusion, are legitimate and which are not, and hence which may validly be pursued and which may not.

As long as these conditions are met, any image of the subject, and hence any form of separation and exclusion of the Other, is legitimate as far as Cornell is

---

[28] Cornell believes that deconstruction embraces both these impulses in what she calls a double gesture. I do not wish to challenge this description, and discuss the double gesture in some detail below. For the moment, however, for lack of a better term, I use deconstruction to refer to what Cornell herself might prefer to call "the phase of overturning": see *Beyond Accommodation, supra* n. 3, at 95–96.

concerned. The dialogue between subject and Other is free to take any course, as long as the role of each participant in it continues to be recognized. Yet the obligation to recognize and preserve the roles of the participants necessarily constrains the course of the dialogue in terms of those roles. That is to say, the condition of dialogue itself limits both the freedom to establish new images of the subject and the freedom to deconstruct them through recognition of the Other. In particular, it prevents the dialogue from taking a direction that would undermine the existence of either of the components on which its own existence as an image depends.

If the image of the feminine is to serve as a framework for the impulse to deconstruction and recognition of the Other, to preserve the character of the subject as a dialogue, that framework cannot itself be subject to deconstruction. On the contrary, it must resist deconstruction to whatever degree is necessary to maintain its role in preserving the character of the subject as a dialogue. Any lesser degree of resistance would permit one component of the subject, namely, the impulse to recognition of the Other, to stand in for the meaning of the subject as a whole, and so foreclose any possibility of dialogue. Conversely, of course, any greater degree of resistance would permit the framework of the feminine to do the same, by repressing the Other and refusing to engage in dialogue with it.

At one level, Cornell clearly recognizes this,[29] offering an account of the feminine that has two aspects: the first she calls a philosophy, designed to force recognition of the Other and its utopian possibilities; the second she calls a programme, designed to serve as the vehicle within which those possibilities can be ethically pursued. These aspects of Cornell's account mirror and respond to the challenge of feminism as she poses it at the outset of *Beyond Accommodation*, namely, that any account of the feminine must acknowledge women's oppression without endorsing its status as truth, and must offer the opportunity of a new feminine reality without enclosing women, or any portion of them, in its description.

Yet at another level important questions remain unanswered by Cornell's presentation of the feminine in this form. The first of these is what ethical standard she intends to call upon in order to establish the validity of the relationship between the two components of the subject addressed by her philosophy and her programme, respectively. That standard cannot merely be, as she sometimes seems to suggest, the compliance of her programme with her philosophy,

---

[29] See *The Philosophy of the Limit, supra* n. 12, at 100–107. It may be noted here that Cornell's Lacanian view of nature of the symbolic order makes her assessment of present social reality superficially similar to that of Catharine MacKinnon. Where Cornell parts company with MacKinnon, however, is in the conclusion that that reality constitutes the truth of the feminine: see *Beyond Accommodation, supra* n. 3, at 119–64, and particularly at 129–30. As she puts it, *id.* at 116: "Catharine MacKinnon's task is best understood to give us a relentless genealogy of our current conceptions of justice so that we will finally see the masculine bias that undermines the claims of our legal system. As important as this genealogy is for feminism, it is not enough."

because the role of the latter is to resist and balance the former, which it cannot do through compliance with it. The second and consequent question is to what extent the stability offered to the subject by Cornell's programme is achieved by determining the content of the image of the feminine. To the extent that her programme does this it necessarily defeats her attempt to describe an indeterminate account of the feminine.

III. The Renewal of Gender

A. Deconstruction of the Masculine Subject

In the first aspect of her account, that of deconstruction, Cornell argues that we must revise our understanding of human identity so as to acknowledge the presence of the Other and give effect to the full implications of our interdependence with it. This means that we must deconstruct the story of sexual difference as it is given to us, expose the false status of the masculine subject, and reveal the fundamentally undecidable character of our existence as images in language and culture. In Cornell's view it is essential that feminists, as much as the society whose mythology they seek to disrupt, refrain from any attempt to determine the content of the feminine, for all attempts to determine existence have the effect of denying the Other. Only by recognizing the Other, she contends, and showing existence to be undecidable, can women escape their present disability, a disability that she believes to be entirely the product of determinate thinking. It is thus a reimagined and yet undecidable conception of existence that Cornell seeks to describe through what she calls the philosophy of the limit.[30]

According to Cornell, any attempt to establish the meaning or content of an image of existence denies the interdependence of that image and the Other, and so contravenes the ethical relation, for the simple reason that the establishment of an image necessarily forecloses its openness to the Other. In the world she calls for, it will never be possible, consistently with the requirements of the ethical relation, to conceptualize or otherwise determine the content of an image of existence. As a result, we can never know once and for all what it means to be a woman, for any content that the image of the feminine may from time to time appear to have can only be provisional, since it must always already be engaged in the process of its own deconstruction in favour of what the provisional determination of its content has temporarily rendered Other, an Other to which it is bound to be completely open by the requirements of the ethical relation.

Any attempt to reconcile an image of existence with the loss implicit in its Other, therefore, has the effect of establishing what Cornell describes as an

---

[30] "The philosophy of the limit" is the phrase that Cornell uses to describe her conception of deconstruction as a philosophy that "exposes the quasi-transcendental conditions that establish any system . . .": *The Philosophy of the Limit, supra* n. 12, at 1.

imperialistic relationship to the Other in which its status as Other is ultimately denied. What must be envisioned, she argues, is a dialogic relationship between subject and Other whose structure and outcome is ultimately undecidable. In this picture the truth of reality lies not in a determinable subject, nor in its Other, nor in some concept that could be said to structure the relation between the two, but in their undecidable relationship. The product and expression of this relationship is a world without either certainty or closure.

B. Affirmation of the Feminine Other

As indicated above, Cornell appears to accept that this account of deconstruction cannot be taken as a programme for social change in itself, but must be pursued within the framework of some organizing theme such as the feminine.[31] Perhaps because she readily endorses this conclusion, however, she does not develop an argument for it at any length. Nevertheless, I believe that it is essential to fill this gap in the presentation of her argument by exploring in detail the basis of what she describes as the need for thematization, that is, the need to provide a framework for the process of deconstruction. The character of this need, and its relationship to Cornell's ethic of deconstruction, has a critical bearing on the success or failure of her project of affirming an image of the feminine as the vehicle for realizing a deconstructed approach to existence. If the feminine is to be regarded as the embodiment of a fresh understanding of existence, one that eschews the features of identity as we now know it in favour of a condition that is fundamentally undecidable, forever engaged in the process of its own revision, we must understand the meaning of the deconstructive impulse that it seeks to embody.

In what follows, therefore, I propose to examine the intelligibility of what Cornell calls the philosophy of the limit, namely, the pursuit of deconstruction within the framework of a theme such as the feminine. Exactly what contribution is deconstruction expected to make to the content of feminine difference, by rendering that difference indeterminate? Conversely, what contribution is the image of the feminine expected to make to the coherence of deconstruction, by establishing and so determining the frontiers of its operation? This will involve examining, first, the implications of an unqualified commitment to deconstruction, and second, the impact of the constraints placed on that commitment by a framework such as the feminine. Through this examination I hope to provide an answer to the questions left unanswered by the bare description of the feminine as a subject of dialogue: first, what ethical standard will be used to establish the validity of the relationship of the components of this subject of dialogue, and second, how will use of that standard avoid determining the content of

---

[31] *The Philosophy of the Limit, supra* n. 12, at 181–82; see also *id.* at 103ff.

the feminine, and so frustrating from the outset the search for an undecidable account of the feminine?

In brief, I believe Cornell is correct in her conclusion that to be coherent, deconstruction needs the discipline of a theme such as the feminine. Yet I further believe that once this need for discipline is admitted, deconstruction is robbed of its radical and ethical power, so as to make its ethical authority and transformative capacity entirely derivative of the theme that is called upon to structure it. In other words, any claim that a deconstructed account of the feminine may make upon us flows from the concept of the feminine that is used to frame it, or to use Cornell's term, to thematize it, and not from deconstruction itself. To paraphrase Luce Irigaray, the problem of sex is a product of the determination of sex, and it is in that determination that we must look for its resolution.[32]

i. REJECTION OF UNQUALIFIED DECONSTRUCTION. To begin with the implications of an unqualified commitment to deconstruction: a world without either certainty or closure, as an unqualified account of deconstruction contemplates, is clearly a world that courts chaos, as Cornell herself acknowledges.[33] A concept that is fully open to the Other, and infinitely permeable, whether a concept of the feminine or some other, is so insubstantial and unstable as not to exist at all. From the point of view of Cornell's project, this is an unacceptable outcome, as she herself recognizes, not merely because it imports chaos and so threatens the coherence of the symbolic order and hence any possibility of the pursuit of the feminine there.[34] More tellingly, the elimination of all concepts is an outcome that is not consistent with an act of acknowledgment of the Other, for it is only in achieving and establishing concepts that the Other is brought into being.[35] More precisely, chaos of this kind is to be resisted not simply for the sake of order, but for the sake of the Other.

According to Cornell's analysis, which in this respect she shares with Lacan, concepts such as identity and gender can be grasped only through an act of closure that in the very moment of its definition excludes the Other, and by so doing brings the Other into existence. Cornell's reference to the Other, therefore, and her call for its recognition, is not a reference to some prediscursive reality that is imperfectly represented in our present account of human existence. On the contrary, it is a reference to that dimension of reality that is brought into being only as a result of its exclusion in the embodiment of concepts such

---

[32] Luce Irigaray, "Equal or Different", in *The Irigaray Reader*, ed. Margaret Whitford (Oxford, 1991), 32, quoted above in Chapter 2, section IV, at text accompanying note 124.

[33] *The Philosophy of the Limit, supra* n. 12, at 61, 100–104.

[34] The existence of a concept of identity, whether seen as inevitable or as desirable, entails the exclusion of the Other: see section II.B., "The Ethical Relation to the Other". The argument here is that respect for the Other further entails preservation of the concept of identity.

[35] *The Philosophy of the Limit, supra* n. 12, at 71–72.

as identity, as images in the text of language and culture that Lacan calls the symbolic order.

It follows that the realm of the conceptual and the realm of the Other are dependent upon one another for their very existence. Just as the existence of concepts is contingent upon the existence of the Other, so the existence of the Other is contingent upon the existence of concepts. Any acknowledgment of the claims of either realm, therefore, must be undertaken in a manner that safeguards the existence of the other. For human beings to deny, or otherwise seek to transcend, this implication of the achievement of their existence as images, is for them to refuse to acknowledge the Other, and hence to reprise the fantasy concerning the nature of the human subject that currently defines the masculine and establishes the pattern of dominance that we know as sexual difference.

Given this interdependence of the existence of a concept and the existence of the Other, the result of infinite openness to the Other would be not only the elimination of all concepts but the elimination of the Other. Indeed, any action that threatens the fundamental coherence of the symbolic order, and so threatens the realization of any concept or image there, is for that reason a threat to the existence of the Other. It follows that it is not possible to be infinitely open to the Other for the sake of the Other; to do so would in fact be to betray the Other in the guise of securing its recognition. Paradoxically, some degree of commitment to structure, sufficient to secure the coherence of the symbolic order and the preservation of images and concepts there, and thus sufficient to exclude the Other and so bring it into existence, is a necessary part of any commitment to the recognition of the Other.

It might be thought, against this conclusion, that endless openness of a concept to the Other would produce a transient, continuously evolving understanding of that concept, one forever prepared to surrender itself to the forever shifting claims of the Other. On this account, an unqualified commitment to the Other might be thought to have a progressive character, something like an unfettered commitment to innovation and change. The effect of such a commitment would be to dissolve the boundaries of a concept continuously, even as they are established and reestablished, without being so profound or corrosive as to prevent the boundaries from ever forming. A commitment to acknowledge an infinite openness to the Other might thus be understood as an endless readiness to submit to the claims of the Other, rather than as an endless, unrestrained process of submission to those claims.

In fact, however, any concession of stability that is sufficient to define and establish a concept, no matter how transiently, is acceded to only at the price of a corresponding, albeit equally transient, exclusion of the Other. It follows that an ethic of infinite openness to the Other, by invalidating any kind of establishment of the Other's exclusion, however transient, invalidates any concession of stability sufficient to establish a concept and leads, therefore, not to the constant evolution of our images of existence but to their total dissolution, and hence to the total dissolution of the Other. The very existence of the Other, in other words, is a function of the existence of a concept that its full recognition would destroy. Some qualification of the commitment to deconstruction, therefore, which would permit some limited establishment of the Other's exclusion, is necessary if any concept, and hence any existence of the Other, is to be preserved.

A concept cannot hold itself in readiness to surrender to the claims of the Other if it has no basis upon which to distinguish between those claims, and hence no basis upon which to resist some portion of them. It can only surrender to each in turn as they present themselves, however rapidly, however comprehensively. Infinite openness to the Other results, therefore, not in an evolving understanding of form, but in a state of formlessness, in which a concept and its Other are returned to the void of infinite possibility from which they were drawn. It follows that an unqualified commitment to deconstruction is literally incoherent, in the sense that it destroys the coherence that brings both a concept and the Other into being, and thus destroys the coherence on which the very commitment to deconstruction, or in Cornell's term, the philosophy of the limit, depends. Without the establishment of images and concepts there can be no difference between those images and what they might have been, and hence no Other to recognize, with the consequence that absolute openness to difference ultimately betrays the difference that it is committed to honour, and so ironically becomes, in Cornell's terms, unethical. More simply, because the Other exists only through its exclusion, to invalidate that exclusion is simply to invalidate the Other's existence.

If Cornell intends to affirm an image of the feminine as the vehicle for a deconstructed approach to existence, therefore, it is clear that she must grant that image a form substantial enough to shape and constrain the process of deconstruction, at least provisionally, so as to preserve the existence of the Other. To the extent that she fails to do so, her account of the feminine is indeterminate and unknowable, without any basis upon which to sustain the very existence of an image of the feminine, and hence without any basis that could give rise to an Other to which that image could be ethically obliged. It follows, as suggested above, that the ethical obligation to recognize the Other in its full character as Other can be only one aspect of the rehabilitation of the relationship between subject and Other that Cornell seeks to redefine through the ethical relation and to embody in the image of the feminine. That basic obligation to the Other must be supported and constrained by an independent ethic, one that is capable of determining which forms of exclusion of the Other are legitimate and which are not, and hence of determining what constitutes a legitimate relationship between subject and Other, and by extension, between the sexes.

And yet on Cornell's understanding of deconstruction neither the content of an image such as the feminine nor its relationship to the Other can ever be conceptualized or otherwise determined. Any attempt to do so once again establishes what she describes as an imperialistic relation to the Other, by reducing the possibilities that the Other represents to those that are a function of the image in question. More important, any concept or image of the feminine that is to some degree secured from deconstruction by its role as a theme is thereby made determinate, with all that that entails. It follows that for Cornell, an ethic that seeks to supplement the practice of deconstruction, albeit in order to sustain the intelligibility of the practice, violates the very commitment that it claims to preserve. This paradox, in which we are ethically obliged to establish a context of meaning that we are as ethically obliged to disestablish, she calls, using Derrida's term, the double bind.[36] She maintains that the paradox can be addressed only through a practice that Derrida describes as the double gesture, in which meaning is established and its status undermined in a single deconstructive movement.

ii. THEMATIZATION AND THE DOUBLE GESTURE. It is clear that Cornell recognizes the presence of a dilemma here, though a good deal less clear exactly how she hopes to resolve it. Three possible resolutions appear to be present in her work, each of which I outline briefly before examining in detail. The first lies in Cornell's belief that the process of giving shape to deconstruction through an independent ethic, the process she calls thematization, is self-governing, in that it takes place through a double gesture of deconstruction and affirmation, in which each element acts as a check upon the other, so as to prevent an image or concept from ever becoming either determinate or indeterminate. The second possible resolution builds on the first, stipulating that the practice of this double gesture must ensure that any affirmation of a theme such as the feminine is no more substantial and determinate than necessary to sustain the commitment to deconstruction itself, by securing the existence of some kind of social order that deconstruction is intended to serve by continuously transfiguring. The third possible resolution qualifies the second, stipulating that any affirmation of a theme such as the feminine must be sufficiently indeterminate, or transparent, as not to give rise to those consequences of determinacy, namely, rigidity and exclusion, that Cornell deplores and seeks to escape.

In effect, and as Cornell may intend, these three positions are no more than variations on a single idea, namely, that the shape that is given to deconstruction by a setting such as the feminine must itself be deconstructable. Yet to the extent that the image of the feminine is indeed deconstructable it cannot perform its function as a theme, and to the extent that it performs its function as a theme it does so only by insulating itself from deconstruction, thereby determining its content. The several solutions that Cornell proposes to her dilemma, therefore, merely reproduce and redescribe rather than resolve it. As a result, her account of the feminine is ultimately determinate to the extent that it has any content at

---

[36] *Id.* at 111–13. See also *id.* at 181, quoting Thomas McCarthy: "[H]ow is tolerance of difference to be combined with the requirements of living *together* under *common* norms?"; and *id.* at 133: "... justice is the refusal to accept as valid the system's own attempts at 'deparadoxicalization'."

all, and indeterminate to the extent that it is subject to deconstruction, with all the consequences that determinacy and indeterminacy entail.

At the heart of Cornell's dilemma is the difficulty, indeed, the impossibility, of providing an account of the feminine that is in every respect at once determinate and indeterminate, in the hope of avoiding, on the one hand, the limitations imposed by determinacy and, on the other hand, the anarchy and lack of meaning that would flow from indeterminacy. This difficulty arises from the fact that the very existence of an image of the feminine, and the understanding of language and culture upon which it depends, presupposes that whatever that image might come to mean in the future, at any given moment its meaning and content are determinate in some respects – those that the image describes, directly or indirectly – and indeterminate in others – those that the image excludes. Because Cornell accepts this presupposition, as indeed she must, she is forced to treat her image of the feminine as determinate and indeterminate in separate dimensions, with the consequence that the image as she describes it is determinate in all those respects in which it is not subject to deconstruction and indeterminate in all other respects, and so suffers from the limitations of both determinacy and indeterminacy, rather than transcending each in some new understanding of existence. This bare assertion requires a good deal of explanation and support, and in order to provide that it will be necessary to review each of Cornell's suggested resolutions to her dilemma in somewhat more detail.

a. Self-Effacing Feminism. The first possible resolution to the dilemma that Cornell calls the challenge of the double bind is to understand the ethical relation as requiring us to pursue certain themes, such as the image of the feminine, the status and content of which we simultaneously dissolve through continuous transformation. She calls this process, after Derrida, the double gesture. Thus deconstruction as Cornell interprets it takes place within the framework of themes, the basic outlines of which are not themselves subject to deconstruction. In particular, a deconstructed approach to our existence as human subjects, one that is capable of displacing the social and psychological reality that Lacan describes, can and must take place, Cornell argues, within the framework of an image of the feminine. It is in this respect that she parts company with interpretations of deconstruction and its application to feminism, such as certain of readings of Derrida, which refuse to affirm a renewed image of the feminine and opt instead for what Derrida calls a polysexual choreography of sexual difference.[37] Those readings, in her view, would be unlikely to overturn present social reality, and if they did would lead only to anarchy.

---

[37] The work Cornell is referring to here is Jacques Derrida and Christie McDonald, "Choreographies", in *The Ear of the Other: Otobiography, Transference, Translation*, ed. Christie McDonald, trans. Peggy Kamuf (New York, 1985) 169 at 183, where Derrida invokes "a chorus . . . a choreographic text with polysexual signatures". Cornell argues that this must be read in such a way as to permit the affirmation of the feminine: see *Beyond Accommodation*, *supra* n. 3, at 93, 96, 100–102. The readings Cornell is rejecting include those offered by Luce Irigaray and Jacqueline Rose, in the works cited at note 27.

Cornell's first answer, then, to the problem of imagining and describing a condition of simultaneous determinacy and indeterminacy is that the ethical relation can be given effect only by means of a gesture whose ambiguity is an authentic reflection of the ultimate undecidability of the relationship between subject and Other. In its first dimension, that of deconstruction, the practice of this gesture requires that we refuse to take deconstruction as a programme in itself, but instead pursue its implications in the context of certain themes that are derived from the present shape of our culture.[38] The determination of those themes defines an ethic that supplements and sustains the ethical relation, and tentatively describes which forms of exclusion of the Other are legitimate and which are not. It is the practice of this ethic that qualifies the pursuit of deconstruction, and so saves it from incoherence and a betrayal of the very ethical relation that it is committed to secure.

However, this establishment of the themes within which deconstruction is to take place must itself be deconstructable if it is not to determine the content of those themes, and so frustrate the purpose of deconstruction. Cornell contends, therefore, that the practice of the double gesture entails a search for themes that, although established in their structure, are open to deconstruction in their status and content. It is a gesture, in other words, that is designed to redeem its endorsement of certain themes, and hence its apparent violation of the ethical relation, by making that endorsement provisional, and hence deconstructable. It follows that if deconstruction, as Cornell understands it, is to take place in the context of the affirmation of certain themes, the affirmation of those themes must take place in the context of their deconstruction. The double gesture thus affirms even as it deconstructs, and deconstructs even as it affirms. In this way, Cornell contends, it avoids the twin perils of indeterminacy and determinacy, and so offers an entirely new, ethical understanding of existence.

In ensuring this, of course, the double gesture must also ensure that the acknowledgment of contingency upon which it insists is neither so comprehensive nor so corrosive as to dissolve the basic structure of the themes in question. To pursue deconstruction that far would be to frustrate the whole purpose of thematization, and so remit the philosophy of the limit to the problem of its coherence. In attempting to affirm the themes in light of which deconstruction is to take place, and yet at the same time to insist upon their contingency, the role of the second dimension of the double gesture is simply to reveal and keep open the possibilities for transformation that are latent within those themes, so as to secure the realization of what Cornell sees as the utopian implications of the ethical relation, without going so far as to overturn their basic structure and conditions.

In this way each dimension of the double gesture is designed to imply and anticipate the other. Only through the double gesture, Cornell maintains, can the

---

[38] *The Philosophy of the Limit, supra* n. 12, at 104–6.

image of the feminine escape the perils of both determinacy and indeterminacy. Only through the double gesture can the feminine be expected to flourish as a setting for the aspirations of all women, one that can serve as the vehicle for the realization of all those possibilities of women's existence that are now repressed within the Lacanian social order, without ever becoming so established as to exclude any of them.

Yet it is clear that Cornell's ambition of striking a balance between determinacy and indeterminacy in this way, in the hope of offering an account of the feminine that is identifiable as such without ever becoming finally determinate, cannot be entirely fulfilled by the conditional affirmation embodied in the second dimension of the double gesture. The fact that the affirmation of the themes upon which deconstruction is to be based is conditional on their subsequent deconstruction does nothing to vindicate the selection of those themes in the first place. It hence does nothing to redeem the status that is accorded to them in the act of securing their structure as themes, that is, in preserving their basic outline against deconstruction. On the contrary, the affirmation embodied in the second dimension of the double gesture must be sufficiently unconditional to secure at least the definitive features of those themes from deconstruction. Otherwise they would cease to be recognizable as themes and so would be incapable of fulfilling their role as constraints upon deconstruction. In other words, without some element of unconditional affirmation, the presence of a theme or set of themes in Cornell's account of deconstruction would serve merely to mark the path to indeterminacy rather than to act as a check against it. It follows that the affirmation of certain themes required by the first dimension of the double gesture, and the determinacy conferred upon those themes by their selection and endorsement as a context for deconstruction rather than the subject of it, cannot be redeemed by the fact that the status and content of those themes is subject to deconstruction in the second dimension of the double gesture.

Cornell's philosophy of the limit must chart a delicate course between two shoals here, those of determinacy and indeterminacy, a course that cannot be established by the practice of the double gesture alone. In itself that practice, operating as it does within the context of a set of themes only the content of which is subject to deconstruction, is incapable of establishing a balance between the conflicting demands contained within the philosophy of the limit, and thus is incapable of resolving Cornell's dilemma. The double gesture cannot be looked to as a means of ensuring that the process of thematization on which its operation is premised does not violate the ethical relation, since it cannot police what it presupposes.

It follows, as indicated above, that if the process of deconstruction is to satisfy the ethical relation as Cornell has described it, the double gesture must be supplemented by a genuinely independent ethic, whose scope of review transcends that provided by the second dimension of the double gesture. The double gesture must be supplemented, in other words, by an ethic that does not simply constrain the affirmation of value that thematization involves, in the manner of the second dimension of the double gesture, but actually justifies that affirmation, by determining which of the themes available in our culture may legitimately be exempted from deconstruction and which must be subjected to it. The challenge for Cornell, of course, is to answer the need for this ethic without determining the content of the feminine and so undermining her commitment to the ethical relation. To meet that challenge, she offers two further, qualified versions of the double gesture.

   b. Skeletal Themes. Cornell's second resolution to her dilemma is to stipulate that the selection and pursuit of the themes within which deconstruction is to take place must be a function of the conditions necessary to the acknowledgment of the ethical relation itself. As a threshold, she reasons that the themes within which deconstruction is to take place must be those that constitute the minimum conditions for the achievement of a social order without which the practice of the philosophy of the limit would be impossible.[39] She contends in particular, in the context of a consideration of the relationship between deconstruction and justice, that a minimal theory of the good, together with the existence of some body of legal principles and a legal system, is a necessary condition of the practice of deconstruction and the enactment of the ethical relation.[40]

   Cornell further contends, within the setting of her feminist project, that the present symbolic order, and the hegemony of the masculine subject there, can be overturned only through a vision of deconstruction that in its positive dimension affirms an image of the feminine. Because the lives of men and women cannot be separated from the metaphors in which they are couched, we cannot simply set aside present gender reality, and its basis in the relationship between subject and Other, through an act of the collective imagination and will. On the contrary, she argues, any attempt to overturn that reality can be undertaken only through the medium of the resources that are now available to us within the symbolic order. We can seek the trace of the Other only by working through the image of the feminine that is given to us and exploiting the slippage that is inevitably present in the language in which the feminine is inscribed.[41] Without such an affirmation, she believes, it is inevitable that we will once again repudiate the feminine and privilege the masculine.[42]

   Cornell explains and illustrates the need to affirm those themes, whose existence is necessary to maintaining the possibility of deconstruction, by using the theme of nondiscrimination as an example. The South African antiapartheid

[39] *Id.* at 106.
[40] *Id.* at 104–6.
[41] *Beyond Accommodation, supra* n. 3, at 95–96.
[42] *Id.* at 171.

movement, she argues, expresses a vision of the good that is consonant with the requirements of the ethical relation, despite the fact that the ultimate success of that movement would necessarily entrench the exclusion of the Other that that success, and the consequent realization of a nonracist society, would make of the doctrine of apartheid and its embodiment in the self-image of its supporters. As she puts it:

> . . . apartheid is wrong, any time and any place. The resistance movement does not then appeal to the cultural good of a specific context, but to the universal Good. Apartheid violates the ethical relation as evoked by Levinas. Apartheid does so now and will do so always. If apartheid were outlawed, the normative view of the whites who enforced their legal sentence on the flesh of blacks would indeed be silenced. And this silencing would be violence to their "difference". But as Derrida, amongst others, has reminded us, it is a deserved and necessary "violence" we are called to by any version of the Good worthy of its name.[43]

For Cornell, the criteria for selecting the themes within which the philosophy of the limit is to be pursued are, or ought to be, fundamentally uncontroversial, since on the one hand they constitute the conditions without which that philosophy could not be pursued, and on the other hand the status and content of the themes that are selected to that end are monitored and regulated by the second dimension of the double gesture. Yet it is clear, as she herself seems to recognize, that without further qualification these criteria cannot satisfy the requirements of the ethical relation as she has described it.

Notwithstanding the constraint, it remains the case that to acknowledge that deconstruction requires the presence of some theme or set of themes to sustain its coherence is not to establish anything about which themes in particular it requires. The coherence required by deconstruction could be supplied by any theme that is capable of securing the existence of an image or concept, and hence capable of securing the correlative existence of the Other. It follows that in itself the need for coherence cannot justify any particular selection of themes within which deconstruction is to take place. It cannot explain or justify our choice of one minimal theory of the good over another, or one body of legal principles over another, and so cannot justify the particular exclusion of the Other that the endorsement of such choices would entail.

By the same token, within the context of identity as a human subject and Cornell's vision of the feminine, it is not demonstrable that the comprehensive image of the feminine that Cornell herself endorses has a peculiar contribution to make to the coherence of deconstruction that could not be supplied by any number of other, rival images of existence. On the contrary, it is clear that such coherence could be supplied by any image of existence, as long as it is not predicated on denial of the Other, as is the image of the masculine subject in

---

[43] *The Philosophy of the Limit, supra* n. 12, at 114.

the present symbolic order, a denial after all that the second dimension of the double gesture is designed to forestall.

The need for coherence, therefore, cannot in itself justify Cornell's decision to deconstruct the present image of the human subject by affirming a single, comprehensive image of the feminine rather than, for example, multiple images of the feminine that could call into question not only our present understanding of masculine and feminine but our binary understanding of gender itself. That being the case, the process of thematization and the ethic that describes it would remain highly controversial if specified solely in terms of the coherence of the practice of deconstruction, since the necessary effect would be to determine which values in our culture generally, and which feminisms in particular, are to be subjected to deconstruction, and which values are to serve as its setting and hence are to be sheltered from its consequences.

More to the point of Cornell's argument, however, the ethic that describes thematization continues to impart a character to the practice of deconstruction that is impervious to the claims of the Other. The fact that some set of themes may be necessary to the coherence of deconstruction does not alter the fact that the endorsement of those themes, and their consequent immunity from deconstruction, determines their content to the extent that it is not subject to the second dimension of the double gesture, as it cannot entirely be if the themes are to perform their function. Cornell suggests that the comprehensive vision of the feminine she endorses is by its nature uncontroversial, as if to suggest that absence of controversy can be equated with absence of determinacy, or at least with absence of what she regards as the vices of determinacy. Yet in itself, lack of controversy does not make an image any less determinate, nor alter the consequences of its determination, namely, the suppression of all the possibilities excluded in the act of determination.

Even were Cornell's vision of the feminine uncontroversial, therefore, which there is reason to doubt, its endorsement as a theme that is not subject to deconstruction necessarily determines it to the extent of the endorsement. In endorsing a particular vision of the feminine, Cornell treats the wrong of our present understanding of identity as something quite different from that which she has argued it to be. The endorsement of one determinate image of the feminine over another, and the insulation of that image from deconstruction, implicitly treats the question of the feminine as a question of the legitimacy of the present exclusion of that particular image, rather than of the legitimacy of exclusion itself, which that image suffers in common with its rivals. In effect such an approach treats deconstruction as an empirical rather than an ethical claim, as an argument about what can be changed, for good or ill, rather than an argument about what ought to be changed.

In other words, the endorsement of any image of the feminine, however minimal its content, and the consequent repression of rivals to that image, contradicts Cornell's argument that gender repression is repression of the Other, whatever the content of the Other may be. It presents instead a picture of gender repression as repression of what ought not to be repressed because it is worthy of inclusion among the images of existence available to us. Yet to know that a given image of the feminine is worthy requires at a minimum that we know what the content of that image is, while the essence of Cornell's argument is that the true meaning of the feminine, as she would reimagine it, is and must remain undecidable. More important, to know that a given image of the feminine is worthy requires that we have an understanding of value based on something other than the fact of exclusion. Cornell's second way of resolving her dilemma, therefore, attempts to redeem her argument by a means that undermines its basic premise.

c. Transparent Themes. It follows that Cornell's second way of resolving her dilemma still fails to strike the required balance between determinacy and indeterminacy, and so makes necessary yet another refinement of the double gesture. Given that affirming certain themes as settings for, and constraints on, deconstruction has for Cornell the undesired effect of determining the consequences of deconstruction, to the extent that those themes have any substance at all, her third way of resolving her dilemma is to stipulate that such themes must be sufficiently transparent that they do not violate the ethical relation. Within the setting of her feminist project, therefore, she contends that the bare existence of a framework of the feminine is not only essential to the deconstruction of the present symbolic order and the role of the masculine subject there, but is transparent enough not to conflict with any other image of the feminine. So understood, she argues, the feminine is inherently compatible with the requirements of the ethical relation, provided of course that the content with which its framework is from time to time infused remains subject to continuous monitoring and regulation within the double gesture, so as to prevent it from ever assuming a status that would violate the ethical relation.[44]

Cornell argues that, understood in this way, the practice of the double gesture makes possible the realization of an infinite range of meanings for the feminine, and thus makes the pursuit of feminine difference compatible with the fullest range of feminine aspirations, as they are understood and felt by all manner of women. It makes possible, in other words, the affirmation of an ideal of the feminine that is compatible with the fullest degree of feminine pluralism, an ideal that has its roots in the present position of women in our culture, but that embodies an acknowledgment that latent and ineradicable within that position there lies an infinite capacity for women's redemption.

And yet the feminine, so conceived, cannot entirely free itself from tension with the obligations embodied in the ethical relation as Cornell describes it. To the extent that the structure and outline of the feminine are identifiable as an image and established as such, as they are by the process of thematization,

---

[44] *Beyond Accommodation, supra* n. 3, at 171.

the feminine is by definition not fully transparent. This is because its structure and outline establish the parameters of an image whose existence, sheltered as it is from deconstruction, precludes the realization of any other image whose structure would compete with it, including all the images of gender we have yet to imagine, as well as those we are already aware of. Indeed, if the image of the feminine did not have this consequence, it could not fulfil its role as a theme within deconstruction. Complete transparency in this situation would be equivalent to indeterminacy.

To the extent that the image of the feminine is rendered transparent by the second level of the double gesture, it lacks any content sufficiently established to be capable of begetting an Other to which it could be ethically obliged, and to which it could accordingly be expected to yield. In other words, any content that the feminine possesses, in Cornell's account, flows entirely from the determination of its structure, so that the feminine character of the content with which that structure is from time to time infused comes exclusively from the terms of the structure that shapes and contains it. That structure, like any other image, is conceived in terms of an Other to which it is ethically obliged, yet an Other in favour of which it, unlike other images, is sheltered from deconstruction as a theme within the double gesture. It follows that the initial decision to affirm the feminine as a theme within deconstruction categorically defines the content of the feminine as feminine, and establishes its ethical character. That decision can neither be derived from deconstruction nor be rendered consistent with it. On the contrary, both its justification and its consequences, to repeat, lie within determinacy, not outside it.[45]

iii. CONCLUSION. None of the three resolutions that Cornell offers to her dilemma, therefore, is successful in striking a balance between determinacy and indeterminacy that could mediate between those two perils without partaking of either, and so could give rise to an account of the feminine that embodies an entirely new understanding of existence. Nor is this failure the result of some flaw in the design of Cornell's argument that could be corrected by yet another description of the double gesture. Rather, it is the result of her recourse to the idea of deconstruction itself, which conflates the fact that our culture is repressive of much that is worthy with the fact that it is repressive of possibilities in its very definition as a culture. What ultimately matters to Cornell, by contrast, and the only thing that could matter to her as a feminist who seeks to affirm the

---

[45] Cornell sometimes uses the word "feminine" to describe the Other itself. However, she cannot be understood to be using the word in that sense when she treats the feminine as a theme within the practice of the double gesture, a theme designed to shape our response to the claims of the Other. Rather, she is using it to refer to a subverted version of our present gender roles, to the possibilities for transformation latent in the metaphors through which she believes our lives are now lived: see *The Philosophy of the Limit*, *supra* n. 12, at 104–6, 174–75; *Beyond Accommodation*, *supra* n. 3, at 3, 198.

experience of being a woman, which cannot be affirmed without repressing its rivals, is the worth of what is repressed, not repression itself.

In each of the three resolutions that Cornell offers to her dilemma, the only character her vision of the feminine possesses that enables it to be called feminine flows from its determination as an image in language and culture, one that despite her protestations to the contrary, Cornell implicitly believes is worthy of recognition by reason of what she sees as its freedom from the taint of the past, its flexibility, and its pluralism. The idea of deconstruction that she seeks to invoke in support of this vision of the feminine might, it is true, radically undermine and so overthrow our present understanding of gender, but in doing so it could not affirm the existence or worth of Cornell's or any other vision of the feminine. Deconstruction's ethical claim, that which would give it its power to revise the prevailing understanding of language and culture rather than merely remind us of their origins, is by its nature foundational to the very idea of language and culture, so that it threatens the stability of any image or concept by reason of its stability alone. As a result, the practice of deconstruction is fundamentally incompatible with the affirmation or reaffirmation of an image of the feminine, whether the content of that image be minimalist or highly developed, comprehensive or specific.

Any scope that is given to the practice of deconstruction yields indeterminacy to that extent, or as Derrida would call it, undecidability, while any meaning and content that is given to the image of the feminine is predicated on its determinacy and resistance to deconstruction. It follows that while deconstruction might appear to serve as Cornell's ally in her attack on the present social order, it in fact serves no agenda but its own. The authority that it undermines is the authority of any image or concept; as a result it cannot be harnessed to the service of the feminine. It is for this reason, one assumes, that Derrida resiles from any affirmation of the feminine, on the ground that it would merely result, in his phrase, in the passing out of new sexual identity cards. More to the point of Cornell's project, it is for this reason that any meaning the feminine is to have must flow from its determination, not its deconstruction.

Ultimately, therefore, Cornell can avoid the indeterminacy that an unqualified account of deconstruction would yield only by determining the content of the feminine, either arbitrarily or by limiting recognition of the call of the Other to what is desirable because of its perceived contribution to social order, human dignity, pluralism, or some other good. What this reveals, however, is that the Other that is excluded in the establishment of an image is not only human potential, emancipation, and liberation from oppression, but also brutality, evil, disorder, chaos, and worse. When we define ourselves in terms of cultural images we often exclude qualities that are desirable and worthy, but we do not exclude only qualities of that kind. On the contrary, we also exclude a great deal that is harmful and wrong. It follows that if the worth of an image is what we ought to care about, exclusion of the Other is as potentially emancipatory an act as its inclusion. Conversely, if ending exclusion of the Other were what we ought to care about, ending the exclusion of what is unworthy would be as emancipatory an act as ending the exclusion of what is worthy. Since Cornell clearly does not believe that ending the exclusion of what is unworthy is in any sense emancipatory, she cannot believe that ending the exclusion of the Other is what we ought to care about, except when to do so coincides with ending the exclusion of what is worthy.

Within the context of the feminine and similar images of existence, exclusion of the Other permits the establishment of forms of solidarity and community from which our lives derive much of their meaning. We can pursue an image of the feminine, or any other image of existence that enables us to identify with other human beings and develop associations with them on that basis, only by repressing and excluding not only competing forms of solidarity, but all those forms of existence not based upon solidarity. To seek to eliminate those determinate images in pursuit of an undecidable image of the feminine is in fact to seek to destroy the possibility of communal identity in the name of communal identity.

And yet to pursue the feminine as a value requires an ability to determine what is and what is not worthy of recognition as a social image, an ability that at the most basic level Cornell denies we possess. According to her account, our fundamental ethical obligation is to acknowledge the Other, so that any form of morality or social value must be predicated on that acknowledgment. Yet what her description of the practice of the double gesture, and particularly her apartheid illustration, reveals is that what she in fact cares about is the worth of what is excluded and hence Other, not the fact of exclusion itself. Despite her protestations to the contrary, what implicitly justifies the recovery of the feminine for Cornell is the worth of what she takes that image to represent. The difficulty for her, of course, is that as long as she remains committed to avoiding a determinate account of the feminine, she can offer no sense of the content of the feminine, other than to identify it with all that is excluded in the place of the Other. If she is in fact to affirm the worth of the feminine, she must abandon her reliance on the Derridean deconstruction of sexual difference and reject the Lacanian analysis of gender on which it is based, for both present a picture of existence in which, to use Lacan's phrase, woman does not exist.

In effect, in Cornell's account, it is an ethic that is both external to deconstruction and not subject to its claims that must carry the weight of defining the feminine and establishing its worth. What she presents as an account of the feminine based on an ethic of deconstruction ultimately derives both its feminine character and its ethical authority from the precepts that are taken to govern and constrain the consequences of deconstruction. To pursue a comprehensive rather than a local vision of the feminine, or to pursue one comprehensive vision of the feminine rather than another, are issues of social value and morality, and must be examined and evaluated as such.

4

Reasons for Feminism

I. The Value of Diversity

It is often said that human beings are complex creatures, who are inevitably betrayed by any attempt to comprehend them in simple terms. Indeed, much of the force of Drucilla Cornell's argument stems from its endorsement of the view, shared by many, that a failure to appreciate the complexity and diversity of human existence is responsible for the predicament that women now find themselves in. According to this view, Western society fails to appreciate diversity sufficiently, and so fails to appreciate fully the difference that women represent. Or, as it is sometimes more skeptically put, Western society denies many of the differences between human beings, including many of the differences between women and men, in order to avoid having to come to terms with those differences. For those who share this view of human complexity and diversity, the release of women from their present predicament is dependent on an escape from the straitjacket of masculine values, and a consequent recognition of and respect for the distinctive meaning of women's existence as women, as one element, if perhaps the most significant element, in a general acknowledgment of human diversity.

This understanding of feminism bears a strong relationship to that offered by Cornell herself. Like Cornell, its adherents are committed to recognizing difference for its own sake. Unlike Cornell, however, they are unidealistic, nonutopian. The differences they seek to honour are those that are already present in the world, not those that never have been and in a very real sense never could be. Their concern is with the many different ways of being that our society has neglected, overlooked, undervalued, and sought to suppress in its ongoing construction of what is normal and what is valuable. Their claim is that society should respect women as it should respect all ways of being, and for the same reason.

This is a distinctive and, on the face of it, somewhat surprising view of sex discrimination. Many if not most women hold an understanding of the disadvantage they experience on account of their sex that is instinctively based on a commitment to a particular view of what it means to be a woman, and the ways in which that meaning has been suppressed by the forms and practices of our culture.[1] By the same token, any affirmation that such women undertake of their distinctive existence as women is based on a sense of the value of that existence. Yet not all those who question the present place of women in society need be feminists in this committed sense, as both MacKinnon's and Cornell's discussions of discrimination demonstrate. Neither of those discussions takes any view about what it really means to be a woman and what value there might be in that.[2]

In particular, a commitment to a particular view of what it means to be a woman and the value of that existence forms no part of the argument of critics of the present social order who do not rely on a specifically female experience for their understanding of women's disadvantage, but regard the oppression of women as one aspect of the oppression of human difference.[3] For critics like these, women's qualities and characteristics are to be affirmed not for their own sake – that is, out of a belief in the value of their particular content and the activities that content makes possible – but out of a belief in the value of human diversity generally, and a corresponding belief in the existence of an obligation on human societies to recognize and affirm that diversity in all its variety and particularity. It is the diversity that women's qualities represent that is valued here, not the female character of those qualities. Advocates of this approach thus rely on the truth of two propositions. On the one hand, they maintain that a society that neglects or otherwise refuses to affirm women's qualities is oppressive of women simply by reason of its failure to affirm the full diversity of human experience. On the other hand, they maintain that a society that affirms

---

[1] See Carol Gilligan, *In a Different Voice* (Cambridge, Mass., 1982). The approach described here differs from Gilligan's in including the view that the content of what it means to be a woman is very largely the same as the content of what it means to be a man, so that the oppression of women is a matter of suppressing their equality with men.

[2] Both would condemn any search for a true answer to the question of what it means to be a woman. MacKinnon castigates Gilligan, and refuses to affirm women's qualities on the ground that there is no value in those qualities as we know them, although she does not rule out the possibility that once the subordination of women is ended it will be possible to develop an understanding of sexual identity that is worth affirming. Cornell endorses MacKinnon's analysis of women's present predicament but insists on affirming the feminine, understood as the unrealized and unrealizable possibilities implicit in the present understanding of sexual difference.

[3] I have in mind here commentators such as Martha Minow, *Making All the Difference: Inclusion, Exclusion and American Law* (Ithaca, 1990) ("When those who have been considered 'different' become the source of information about a critical but previously suppressed perspective on the legal issues affecting them, the social and institutional patterns that ignore this perspective themselves become questionable": *id.* at 218), although I do not wish to suggest that the position I present here is Minow's own. My purpose is not to address the substance of a particular position, such as Minow's, but to use my criticism of the affirmation of difference for its own sake as a way of showing that affirmation of any difference must be based upon the value of that difference and the contribution it can make to the success of some person's life.

human diversity in all its fullness necessarily brings to an end the oppression of women in the very act of doing so.

In my view, however, both of these propositions are false. Neither the oppression of women nor their liberation and redemption can in truth be said to turn upon a question of the unqualified and comprehensive affirmation of human difference, for affirmation of all forms of human difference is neither possible nor desirable. On the contrary, affirmation of any given difference between human beings, including the difference that constitutes a particular conception of what it means to be a woman, and hence a particular conception of sexual identity, takes place only at the expense of nonaffirmation of all those other forms of human difference with which the difference in question is necessarily in conflict. These include most obviously all those conceptions of what it means to be a woman that are either more or less sensitive to the existence of differences among women than the particular conception that is affirmed. That being the case, a failure to affirm human difference cannot be the correct explanation of women's disadvantage. Nevertheless, I believe that the appeal to human diversity, while in itself unsatisfactory as an explanation of or answer to sex discrimination, is indirectly helpful in arriving at that explanation, since the reasons for its inadequacy as an explanation offer the first clue as to where the true explanation lies.

In brief, for I address the issue fully below, I believe more specifically that an examination of the ideas of human complexity and diversity shows, first, that human beings are not unequivocally complex or diverse creatures, for they are both complex and simple, diverse and uniform, depending on our purpose. Second and consequently, it shows that the affirmation of human complexity or diversity in any particular context must be based on reasons that explain and justify both the value of complexity or diversity in that context and the value of the particular forms of difference that are sought to be affirmed there. Finally, it shows that affirmation of all valuable forms of human difference is neither possible nor desirable. It follows that the affirmation of one aspect or the other of sexual identity, whether in general or in any particular context, must be based on reasons that explain and justify the affirmation of that form of difference in that context. It further follows that such reasons cannot be based on the value of difference itself, but must be based on some determinate understanding of the meaning and value of sexual difference in that context, or more precisely, the value of the activities that the acknowledgment of that difference makes possible there.

II. The Character of Disadvantage

It is often thought to be wrong to endorse or accept standards that by their very definition place a certain category of human beings, defined other than by reference to the standard itself, at a disadvantage in relation to other human beings. Indeed, much of the force of MacKinnon's argument stems from the sense that it must be wrong to understand women in terms of *qualities* that ensure their disadvantage in relation to men. If women are caring and men are ruthless; if women are cooperative and men are aggressive; if women are passive and men are active; then men will prevail. That cannot be right, for it cannot be right to understand any category of human beings in terms that ensure their inferiority to other human beings. Or so it is said.[4]

MacKinnon's response to this wrong is to insist upon the transformation of sexual identity as we know it, so that women and men are redefined in terms that preclude the inferiority of either sex to the other, in any respect. According to her, existing sexual differences serve only to subordinate women; they must be abolished in favour of a model of sexual identity that is constructed on strictly egalitarian lines. This is a distinctively radical solution to the problem of sex discrimination. The argument against women's disadvantage is more typically and cautiously presented from the opposite point of view, which seeks to change our understanding of value rather than the qualities of women and men. It must be wrong, it is often said, to judge women by *standards* that ensure their disadvantage in relation to men. If ruthlessness is valued above concern; if aggressiveness is valued above cooperation; if activity is valued above passivity; and if men are ruthless, aggressive, and active, or more likely to be so than women; then men will prevail. That cannot be right, for it cannot be right to endorse standards that ensure the inferiority of women to men, or more generally, that ensure the inferiority of any category of human beings to other human beings. Accordingly, one of the main projects of antidiscrimination law has been to identify and remove any conditions and requirements that have a disparate impact on women or men, unless it can be shown that the cost of that removal is prohibitive.

The difference between these approaches, one seeking to reform human qualities, the other seeking to reform human values, masks a common basis and a common concern. If women and men are redefined in terms that preclude the inferiority of either sex to the other, in any respect, as MacKinnon demands, then the realm of value will cease to include any standards, such as ruthlessness and concern, that engender the inferiority of women to men.[5] Conversely, if our sense of value is redefined so that it ceases to include any standards that have a disparate impact upon women and men, then women and men will cease to differ from one another in any way that matters. In short, distinctions between men and women are ultimately distinctions of value. Accordingly, to redefine sex is to redefine value; to redefine value for the sake of sex is to redefine sex. Antidiscrimination law is in this respect as radical as Catharine MacKinnon.

---

[4] See, for example, *Feminism Unmodified* (Cambridge, Mass., 1987), at 41, 43.
[5] MacKinnon vehemently rejects the possibility that such standards might survive and apply equally to both sexes: *id.* at 4–5.

This is no accident. Underlying both these approaches is the belief that it is possible to comprehend human advantage and disadvantage in the abstract, simply by assessing the relationship between two categories of human being, without reference to the kind of person, and the kind of quality, that is said to be disadvantaged. Sometimes, if truth be told, that belief seems entirely plausible. After all, it cannot be denied that human beings need food when they are hungry, drink when they are dry, shelter against the elements, and treatment for disease, to name but a few. We need to know only that one person has received these things and another has been denied them to know that the latter has been disadvantaged. We need know nothing else about the disadvantaged person. Or so it seems. It is then tempting to conclude that what appears to be true of needs such as these is true of all human needs, and so of human welfare generally.

Yet in fact advantage and disadvantage can never be understood merely in the abstract, or in relation to other people. They are always relative to the person in question, not to some other. A person denied food and drink is disadvantaged by that denial if and only if he or she needs food and drink; so it is only because and to the extent that we know a person's needs by virtue of their humanity alone that we can know that denial to that person of what has been accorded to any other person is a disadvantage. Beyond the realm of such basic human needs, which all human beings share, this is rather more evidently the case. Advantage and disadvantage for any particular person in these further respects is profoundly shaped by the kind of person that he or she is. A reader needs good books and is disadvantaged by their denial; a swimmer needs open water and is disadvantaged by its denial; but the reader is no more disadvantaged by the denial of open water than the swimmer is disadvantaged by the denial of good books, unless of course the reader is also a swimmer and the swimmer a reader. Advantage and disadvantage are principally and fundamentally relative to the person in question, and only secondarily and consequently relative to some other person, who shares that person's qualities and the commitment to a particular application of them.

If that is the case, women are disadvantaged by denial to them of what is necessary to their well-being, given the kind of people they are. To the extent that women are no different from men, the requirements of their well-being will be no different from those of men, so that women will be disadvantaged in respect of those requirements by denial to them of what men have received, not because men have received it, but because women need it. To the extent that women differ from men, the requirements of their well-being will differ from those of men, so that women will be disadvantaged by denial to them of what men have never received, just because women need it, and conversely, will not be disadvantaged by denial to them of what men have received, simply because women have no need of it. To deny this is to deny the significance of sex, or of any other human difference that is capable of engaging value, in the construction of a successful life.

The existence of sexual difference implies the division of certain realms of human experience into male and female aspects, access to which belongs exclusively or predominantly to those whom that division defines as male and female for those purposes. In any context in which sexual difference functions so as to offer an advantage to the qualities possessed exclusively or predominantly by one sex, it necessarily imposes a corresponding disadvantage upon the qualities possessed by the other sex. In this way sexual difference constrains the experience of those defined by it even as it enables, constraint being simply the obverse of capacity in any given respect. It follows that the attempt to affirm a conception of sexual difference that avoids all limitation and disadvantage is flawed in two ways. First, it is inconsistent, since it seeks to affirm a form of human difference while denying what difference means, and second, it is empty, since it seeks to affirm a difference between the sexes while denying any content to that difference.

This is not to say, of course, that women do not suffer illegitimate disadvantage as a consequence of their existence as women, disadvantage that they experience distinctively as women and that is embodied in the understanding of them as women.[6] Rather, it is to say that the disadvantage experienced by women as a consequence of their existence as women, which flows from the perception of them as women and that we call discrimination, cannot be equated with the fact that certain incidents of limitation and disadvantage are present in the lives of women (and correspondingly absent from the lives of men), despite the fact that those incidents are a consequence of their existence as women, for limitation is a function of the existence of any form of difference, and a consequent degree of exposure to disadvantage the inevitable product of that existence.

It follows that the avoidance of disadvantage in this brute sense cannot be the basis for rejecting one conception of sexual identity and affirming another. However, the attempt to make it so offers a second and final clue to the true explanation of sex discrimination, by suggesting what might constitute a morally compelling objection to a particular conception of sexual identity and a morally compelling basis for affirming a different conception as its replacement. To see how and why this is so it is necessary to return to the accepted facts of discrimination, features that attend all descriptions of it and so constitute the necessary basis for its explanation without predetermining the character of that explanation.

[6] This is in addition to the disadvantage they suffer as a consequence of their existence as human beings who are distinguished from others on bases other than sex, which some women experience in common with some men and is embodied in some understanding of human existence other than that of sex.

III. The Role of Sexual Identity in a Successful Life

Any account of feminism and any explanation of discrimination, I have said,[7] must address and answer satisfactorily the two features of women's predicament to which Catharine MacKinnon calls attention. These are the widespread instances of disadvantage that women face in attempting to lead successful lives, and the incorporation of those disadvantages, or at least the qualities that entail them, in our very understanding of what it means to be a woman. The problem facing those who seek to explain discrimination, then, is one of showing how our understanding of a certain image, namely, that of what it means to be a woman, has become so corrupted as to impair the life prospects of certain people, namely, women.

It follows from this description of what I take to be uncontroversial features of discrimination that the question of discrimination that feminism seeks to address cannot be as broad as the question of the disadvantage that is experienced by women in whatever capacity, for not all such disadvantage can be linked to the perception of them as women. It is certainly the case that many of the forms of disadvantage now experienced by certain women on bases such as race, religion, or national origin, disadvantage that those women experience in common with men, are illegitimate and call for redress. Nevertheless, the imposition of such forms of disadvantage can be understood only as sex discrimination, and hence redressed through the redefinition of sexual identity, if and to the extent that the qualities that give rise to them constitute part of our understanding of sexual identity. In other words, it is possible to regard a species of conduct as sex discrimination only if it either picks out women or has a disproportionate impact upon women. It can be necessary to alter our perception of sex, as both feminism and antidiscrimination law ask us to do,[8] only if that perception is in some way implicated in the creation of the disadvantages experienced by women.

Nor can the question of feminism be as broad as the question of the disadvantage that is experienced by women as a consequence of their existence as women. If that were discriminatory, we would have to redefine sexual identity in such a way as to eliminate the disadvantage, which we cannot possibly do, for some such disadvantage is a necessary consequence of the very existence of sexual difference. As the analysis of Drucilla Cornell's arguments showed, any

---

[7] Chapter 2, notes 125–127 and accompanying text.

[8] Some might argue that antidiscrimination law differs from feminism in asking us to change our treatment of sex rather than our perception of it. However, unless it is merely clumsy, treatment is based on perception, so that a change in treatment must ultimately be founded on a change in perception. In its present form, antidiscrimination law asks that men and women be treated as equals. The only explanation for this requirement is that those whom we now treat as different are in fact the same, at least for all purposes addressed by the law. Any differences that appear to distinguish men and women in those respects are merely superficial, and so irrelevant to the ultimate moral assessment upon which the allocation of social goods must be based. It is true, therefore, to say that the law, like feminism, asks us to change our perception of sex.

attempt to eliminate the *limitations* that flow from the fact of sexual difference, however that difference may be conceived, amounts to an attempt to eliminate sex itself, by eliminating the very thing that gives it structure and so defines it. And as the analysis of Catharine MacKinnon's arguments also showed, any attempt to eliminate the *disadvantages* that flow from the fact of sexual difference amounts to an attempt to nullify that difference in any setting in which it is coextensive with a question of value, and hence to nullify the possibilities that sexual difference expresses there, advantageous or disadvantageous.[9]

The question of feminism, put simply, is a question of the ways in which our conception of sexual identity has been misconceived so as to impose an illegitimate set of disadvantages upon the lives of a whole category of people, namely, women. While neither the failure to affirm diversity nor the failure to avoid disadvantage in its brute form can be taken as answers to that question, I believe that the reasons for their inadequacy offer an indication of where the correct answer lies. Each of those approaches suggests the correct explanation of one of the two features of the problem of discrimination, and it is the conjunction of the two features, and hence of the two explanations of them, that in my view makes a practice discriminatory. The first feature brings our conception of sexual identity into issue, while the second makes the role of that conception in the lives of women and the disadvantage it imposes on those lives not merely unwarranted but morally significant.

From the conclusions reached regarding the affirmation of human diversity and the avoidance of disadvantage, it is possible to deduce the character of a genuine commitment to feminism and to a particular conception of what it means to be a woman. First, that commitment must be based on reasons that explain and justify it as a commitment to that form of human difference, rather than to the other forms of difference with which the recognition and pursuit of that difference is necessarily in conflict. Those reasons can be found, I argue, only in the *truth* of any particular conception of what it means to be a woman, in the *relevance* of that conception to the culture in relation to which it is invoked, and in the *value* the pursuit of that conception is capable of realizing within the culture.

It follows that we cannot simply choose which conceptions of womanhood to endorse, for any such endorsement is shaped, on the one hand, by what is genuinely true and valuable, and on the other hand, by what it is rational and possible for us to pursue in a particular cultural setting.[10] Conversely, it follows

---

[9] I am ignoring here the possibility that men and women might occupy a world in which they are never measured according to the same standard. As I noted in Chapter 2, the dominance of men and subordination of women is a problem born of a world in common and its resolution must lie there.

[10] I should emphasize that despite my singular description of it, what it means to be a woman is not singular but plural in form. There is an enormous variety in the content of what it means to be a woman, a variety that is expressed in the lives of different women and the different experiences

that we have reason to reject certain conceptions of what it means to be a woman on the basis that they are false or irrelevant to our culture, without entering into the question of their value. Again, this is not to suggest that the question of value is not part of feminism. On the contrary, I believe the question of the value of the qualities that genuinely describe women, or more accurately, the value of the activities that those qualities make possible, is an essential aspect of feminism. That being the case, value will constitute a further basis for rejecting one conception of what it means to be a woman and affirming another in its place. What is significant here is that there is reason to reject a conception of what it means to be a woman before any consideration of the value it gives access to, that reason being that the conception in question is either false or irrelevant to the culture in which it is invoked.

Second, feminism does not acquire its moral dimension, the dimension that imposes an obligation on society to correct the misconceptions it holds concerning sexual identity, from the mere existence of a misconception of sexual identity, for misconceptions are not in themselves morally significant. Nor is this moral dimension derived from the mere presence of instances of limitation and disadvantage in the lives of women, for limitation and disadvantage attend all forms of difference, including those that define men as well as women. Nor is it even derived from the presence of what is conceded to be illegitimate disadvantage in the lives of women generally, disadvantage that is experienced in common with men, for such disadvantage is not discriminatory where it does not involve a conception of what it means to be a woman. Feminism derives its moral dimension from the particular forms of limitation and disadvantage that may follow from the widespread promulgation of a false or irrelevant conception of what it means to be a woman. Such a conception, if comprehensively endorsed, renders it impossible or virtually impossible for those defined by it to gain access to the goods to which all human beings are entitled, whether those goods are understood as opportunities, as resources, as an adequate range of valuable options, as the satisfaction of needs, or as anything else *that is sensitive to the condition of those to whom it is addressed.* Any such good depends for its realization on a genuine understanding of those to whom it is allocated. No such good is genuinely accessible therefore to those who are known either exclusively or very largely in terms of an image that is false or irrelevant to their existence, and that as a result misrepresents the options and resources they find valuable, and the needs they seek to fulfil. Indeed, for those who believe that all human beings are entitled to an adequate range of valuable options,[11]

---

and aspirations to which those lives refer, a variety that those lives interpret and renew as a consequence of the different courses they take. When I speak of what it means to be a woman, therefore, I do so simply for ease of expression, not because I take a fixed or limited view of the content of that way of being.

[11] I have in mind here, of course, the views of Joseph Raz, particularly as they are expressed in *The Morality of Freedom* (Oxford, 1986) and *Ethics in the Public Domain* (Oxford, 1994). As

a misconception of human difference may be illegitimate even though neither profound in its error nor broadly endorsed in social practices, as long as that misconception plays a critical role in denying those who are subject to it an adequate range of valuable options, as it may if those people are dependent for their well-being on access to certain options that the misconception of their difference renders inaccessible to them.

It follows that the existence of a widespread and comprehensive misconception as to the nature of sexual identity does not simply give one sex more goods than the other, be they opportunities, resources, or the satisfaction of needs, or give one sex the goods that it deserves while denying them to the other, although it may well do just that. If and to the extent that the truth of sexual identity reveals that the sexual differences we now subscribe to either do not exist or exist only in a form that has no relevance to our culture, so that men and women are in fact equal in all respects that may concern us, it is entirely possible and, indeed, seems to have been very largely the case that one sex, namely, men, has been justly accorded what ought to have been accorded to both sexes, and so has obtained not only the goods it deserves but more of them than the other sex, namely, women. In this situation, only women are denied what they deserve, and it is accordingly the task of feminism to expose the inauthenticity of these aspects of sexual difference as a distinction that is relevant to our society, and to establish the truth of sexual equality in its place. In the execution of this task, both sexes have an obligation to correct the misconceptions on which the presence of sexual difference in our culture has been founded, although only women will have a direct interest in doing so.

However, to the extent that the truth of sexual identity reveals that sexual difference is real and relevant but other than we have taken it to be, the prevailing misconception of the character of sexual difference will have ensured that neither sex has received the goods it is capable of enjoying. As I have said, goods whose allocation is based on a false understanding of the people to whom they are directed offer opportunities that those people cannot use and purport

I have already suggested and argue more fully below, an adequate conception of what it means to be a woman, one that is not false, or irrelevant, or incapable of valuable application, plays an essential role in the implementation of any account of the goods to which all human beings are entitled. This means, however, that those accounts of the goods necessary to a successful life that lack the capacity to register the differences between people, such as accounts of equality, which by their very nature lack the capacity to register the differences between people in the dimension that they seek to equalize, are to that extent flawed, and profoundly so, for they necessarily assign to people goods that they cannot value and so are empty in their hands, and thus impose upon people the futile task of attempting to live up to the conception of themselves that would make possession of those goods valuable. Conversely, a description of the goods necessary to a successful life that has the capacity to take into account the critical impact that a failure to understand even a limited portion of the difference between one person and another may have upon both those persons' lives, such as that provided by Raz as I understand him, is to that extent vindicated. It follows that although what I have to say is not dependent upon acceptance of Raz's views, it is undoubtedly more congenial to those views than to some others.

to satisfy needs that they do not have. At best they are empty in the hands of those to whom they are assigned; at worst they impose upon those people a futile task, that of attempting to live up to the misconception of themselves that would make possession of those goods valuable. In this situation, neither sex is offered the goods that it deserves, and it is accordingly the task of feminism to expose the false character of our present conception of sexual identity and to give effect to the true meaning of sexual difference. In this task both sexes have not only an obligation to rectify our present conception of sex, but a common interest in doing so.

In conclusion, therefore, I believe that sex discrimination arises when we mistake the meaning of sexual identity, so that the conceptions we hold of men and women are either false or irrelevant to our culture, and then invoke that mistaken picture either comprehensively or in realms of activity that are critical to the success of women's lives. When this happens, the misconception we hold of what it means to be a woman, for example,[12] comes to dominate the lives of women, forcing them to live in terms of an image of themselves that is either false or irrelevant, and which, governing as it does their access to options in life, and the resources with which to pursue them, denies women access to those options in terms that they can genuinely value. It thus denies them what all human beings are entitled to, thereby exposing them to a form of disadvantage that is morally illegitimate. Discrimination so understood depends upon the presence of a causal connection between two sets of social circumstances: first, a profound misconception of the character of a form of human difference, and second, the inability of certain people, namely, those understood in terms of that misconception, to lead successful lives. A misconception about the meaning of sexual identity is not discriminatory unless it has a critical bearing on the success of the lives of those who are subject to it. Conversely, the presence of disadvantage in women's lives is not discriminatory, even if it has a critical bearing on the success of those lives, unless that disadvantage is caused by a misconception of the meaning of sexual identity. This analysis and explanation of discrimination offers an important reason why certain lives are unsuccessful in our culture, important because that reason is entrenched in the very fabric of the culture and the conception it holds, in the case of women, of half its members, and at the same time suggests how and why that reason might be removed and those lives might be made successful.

It remains to be established, at least partially and provisionally, what misconceptions of sexual identity we now hold and what impact they have on the

---

[12] We can misconceive what it means to be a woman without misconceiving what it means to be a man if we correctly perceive the character of men's experience but falsely believe that women's experience is different; that is, if we perceive a sexual difference where in truth there is none and in addition correctly perceive the attributes of one component of that supposed difference. In short, if women are in truth equal to what men are correctly taken to be, a mistaken perception of sexual difference misconceives the existence of women only.

capacity of women to lead successful lives in our culture. Once that is established, it remains further to establish what role the law has to play in correcting such misconceptions and whether the present laws against discrimination legitimately fulfil that role. That, in turn, will depend upon whether the societies in which antidiscrimination laws have been enacted now hold conceptions of sexual identity that are both so profoundly misconceived as to be morally objectionable (and hence discriminatory on the test of discrimination that I have just outlined), and so entrenched, in certain domains at least, as to require the intervention of the law to correct them.

If there is, indeed, entrenched sex discrimination in those societies, as few would deny, the legitimacy of the laws that have been enacted to correct it in domains such as employment, accommodation, and the provision of services will depend upon whether the revised conception of sexual identity that those laws implement, that of sexual equality, is true to the meaning of sexual identity for those societies. It clearly will be if none of the differences that genuinely distinguish the sexes has any possible relevance to employment, accommodation, or the provision of services in those societies. If, however, any of the differences that genuinely distinguish the sexes is relevant in any of those domains, then the legitimacy of antidiscrimination law will ultimately depend upon whether the conception of sexual equality that it promotes is so deeply misconceived as to be morally objectionable and hence itself discriminatory, as it will be if at least some women or some men need to call upon the differences between them that the law declares to be irrelevant if they are to lead successful lives in those domains.

To establish that antidiscrimination law's imposition of sexual equality is legitimate and not itself discriminatory, therefore, it is necessary to show either that sexual difference has no relevance in any of the domains to which the law applies or that any sexual difference that is relevant in those domains may be denied without denying women and men that to which they are entitled, namely, the ability to lead successful lives, and so may be denied without discriminating against them. To establish the latter, it is necessary to consider more fully the question of value, for access to a conception of sexual identity is morally required only if that conception is necessary to the capacity of women to pursue valuable goals that are critical to the success of their lives. To put it from the opposite perspective, it is only if equality (or absence of sexual difference) is the truth of sexual identity in domains such as employment, accommodation, and the provision of services, as antidiscrimination law maintains, that antidiscrimination law can be justified simply on the basis that the existing conception of sexual difference is false. If, on the contrary, sexual difference is not only true but relevant to our culture, albeit other than we have taken it to be, then antidiscrimination law is mistaken and potentially illegitimate. Whether it is actually illegitimate depends upon the value of sexual difference and the critical role it may play in the construction of a successful life, a role that would be a ground for affirming a particular conception of sexual difference, and for concluding that the law's present imposition of equality is morally objectionable.

Before it is possible to consider antidiscrimination law and the question of its success or shortcomings, however, it is necessary to actually make the arguments for the theory of discrimination whose outline I have sketched in this chapter, or at least to provide a fuller account of those arguments. I do so under three headings, the import of which should be clear from the outline: the value of diversity, the character of disadvantage, and the role of sexual identity in a successful life.

5

The Value of Diversity

Those who would affirm women's existence as a facet of human difference rely on the suggestion, as I have said, that human beings are complex creatures,[1] who are inevitably betrayed by any attempt to comprehend them in simple terms.[2] I believe there is an element of truth in this suggestion, or perhaps I should say in the intuitions that underlie it, since I have already expressed my belief that the propositions it rests on are false. What truth there is in the suggestion lies in the perception that in some measure at least a failure to acknowledge the distinctive features of women's existence, and the possibility that certain of those features are relevant to our culture, despite the fact that they have been suppressed and concealed by the present social order, may well be a crucial element in the problem of sex discrimination and its remedy. However, when framed in such a manner as to suggest that the suppression of women's existence is but an instance of the suppression of human diversity, so that its remedy is merely a matter of affirming that diversity, the appeal to human complexity and diversity is highly misleading, in three ways. It is misleading, first, because it treats diversity as if it were simply a fact about human existence; second, because it assumes that human differences can be detached from the purposes that make those differences matter to certain people and not to others; and third, because it takes the affirmation of all differences to be a rational and desirable goal when in fact it is neither.

---

[1] A concept is sometimes called complex if some people have difficulty in mastering it; so understood, its description as complex expresses a comment on the character and capacities of certain people rather than on the concept itself. What is I have in mind here is a concept that is complex because its structure is complex, so that it has different implications when considered for different purposes. See the discussion below.

[2] I do not wish to overstate the degree to which this argument has been endorsed by feminist scholars. In particular, I should note that it is specifically rejected by Drucilla Cornell, *The Philosophy of the Limit* (New York, 1992), 105.

I. The Nature of Diversity

The appeal to complexity[3] is misleading, first, because human beings are not complex or simple, any more than are trees or rocks or anything else. They merely are what they are; what we take to be their complexity or simplicity is not a quality inherent in them, but a product of the concepts that we from time to time bring to bear upon them, and the purposes that those concepts serve. Those concepts may treat the same set of human qualities as either complex or simple, depending upon the purpose or purposes for which the qualities in question are invoked.

This is not, as might at first appear, to make a skeptical point about the nature of reality; it is not to say that human beings are complex as we perceive them yet nevertheless not "really" complex. It is, first, to say something about concepts in general, and second, to say something about the particular concepts of complexity and simplicity and the relation between them. Human beings really are intelligent, two-legged creatures who can laugh, among a host of other things. They are also, it follows, complex creatures, in the sense that they are susceptible to complex understanding, as perhaps an amoeba is not. But complexity, unlike intelligence or the capacity for laughter, for example, is a concept that implies rather than excludes the existence of its correlative, so that what can be understood in complex terms can also be understood, just as accurately if less completely, in simple terms. Human beings, in short, are both complex and simple creatures, and that is no more than a fuller account of what it means to say that they are complex.

It is necessarily the case that a determination of complexity for one purpose precludes a determination of simplicity for the same purpose. Yet it is also the case that a determination of complexity for one purpose does nothing to preclude a determination of simplicity for some other purpose. Those who regard human beings as complex in terms of the purposes that contrast them to amoebae, therefore, may also legitimately regard human beings as simple for other purposes, such as the ascription of basic human rights, and may indeed regard human beings as no more complex than amoebae for still other purposes. It follows that a determination of our complexity as human beings implies rather than precludes the existence of dimensions of understanding in which we may be seen in simple terms. The same is true, of course, for those contexts in which we are seen as simple creatures, for a determination of our simplicity there does nothing to preclude a determination of our complexity in other contexts and for other purposes.

This is a rather compressed way of describing a very complicated state of affairs, one that raises issues about the character of human existence, about the

---

[3] For the sake of clarity, I consider the complexity of human beings first and then return to the question of their diversity. I take the two to be closely connected in that human complexity is understood to be the source of the human diversity that those who would affirm diversity have in mind.

nature of concepts and their role in representing that existence, and about the nature and role of the particular concepts of complexity and diversity. Those issues will have to be untangled if I am to explain the basis for my claim that the appeal to both complexity and diversity is highly misleading. My purpose in this section, therefore, is to offer an overview of the relevant aspects of what I take to be the relationship between reality and our conceptions of it, and more particularly, of what I take to be the relationship between what it really means to be a woman and our conceptions of that reality. In the course of this overview I address four issues: first, the variety in the world; second, the dependence of any concept of the world upon the purposes that make that concept, rather than some other, matter to us; third, the role played in human lives by concepts and conceptions; and finally, the complexity and diversity of human beings, in terms of the reality of their lives, the concepts in and through which those lives are understood, and the dependence of those concepts upon the different purposes that make them relevant.

A. *Nature, Nurture, and Variety in the World*

We live in a world that is in part the product of natural forces and in part the product of human action.[4] As far as we know, much if not all of that world is in a state of continuous evolution in which we play a prominent and, perhaps for the time being at least, a leading role. The shape of our lives, the culture within which those lives are pursued, and the physical world that is the theatre for both, all bear the heavy imprint of human behaviour. It follows that the different course of human affairs in different cultures, in different times and in different parts of the world, has both compounded and created significant variations in the content of universally recognized differences between human beings, including significant variations in the content of the difference between men and women. What it means to be a man and to be a woman is not the same the world over, therefore, any more than it is now what it always was, and part of the reason for that variation is that different cultures have over time made different contributions to the meaning of sexual identity, so that sexual identity is not simply conceived and expressed differently in different cultures, but as often as not is experienced differently there. Both nature and nurture have shaped sexual identity as we know it. One important reason, then, for us to be concerned about the content of what it means to be a woman is that that content may not be the same for some of us as it is for others, precisely because we and they have helped to make it different.

Just because we have made the world does not mean that we can change it. On the contrary, we are constrained by the limits of our knowledge and by the

---

[4] I do not mean to suggest that human action is other than natural. Rather, I want to distinguish human and nonhuman forces, and it is to that end that I have called the latter natural.

limits set by the various contexts in which we find ourselves, limits that shape what is rational and possible for us to pursue. For those who doubt this, there is ample evidence of the constraints upon us, and of the effects of ignoring them, in the mixed fortunes of our attempts to predict and control the natural world and to direct the course of human affairs, attempts that demonstrate all too clearly the limits of our understanding, our authority, and our grasp of what is rational for us to desire and pursue.

Unfortunately, the lessons in modesty this experience ought to have taught us are not lessons that human beings have ever quite appreciated or taken to heart. As the familiar debate over the roles of nature and nurture in the construction of sexual identity makes plain, we are prepared to accept our inability to alter the facts of nature, despite the overwhelming record of our impact on the natural environment, yet are oddly confident of our ability to alter the facts of culture and society, despite the just as overwhelming record of our inability to remedy the most significant of our social ills, and the disastrous effects of many of our attempts to do so, particularly when they have been based on assumptions about the plasticity of a society and its citizens. In this regard, both MacKinnon's and Cornell's accounts of feminism not only urge the desirability of changing the meaning of sexual identity, but assume, wrongly in my view, that if that identity has been socially constructed it can be reconstructed simply through social decision.[5] We cannot, simply by decision, make women something they are not, and more profoundly, we cannot even want to do so, although we can and must understand far better than we do what women are and what that makes possible.

B. Objectionable Concepts, Objectionable Purposes

Variety exists not only in the world but in the concepts that we apply to the world, the concepts we use to understand and come to terms with the world. Concepts are ways of dividing up the world, of organizing, editing, and focusing the myriad features of the world and so linking them to a set of purposes that arise from the particular circumstances in which we find ourselves, the ambitions and concerns that those circumstances give rise to, and what in the features of the world those ambitions and concerns make significant. In other words, concepts function as ways of mediating between ourselves and the world of which we are a part, ways that are so fundamental to our thought that it is impossible to

---

[5] Catharine MacKinnon, *Feminism Unmodified: Discourses on Life and Law* (Cambridge, Mass., 1987), 23: "... what it means to be a woman or a man is a social process and, as such, is subject to change"; Drucilla Cornell, *Beyond Accommodation: Ethical Feminism, Deconstruction and the Law* (New York, 1991), 13: "... the slippage inherent in the so-called achievement of sexual identity – because this identity takes place within mythical fantasy projection and is not given in biology – is what makes possible rewriting from the position of the feminine that denies its current definition as the whole truth."

contemplate the world without calling upon them. That being the case, however, the various circumstances in which human beings find themselves and the various purposes they endorse mean that there is as much diversity in the concepts that can be applied to the world as in the world itself, so that any affirmation of diversity is as liable to be conceptual as it is to be real.

Conceptual diversity has two dimensions, *scope* and *purpose*, each of which is a product and reflection of the different contexts in which a particular concept may be invoked. First, the same concept, invoked for the same purpose, may pick out different features of the world in different cultural settings, either because different conventions govern the use of the concept in those settings or because different circumstances exist there. For example, the socioeconomic concept of the family may pick out different people in different cultures. If grandparents form part of the socioeconomic concept of the family in a particular culture, it may be because the convention as to what constitutes a family in that culture deems them to, or it may be because grandparents in that culture actually support children in ways that a cross-cultural convention takes to confer family status. Either way, the socioeconomic concept of the family in that culture is related to but also different from the socioeconomic concept of the family in those other cultures in which grandparents are not family members. This dimension of conceptual diversity by and large simply reflects the variety in the world.

Second, however, and more relevant to women, the same concept with the same scope may be invoked for different *purposes*. The concept of the family, now understood to embrace grandparents, parents, and children, may be used for legal purposes as well as for socioeconomic purposes. When that is the case, the same people are picked out by the same concept, but for different purposes. We often have different reasons to be interested in the relationships that the concept of the family describes, and so employ different versions of the concept to describe the different aspects of the family that those reasons pick out.

What this shows is that the use of concepts is dependent upon the purposes that make them matter to us. This dependence upon purposes does more than increase the variety in the world, though it does that too. Given that our concepts of the world are as various as our purposes, no concept, such as the concept of a woman, can ever be thought to have exclusive access to the features of the world that it describes, so as to bind those features to the particular purpose that the concept embodies, for those features and, indeed, the concept itself can always be invoked for a different purpose. It follows that while there are a number of reasons to reject particular concepts, they cannot, contrary to what is claimed by Cornell and others, include the notion that those concepts determine and so limit our access to the world, so as to invest the features that they describe with their particular purposes, and thereby exclude rival concepts and the rival forms of access that those rival concepts would offer.

Concepts may be *objectionable*, if they reflect purposes that are objectionable, or be *without instantiation*, if they reflect purposes that do not pick out anything in the world, or be *irrelevant*, if they reflect purposes that have no significance for a culture such as ours, purposes that are based upon a set of beliefs or a way of life that we do not subscribe to. We may *object* to the concept of virginity, therefore, or to the concept of purdah; we may believe that the concept of the unicorn and of the philosopher's stone are *without instantiation*, or that the concepts that defined feudal societies, such as that of knight service, are without instantiation in a culture such as ours; we may take it that the religious concept of pollution, which some cultures attach to menstruation, has *no relevance* in secular cultures. We may reject concepts for any of these reasons, but we do so because we regard those concepts as inapplicable to us, not because we regard them as exclusive of their rivals, or false.

It further follows that features of the world that have come into being to serve certain purposes are in no sense bound to reflect the purposes that brought them into being, for they may be conceived of and exploited in any number of different ways. In particular, human qualities that were acquired in circumstances of degradation, such as a heightened capacity to show concern for others if acquired as the product of a prolonged commitment to the service of one's superiors in a hierarchical social structure, are as apt to serve valuable purposes as degrading purposes, contrary to what Catharine MacKinnon assumes. To seek to reject such qualities on the ground that they are necessarily degrading, therefore, is simply mistaken. What we need to do instead, as I argue below, is to discover and pursue the valuable purposes to which such qualities can be put.

However – and this is of critical importance to the understanding of sex discrimination – confusion can arise from the fact that concepts are typically the setting for beliefs about the world, which we call *conceptions* of the world. These beliefs are sometimes isolated but more often come in packages, the content of which we tend to associate, wrongly, with the content of the concepts within which those packages are set. For example, the concept of sexual identity is typically the setting for a package of beliefs that constitute a particular culture's conception of the content of sexual identity. Unlike the concept of sexual identity itself, those beliefs may well be false, and any reference to them that assumes their truth may, in certain circumstances, have crippling consequences for the people they misrepresent. I have already suggested that it is the falsity of our present conception of sexual identity that is responsible for women's disadvantage. I wish to make clear here that the falsity of our present *conception* of sexual identity, if false it is, should not be equated with the falsity of our *concept* of sexual identity, which is not and cannot be false, and correspondingly, to make clear that my reference to a true conception of what it means to be a woman is not to be equated with a reference to a true concept of sexual identity, or essence of what it means to be a woman or a man.

C. Enabling Concepts, Disabling Misconceptions

A great many aspects of human life are accessible without any reference to concepts. We do not need to refer to the concept of hunger in order to be hungry. We do not need to refer to the concept of the family in order to be part of one. This is because in neither situation do we need to see ourselves as having the feeling in order to feel it, as engaging in the relationship in order to engage in it. Certain aspects of human life, however, have the special feature that they are inaccessible to us other than by reference to the concepts that define them. So, for example, it is impossible to make promises other than by referring to the concept of a promise; it may be impossible to fall in love without referring to the concept of love; many argue that it is impossible to be a homosexual without referring to the concept of homosexuality, here understood as a way of life and not merely as a tendency to engage in certain sexual practices. The same may be true of certain aspects of being a woman, which may be inaccessible except by reference to the concept of a woman. In these situations we need to see ourselves as having the feeling in order to feel it, as engaging in the relationship in order to engage in it, as gendered in a certain respect in order to be gendered in that respect. Access to these aspects of life requires reference to the relevant concept because they are ways of being that can be engaged in only self-consciously, by reference to the idea of themselves that the concept defines. If these aspects of life are valuable, as they often are, then concepts of this enabling kind do more than increase the variety in the world; they increase the scope of what it is possible for us to value.

Concepts of this kind can constrain as well as enable, however, if the aspects of human life that they define (such as the condition of slavery) are without value, and if the endorsement of those concepts in any particular culture is so profound that the concepts come to govern certain people's sense of who they are and what their lives should look like. If women are raised to see themselves as women, and moreover, to see women's role in life as nothing more than one of supporting men, their lives will undoubtedly be diminished. But the constraint upon women's lives in such a case, and the disadvantage that it would give rise to, is not the product of the fact that a concept of a woman's role defines a nonvaluable way of life, but of the belief that the qualities of character that women possess do not enable them to live a life other than that defined by that concept. In short, in such a case it is a *misconception* of the capacities that women possess, and of the lives that they might wish to lead, and not the limited *concept* of a woman's role, that confines the lives of women to the nonvaluable activity that the concept describes. The tendency to hold the concept responsible for the disadvantage that the invocation of it gives rise to is a product of the fact that the limited concept of a woman's role is the setting for a conception of women's character and capacities that not only sustains the concept, by establishing its aptness for women, but confines women's lives to the role that the concept defines, by inculcating in both men and women the belief that women are incapable of any other role. How we are to recognize and correct such misconceptions, and how far they themselves can be self-fulfilling, are issues that I consider below. What matters here is to note that while concepts can enlarge the palette of possibilities the world offers us, only misconceptions can restrict that palette.

D. Affirming Complexity and Diversity

It is against this background that we speak of human complexity and diversity. The content of reality and the role of concepts in portraying that reality give rise to three sources of human diversity, and thus to three realms of difference that the affirmation of diversity might be thought to be directed at. As I have already suggested, however, we can affirm human difference only where we have reason to do so, and we have reason to do so only where a difference is relevant to the practices of a particular culture, and its recognition in that culture would contribute to the realization of certain valuable goals there, and thus to the success of certain human lives. Let me explain briefly, before going on to consider the details.

The first source of diversity is the varying reality upon which concepts such as sexual identity are based. As I have already indicated, life is not only understood differently in different parts of the world, but often really is different there. Being a woman may actually mean something different in India and Japan, Canada and Kiribati. Yet even assuming that this is the case, it is a difference that it is only possible for a woman to live, not to affirm, for it is impossible to affirm a difference as a difference until one has formed a concept of it.

This is what I meant in arguing earlier that human beings are not in themselves unequivocally complex or diverse, for the truth is that they may be either. The set of experiences that we sometimes describe as constituting the concept of a human being may be regarded as simple or uniform for some purposes, by those who see the experiences as characteristically human for example, and yet may be regarded as complex or diverse for other purposes, by those who see the experiences as characteristic of some human beings but not of others. Reality itself is not diverse, strictly speaking, although it is susceptible to diverse interpretation. Rather, it is concepts that are diverse, and accordingly it is only the diversity of concepts that we can contemplate the affirmation of. The first way in which I regard the appeal to diversity as misleading, then, is in its assumption that diversity is a fact about reality that is available for us to affirm.

The second source of diversity is in the concepts that can be applied to any given portion of reality. As I have also indicated, even where reality is uniform in content there is often great diversity in the concepts through which we organize and understand that reality. In particular, two cultures may hold very different concepts of what it means to be a woman despite the fact that there is little or no difference in the reality upon which those concepts are based.

Yet once again this form of conceptual diversity is not a form of diversity that it is possible simply to affirm in itself. We cannot affirm all concepts of human difference, or even all concepts of what it means to be a woman, first, because concepts are linked to purposes and cannot be affirmed in isolation from them; second and consequently, because not all purposes are relevant in any particular culture; and third, because not all purposes that are relevant are valuable. This is the second way in which I believe that the appeal to diversity is misleading, and it is one that I take up in the next section.

The third source of diversity is again in the concepts that can be applied to any given portion of reality. Different cultures often have different ways of conceiving the experience of what it means to be a woman, even where there is no difference in that experience. One way in which cultures do this is by developing subordinate distinctions, so that they see women in terms of their race, or sexual orientation, or income, or political affiliation, or artistic inclination, or otherwise, rather than in terms of an undifferentiated picture of womanhood. In light of this possibility, the appeal to diversity might be understood as an appeal for the affirmation of as many distinctions as possible, within the concept of a human being in general and within the concept of what it means to be a woman in particular.

This, again, is not a form of diversity that it is possible simply to affirm. On the one hand, the attempt to do so would initiate an endless process of particularization that would destroy the solidarities upon which much of our life together is based. On the other hand, the attempt to do so would do as much to destroy difference as to honour it, given that every form of solidarity is as much a form of difference as any of the distinctions that can be found within it. This is the third way in which I believe the appeal to diversity is misleading, and it is one that I take up in the final section of this chapter.

II. The Relevance of Diversity

To return to the second way in which I regard the appeal to diversity as misleading, the choice between complex and simple approaches to the understanding of human beings and the lives they lead cannot, as I have argued, be resolved by appeal to the facts of human existence, since every aspect of that existence is open to both simple and complex understanding. On the contrary, the choice between those approaches in any particular social setting can be resolved only in light of a proper appreciation of what it means to understand human beings in simple or complex terms, an awareness of the role that such modes of understanding play in the formation and development of a successful human life, and an argument that would warrant the adoption of one understanding rather than the other in the setting in question.

It is true that certain understandings of human existence and the qualities that constitute it are endorsed by many, perhaps most, societies. Yet the fact that endorsement of those understandings is widespread is evidence not that their endorsement is compelled by the facts of human existence, but that a number of societies have purposes in common. It remains the case that it takes a social purpose, whether widely or narrowly held, to make particular understandings of existence matter in any of the cultures in which they matter. The endorsement of certain social purposes, and the simplicity and complexity about human beings that it establishes, are facts about a culture and its objects, and hence about the understanding of human beings in that culture, not brute facts about human beings or the necessary consequence of such facts.

The appeal to diversity is misleading, then, because to state that human beings are complex is unintelligible without some point of reference against which it is possible to assess complexity, that will enable us to know in what respects and for what purposes human beings are said to be complex. It is also misleading because that point of reference cannot be discovered by looking to the facts of human existence or to the concept of complexity. Any assertion of human complexity that is intelligible involves taking a position in an argument about how human beings should be understood in a particular setting. It cannot pretend to transcend that argument through an appeal to complexity as a fact about humanity.[6] As far as women are concerned, this means that sexual difference can be rationally affirmed only where there is reason to do so, that reason being the relevance and value of the recognition of that difference to the success of some woman's life.

The relation between these interconnected criticisms of the appeal to human diversity may be illustrated with a familiar image, namely, the concept of snow, for which it is popularly although probably inaccurately said that the Inuit have no general understanding but rather a wide range of separate understandings, each of which distinguishes a particular kind of snow with a particular significance for the Inuit way of life. In contrast to the Inuit, people whose lives are led in climates that are snow-free for much of the year, such as those who live in southern rather than northern Canada, are likely to have only a limited range of understandings of snow, those necessary to decide on the right ski wax, perhaps, and indeed would probably more commonly think of snow in a general sense, as snow. And at the opposite extreme from the Inuit, as an exile from the southern United States living in Montreal, Jesse Winchester complained that all snowflakes looked alike to him, and that every one was a dirty shame.

---

[6] Of course, even were it possible to establish that human beings are complex by nature, it would still need to be established that there is an obligation to honour that complexity in all its detail, even were it coherent to do so. On that issue, see the final section of this chapter.

None of these understandings is false to the nature of snow, which is clearly susceptible to both complex and simple description. Rather, each accurately expresses the role that snow plays in the lives and culture of those who variously describe it in simple or in complex terms. That is to say, in each of these settings what matters is not the fact of snow as a physical object and the question of fidelity to its nature, but rather the community within which and for which snow acquires significance, and the particular meaning and value that snow consequently has and ought to have within that community.

What is true of snow in these settings is also true of the human beings for whom snow has its significance, who not only can be but are understood in both simple and complex terms according to the role that their simplicity and their complexity play in the cultures in which those understandings arise. What matters in the ongoing construction of those cultures is not so much the physical facts of human existence, but the meaning and value that we believe those facts have and ought to have in a particular culture. The facts of existence set conditions for the establishment of concepts, which once created become facts of existence themselves, but facts that matter to a particular culture only if they have some bearing for the kind of people who make up that culture and the kind of society that they inhabit.

It might be objected at this point that I have treated human diversity and complexity as if they are equivalent to one another, whereas in fact they have rather different meanings. The most straightforward response to the objection is to point out that although complexity and diversity are indeed independent concepts, what is true of complexity in this regard is also true of diversity. Human beings are not in fact inherently diverse any more than they are inherently complex. It is true, of course, that they can be distinguished from one another and therefore regarded as different from one another, qualitatively as well as numerically, where there is reason to do so, as when we seek to respond to their individual needs or aspirations. It follows that human beings are susceptible to diverse understanding in a way that manufactured goods are not, in the same sense that they are susceptible to complex understanding in a way that an amoeba perhaps is not.

It is also true, however, that human beings can be assimilated to one another where there is reason to do so, as when we seek to affirm their solidarity as members of a species, as citizens of a nation, or as contributors to a culture. Just like complexity, in other words, diversity is not a quality inherent in human beings but a product of the concepts that we use to understand them and the purposes that those concepts serve, which make certain facts about human beings relevant and meaningful and so make possible the recognition of diversity. It follows that human diversity, where it exists, is as apt to be the product of a spectrum of social purposes as it is to be the product of the spectrum of physical or psychological facts about human beings that those social purposes make relevant. In other words, there is as much human diversity in the recognition of fifty ways to appreciate a human quality as there is in the recognition of fifty human qualities to appreciate in a particular way.

A second objection might be put forward here, one that I have already referred to but have yet to address fully. It might be argued that over the course of history certain social purposes have been so powerfully and comprehensively linked to certain human features that have consistently mattered to societies of all kinds that those purposes ought to be regarded as implicit in the features in question. Such features, it would then be claimed, possess a necessary import that makes a particular meaning and no other relevant to the conduct of life in human societies. It would follow that societies that neglect or suppress that meaning neglect or suppress what every human society must acknowledge as fundamental to human existence. On this kind of reasoning it could be argued that the appeal to diversity is an appeal for the affirmation of features of this kind, with established connections to certain social purposes.

Understood in this way, however, the appeal to diversity would be intelligible but would also lack any transformative power. It would be an appeal no longer to forms of human difference we have failed to notice but to forms of human difference we have always noticed and in the same way. As a basis for a feminist argument, one that seeks a transformation in our present view of sexual identity, the objection needs to be understood somewhat differently. It should be understood not as a claim about certain historical patterns of social understanding that have established the inevitability of the social meanings that history has endorsed but as a broader claim about human character, one that takes those historical patterns to constitute evidence that social purposes are implicit in all significant aspects of that character, only some of which we have historically acknowledged and the rest of which we have suppressed.

The claim would then be a claim that the significant differences between human beings, including sex, are unlike other differences, such as those to be found in snow, in that their relevance does not derive from the needs and purposes of a particular social order. On the contrary, those facts of our character determine the ways in which they ought to matter to us and hence determine the kind of society we ought to have, rather than the kind of society in which we live determining what in the facts of our character might possibly matter to us, in the way that it determines what in the character or composition of snow might matter to us. Proponents of this point of view would acknowledge that we have in practice often ignored what they see as the necessary import of human differences such as sex, but they would argue that in doing so we have erred. In fact, they would say, we have no distinctive choice to make about sex or any other significant form of human difference. There are no two ways to understand such differences, and no legitimate way to ignore their significance.

Even assuming, however, that so understood the appeal to diversity would possess the kind of transformative power that would make it attractive to feminists, it would no longer be an appeal to diversity as such, but rather an appeal to a set of differences that have been labelled as significant. The labelling of those differences as significant, or as natural, is no more than a covert way of expressing the purposes of the society that creates the label and applies it to the purposes that are important to it and the differences that they make matter. It is not a way of avoiding the need for purposes. On the contrary, it is a way of assuming the priority of certain purposes without arguing for it, argument being subverted by the use of the term significant. It remains the case, therefore, that it is impossible simply to affirm diversity. We can affirm only those forms of difference that are made relevant to us by the character and commitments of our society and the purposes they engender.

III. The Value of Diversity

This brings me to the third way in which I believe the appeal to diversity is misleading, which may be no more than another way of formulating my first two objections to it. Let us assume that the appeal to diversity is understood as a call for the creation of as many forms of human difference as possible, on the ground that there is some value in their multiplication. In support of this view it might be argued, perhaps, that variety is desirable in human beings and a virtue in the arrangement of human societies. It would then be argued that the neglect of variety, variety of any kind, is in and of itself an oppression of human possibilities, and that if oppression is to be avoided, as it must be, human differences should be sought out and unreservedly affirmed. In response to those who would reply that social settings and social purposes are required in order to establish the points of reference that make human variety real and intelligible, supporters of diversity might simply reformulate their position in terms of such purposes, so as to present that position as a call for the endorsement and pursuit of whatever range of social purposes is required to engender the fullest degree of human variety. The variety sought is neither that revealed by awareness of a particular realm of human difference, be it sexual, racial, or cultural, nor that constituted by the pursuit of a particular degree of human difference, such as the degree of biological diversity sometimes thought necessary to maintain the health of ecosystems. It is the variety that consists in as much human difference as it is possible to imagine, a variety whose pursuit is predicated on the idea that the neglect of any difference is an unwarranted oppression of that difference.

So understood, however, there is compelling reason to reject the affirmation of diversity on its own terms. The third and most telling of the objections to the appeal to human diversity, in my view, is that when framed in this comprehensive and undiscriminating manner, it is not only misleading but false in the promise it offers. The oppression of any given form of human difference cannot be ended through the unqualified affirmation of human diversity for the same reason that deconstruction cannot be affirmed in its unfettered form. It is simply not possible to affirm all forms of human difference, or to suggest that release from oppression can be found in doing so, not merely because many forms of human difference are in conflict with one another, although they are, nor because many forms of human difference are themselves oppressive or otherwise undesirable, although they are, but because the very possibility of our existence as human beings in human societies depends upon our establishing and maintaining a degree of coherence in our existence that necessarily excludes a wide, indeed, an infinite range of human differences from recognition.

Were human beings to try to affirm all forms of difference that might be thought to lie within and between them, those that go unrecognized in the present social order as well as those we already acknowledge, they would destroy the solidarities upon which their individual and collective existences depend, solidarities in and through which their very existences are conceivable and thus consist. Difference and solidarity are mutually exclusive, at least in any given dimension. Where difference is recognized, solidarity is denied. Where differences are acknowledged in women's experience and understanding of sexuality, or in their experience of race and its consequences, as many lesbians and black women contend they should be, the solidarity of women's experience in those dimensions comes to an end. It is of course possible that solidarity would survive in other dimensions and for other purposes, that is, in settings in which a less diverse or less detailed understanding of women continued to apply. That would depend upon the profundity of the acknowledgment of the distinctiveness of the experience of lesbians and black women. But it would not be possible for solidarity among women to survive in any setting in which the differences of sexual orientation and race were recognized and affirmed. The more profound and comprehensive the pursuit of difference in any setting, the less tenable will be any kind of solidarity and social value there.

As indicated in the discussion of diversity above, it is possible to maintain a diverse understanding in one dimension and a uniform understanding in another, whether of human beings in general or of women in particular, but it is not possible to maintain such understandings in the same dimension at the same time. Women cannot be in the same respect or dimension both women generally, that is, without distinction as to sexual orientation, and also lesbians; they cannot be women without regard to race, and also black.[7] To the extent that human differences are multiplied, therefore, and forms of human diversity are affirmed, the forms of solidarity within which those differences are acknowledged and affirmed are brought to an end. Those forms of solidarity include not only humanity but sexual identity, sexual orientation, race, and any other distinction that assimilates and identifies, however briefly and contingently, the experiences

---

[7] This depiction of womanhood is designed for the purposes of the present discussion; it is not entirely true to the relation between the category of sexual identity and those of race and sexual orientation. Womanhood need not be understood as a set of qualities that all women enjoy, and so is capable of embodying distinctions of race and sexual orientation. For fuller discussion, see the next chapter.

of more than one human being. Ultimately, a commitment to recognition of all forms of difference would undermine individual identity itself, that is, the identification of a set of experiences with the constitution of our existence as individuals who have an ongoing history, past, present, and future.

Furthermore, and more to the point here, since all these forms of solidarity are themselves forms of human difference, the recognition of difference by its very nature suppresses other differences, superordinate and subordinate, as well as undermining the coherence on which our existence, individual and collective, depends. In short, the unqualified affirmation of difference has as great a tendency to undermine any particular difference, such as sex, sexual orientation, or race, as to affirm them. The attempt to recognize all forms of difference, therefore, is not merely threatening to our capacity to sustain social value and ultimately personal identity, but is internally inconsistent: it undermines the very categories it purports to affirm. That fact alone is reason enough to reject the simple affirmation of difference, not only as a basis for the affirmation of women's existence but as a basis for affirmation of any form of human difference.

This is not to say that diversity can never be affirmed, or that women's present predicament is not the product of a neglect of their difference. On the contrary, as I have already indicated, I believe it may well be the case that women's predicament is at least in part the product of a failure to recognize the true significance of being a woman, a significance suppressed and concealed by the present social order. However, it is possible to establish the correctness of that belief only by showing what it is that might make sex matter in a culture such as ours. We need a reason to notice sex in any given setting, and hence a reason to know whether it can matter to us at all, and if so, where and when. In short, we need to discover what reasons we have to notice someone's sex rather than to overlook it, or to notice one conception of sex rather than another, so as to know why we might reject the present conception of sexual difference and seek to affirm either another or sexual equality in its place.

6

The Character of Disadvantage

I. Introduction

It is a common thought that women must change if they are to escape their present disadvantage. The thought is not confined to feminists. On the contrary, it has a counterpart in the general belief, widespread among social reformers, that improving the lives of people, and ensuring that they are no longer disadvantaged in relation to others, necessarily involves improving the capacities of those people, intellectually, physically, psychologically, or otherwise. Among feminists this thought has given rise to a familiar and prolonged inquiry into the question of whether the qualities and characteristics that constitute sexual identity, and so describe what it means to be a woman or a man, are the product of nature or nurture. This inquiry matters to feminists because the source of sexual identity is supposed to make a difference to whether that identity can be changed.

Two assumptions are at work here. First, that what is the product of nurture is subject to change through nurture. What we have made we can unmake; what we have done wrong we can now do right. Second, and more fundamentally, it is assumed that such change is not merely possible but desirable. Women's success in life, it is said, is limited by the very capacities that define them as women. What makes a woman a woman also makes her less. It follows that women must become something other than they now are, something better than they have been permitted to be, if they are to escape their present disadvantage and begin to lead successful lives. We must raise our daughters, and our sons, to be different from ourselves.

Change of this kind is typically thought to be desirable for reasons of equality. It is often suggested, most famously by Catharine MacKinnon, that women and men should not differ from one another in any way that could give rise to disadvantage to either.[1] If it is the case, as MacKinnon further claims, that

---

[1] *Feminism Unmodified: Discourses on Life and Law* (Cambridge, Mass., 1987), at 43.

the existing differences between the sexes serve only to privilege men and subordinate women, then those differences must be eliminated, for the sake of equality.[2] In the short run that would leave men and women with identical capacities, and so would end the difference between the sexes. In the longer run, however, it is possible that sexual difference might be reinvented in a nonhierarchical form, one that does not threaten disadvantage to either sex.[3] Equality demands that we eliminate the disadvantage that now flows from sexual difference. It does not thereby demand that men and women cease to differ from one another, for the achievement of equality is compatible with the recognition of difference. Men and women can differ from one another without being disadvantaged in relation to one another. Or so it is said, not only by MacKinnon herself but by most egalitarians.[4]

Other feminists, more respectful of the present content of sexual identity, perhaps, or more skeptical of the possibility of changing it, seek change not in the character of women but in the standards by which they are judged.[5] If the standards that a given society subscribes to favour the qualities of men over those of women, thereby placing women at a disadvantage in relation to men, then those standards should be eliminated, again for the sake of equality. If, for example, society expects combativeness in candidates for executive office, and if women are less combative than men, then society should find another standard of executive excellence.

The apparent opposition between these two strategies masks their underlying similarity. As I have pointed out above, the difference between changing the standards by which people are evaluated and changing people themselves is largely one of emphasis, given that the distinctions between people, here between men and women, are ultimately distinctions of value. To redefine sex so as to escape certain valuations is to redefine the realm of value, for it is to eliminate from sexual identity features that register certain values that favour one sex over the other, leaving those values unrecorded. If combativeness, for example, were to be eliminated from sexual identity (on the ground that it favours men),

---

[2] *Id.* at 173, 36, 41.

[3] *Id.* at 45.

[4] See, for example, Catharine MacKinnon, *Sexual Harassment of Working Women: A Case of Sex Discrimination* (New Haven, Conn., 1979), at 140; Deborah Rhode, *Justice and Gender* (Cambridge, Mass., 1989), at 304; Christine Littleton, "Reconstructing Sexual Equality", 75 *California Law Review* 1279 (1987), at 1297. Put positively, it is often claimed that what is different can also be equal, typically because differences in treatment can be so tailored as to ensure that they have an equal impact on different people. This is true, of course, only if the differences in treatment are ultimately differences in degree rather than in kind.

[5] I have feminists such as Carol Gilligan in mind here. See her *In a Different Voice: Psychological Theory and Women's Development* (Cambridge, Mass., 1982). See also Martha Minow, *Making All the Difference: Inclusion, Exclusion and American Law* (Ithaca, 1990), and Littleton, "Reconstructing Sexual Equality". Their approach is supported by the requirements of current legislation against indirect discrimination, which call for the elimination, wherever possible, of conditions that either sex finds it significantly more difficult to meet than the other.

it would be correspondingly eliminated (in effect) from the realm of value, for there would no longer be any such characteristic to value, in men or in women.[6] Similarly, and more to the present point, to redefine value for the sake of sex is to redefine sex, for it is to eliminate from the realm of value those standards that enable us to register sexual difference. If combativeness were to be eliminated from the realm of value, it would be correspondingly eliminated (in effect) from sexual identity, for its (relative) presence in men and its (relative) absence in women would then go unrecorded. It follows that both strategies seek to change people, directly or indirectly, and in every way that matters, in order to secure women's escape from disadvantage.

There is an element of truth in all this, but the underlying idea, that escape from disadvantage is dependent upon a change in the qualities and characteristics of the disadvantaged, is false. By and large we do not need to change ourselves, to become something other than we are, in order to lead successful lives. Disadvantage in life is a matter of lacking the ingredients of a successful life, which are by and large relative to the person whose life it is.[7] No person is ever disadvantaged except in terms of the ability to become the kind of person that he or she should be, and the kind of person that he or she should be is a function of the kind of person that he or she is – in some respects the same as other people, in other respects different from them. Contrary to what is popularly assumed, therefore, we are never disadvantaged merely by our inability to be someone else, and so to possess the qualities and characteristics that distinguish that person, and their forms of flourishing, from our own.

The point should not be overstated. It is true that a successful life involves the development of the capacities that people have, so as to bring out the richness of those capacities, or at least as much of that richness as is necessary in order to make life successful. In this sense, it clearly asks us to change. From infancy onward we must learn in order to live well, be it to walk, talk, run, dance, swim, sing, read, think, and so on until death. Learning means growth, and growth means change, not only in the capacities that one has, but in the capacities that one acquires in the course of developing the capacities that one has.

It is also true that a successful life involves elimination from one's character of qualities that amount to moral vices, and correspondingly, development in one's character of qualities that amount to moral virtues. In this sense, too, it asks us to change. We must cease to be dishonest, if that is what we are, to be cruel, or cowardly, or proud, or selfish, and so on. We must learn instead, and

---

[6] And correspondingly, if noncombativeness were to be eliminated from the character of women, so the sexes were neutral with respect to combativeness. That is, of course, unless combativeness were to be simply displaced, so its burdens and benefits fell equally on men and women, enabling certain women to escape the disadvantage it gives rise to at the expense of other women and certain men. According to Catharine MacKinnon, "if this is feminism, it deserves to die": *Feminism Unmodified, supra* n. 1, at 5.

[7] To be precise, the ingredients are relative, though their value is not.

correspondingly, to be honest, kind, brave, modest, and selfless. As I have said earlier, we lead good lives not merely by realizing ourselves, so as to give effect to our qualities in our actions, but by ensuring that our qualities and our actions conform to what goodness requires.

There is no doubt that the lives of some women are unsuccessful for just these reasons. Some women, like some men, fail to develop the valuable capacities that they know themselves to have, and that others recognize in them. Some women, like some men, suffer from moral vices, or fail to develop moral virtues. Such women must change in order to lead successful lives. But neither of these things is true of women as a whole. Most obviously, and contrary to what has often been pretended, moral vice is no part of what it means to be a woman as distinct from a man. Women are not scheming, deceiving, conniving, or cheating, whatever country music may say. Few if any would dispute this.

Less obviously, perhaps, women's lives are unsuccessful, in ways that are the result of sex discrimination, not because women have been denied the opportunity to develop capacities they are recognized to have, but because women are said to be something other than they actually are, so that they are said to lack capacities they in fact have, and to have capacities they in fact lack; or to put it in comparative terms, to be different from men when they are in fact equal, and equal to men when they are in fact different. This is a more controversial claim and I return to the question of its defence below.

What matters at this point, however, is that those who seek to change the qualities and characteristics of women, in order to secure women's release from disadvantage, do not seek change in this respectful, developmental sense, of enabling women to bring out the full richness of the capacities they are recognized to have. Their goal is not to make the best of what women now are, for as they see it, to do so would merely be to confirm women's present disadvantage. It would be to make women better than they now are at playing the subordinate role that women have been assigned, the subordinate role that women's capacities have been designed to serve. As I have said, such people assume that what women are now is responsible for the predicament women now find themselves in, so that women must change what they are now if they are to lead successful lives.[8]

That assumption would be correct if the qualities that defined women, in the sense of distinguishing them from men, constituted moral vices, so that to pursue the implications of those qualities would be to ensure that women led bad lives. Yet that is simply not the case, as I have emphasized. The distinction between the sexes is not a moral one.[9] Moral qualities aside, however, one does not need to

---

[8] The best known example of this way of thinking is MacKinnon's *Feminism Unmodified*.

[9] In fact, there may be certain moral distinctions between the sexes. Perhaps men are violent, or at least more so, or more often so, than women. In the argument that follows I have suppressed this possibility as marginal and so distracting. It is true that MacKinnon implicitly regards women's

change what one is in order to flourish in life. On the contrary, one must identify and understand what one is in order to identify and understand what would make one's life successful or unsuccessful. If the qualities and characteristics that define women as women, and men as men, are not in themselves virtues or vices, but qualities that are capable of being used for good or ill, the question must be what those qualities and characteristics are, what goods they might yield, and how it is that those goods have come to be denied to women. That is the subject of the argument to follow.

I should begin with a brief caveat. While it is true that it is possible to be disadvantaged only in terms of the qualities and characteristics that one actually has, it is also true that many have sought success in life, and some have found it, through changing those characteristics in favour of something more socially advantageous. Where a society refuses to permit people to flourish in life as the people that they are, those people will sometimes, as a matter of survival in a discriminatory setting, seek to turn themselves into the kind of people that a discriminatory society will permit to flourish. In this way homosexuals have sought to live as heterosexuals, and women have sought to live like men. Such people pass themselves off as the people they are expected to be, people other than they are, in order to flourish in life. Sometimes they are successful in this, but only where some aspect of what they actually are forms part of what they seek to become. Homosexuals can live successfully as heterosexuals if and to the extent that they are in fact bisexual. Women can live successfully like men if and to the extent that they do not in fact differ from men. Yet even when they succeed, people who seek to flourish in this way do so only by suppressing all those aspects of themselves that conflict with the kind of person they seek to become, often at great personal cost, one that may be so great as to make their success more apparent than real. What is more, such people neglect the predicament of the bulk of their fellows, who do not share their ability to absorb the qualities and characteristics necessary to flourish in that society, those of heterosexuality, masculinity, or some other.

What is needed, if we are to find an answer to the problem of sex discrimination, is an understanding of the disadvantage that discrimination causes that has moral significance, so as to impose an obligation on ourselves to bring it to an end, and an understanding of sexual identity that has genuine substance. Given the fact that in my view an understanding of disadvantage depends upon a genuine understanding of what is said to be disadvantaged, it is to the question of the relationship between disadvantage and sexual identity that I turn first.

qualities as vices, on the ground that they are the hallmarks of powerlessness, but in doing so she fails to appreciate that the qualities she has in mind, qualities such as concern for others, have manifold implications, good as well as bad, and so are not in themselves vices. See the discussion in note 16.

II. Understanding Disadvantage

It is important to emphasize the skepticism[10] that underpins any attempt to change sexual identity in order to end the disadvantage experienced by women, for ironically, the effect of that skepticism is to undermine the ability to comprehend women's disadvantage. The reason for this is primarily conceptual. Skepticism about sexual identity has a debilitating effect on any feminist project for the simple reason that it is necessary to understand the reality of a woman's life in order to understand what it means for that life to be disadvantaged. It follows that if we are to know what is a disadvantage to women, we need to know first what it means and does not mean to be a woman. We cannot pretend that there is no truth to the matter, for if we do, we will be unable to comprehend, let alone to remedy, women's present predicament.

As I see it, there are three elements to the relationship between women's disadvantage and what it means to be a woman, each of which I address in turn. The first and most important of these is the general conceptual point to which I have just drawn attention, namely, the claim that any assertion of disadvantage necessarily implies the existence and, indeed, the specific character of what is said to be disadvantaged.

A. *The Meaning of Disadvantage*

Let me begin with a contrast. For those who believe in the *fact* of sexual *difference*, the disadvantage women now experience as a result of sex discrimination might be thought to be the product of a betrayal of their difference as women. Such people might believe that women really are different from men in ways other than we take them to be, and that our misapprehension of that difference causes women disadvantage because it imposes on them the burden of living according to terms that are not true to them, thereby frustrating their ability to construct successful lives from the resources available to them and meaningful for them, that is, on the basis of their true character and ambitions. Similarly, for those who believe in the *fact* of sexual *equality*, the disadvantage that women now experience as a result of sex discrimination might be thought to be the product of a betrayal of their equality with men. Such people might believe that women really are no different from men, and that our blindness

---

[10] In speaking of skepticism about sexual identity, I am referring to skepticism about the existence of a genuine sexual identity in terms of which women could be said to be disadvantaged. At one level, those who seek to change what women are now believe that women's present condition is real enough, and that women are disadvantaged because of it. At a more fundamental level, however, such people do not believe that there is any genuine sexual identity that women are bound to attend to in order to understand and remedy their disadvantage. Rather, they believe that the present content of sexual identity is susceptible to unlimited revision to ensure that it serves women's interests, and further, that women's interests can be understood without reference to sexual identity, or more specifically, without reference to what it means to be a woman.

to the equality of the sexes forces women to live in terms of a false image of difference, with the same deleterious consequences for their capacity to construct successful lives. It is also possible to hold some combination of these two views: to believe that women are in some respects different from men in ways other than we have taken them to be, and in other respects no different from men, despite what we have pretended. For those who believe in none of these things, however, and so are skeptical about the existence of all facts of this kind, there is simply nothing to betray. In that case, it is difficult to understand what they can mean when they speak of discrimination on the basis of sex.

As a conceptual matter it is impossible to say that a person is disadvantaged, at least in any meaningful sense, without an idea of what it means to be that person and who he or she is to be contrasted with. Disadvantage is a concept that expresses a relationship between people[11] who have been compared in a given plane and for a given purpose, in light of a proper understanding of their different qualities and capacities. Any assertion of disadvantage is thus dependent upon a claim as to the character of what is said to be disadvantaged, a claim implicit in the character of the alleged disadvantage.

If women are said to be disadvantaged by a denial to them of access to a particular option, for example, the character of the option whose denial is said to disadvantage them expresses a conception of what it means to be a woman, without which the denial could not be said to be disadvantageous. It is disadvantageous to be denied what one would seek and value, given the kind of person that one is. It is not disadvantageous to be denied that which one cannot truly seek, given that it would not be valuable in one's hands. It follows that if promulgation of a false picture of the qualities and capacities of certain people causes them disadvantage, as it clearly often does, it is because it suppresses the true character of the valuable options that might be sought by those whom the picture falsely describes, the pursuit of which is necessary to the success of their lives, and the denial of which is, as a result, a genuine disadvantage.

Two points need to be distinguished, for there are two implications to any given allegation of disadvantage. The first relates to the question of the *character* of an alleged disadvantage, while the second relates to the question of its *threshold*. Where the character of certain people and hence the character of what may disadvantage them is not in dispute, the correctness of any allegation of disadvantage that is made on their behalf will turn on the *threshold* of

---

[11] However, the relationship that disadvantage expresses is only superficially one between different people, for it is ultimately a relationship between a life as it is led and as it should be led. Indeed, as I argue below, the disadvantaging of a life can be understood only in this second, internal sense, for the good of a successful life is something that can be understood only with reference to the character of the person who is to live it, not with that of some other. It follows that the significance of a person's disadvantage relative to some other person in any given endeavour is proportionate to the role that the endeavour, and success or failure in it, plays in the success or failure of that person's life.

disadvantage in their lives and the tendency of any allegedly disadvantageous act or omission to cross that threshold. In other words, in circumstances where we are agreed on the character of what it is that might disadvantage certain people, and where we are also confident that an allegedly disadvantageous act or omission is of that character, and hence are confident that it has the capacity to disadvantage them in life, the only question is whether it in fact does so. The answer will depend upon its impact on their capacity to develop and pursue successful lives.[12]

In contrast to questions of the *threshold* of disadvantage, however, are those regarding the *character* of disadvantage, which arise when one or the other of the above presuppositions does not apply. On the one hand, where we are agreed on the character of what it is that might disadvantage certain people, yet are also agreed that an allegedly disadvantageous act or omission is not in fact of that character, there can be no question of disadvantage, for if an act is not of a kind that could disadvantage the people in question, it is meaningless to ask whether it does so. The character of the act is simply such that it could not possibly have an impact on their capacity to develop and pursue successful lives. On the other hand, less obviously perhaps but more fundamentally, if we are not in agreement as to the character of certain people, and so are not in agreement as to the character of what may disadvantage them, we cannot begin to entertain the question of their disadvantage. In such a case our first task must be to establish what kind of people they are and how they might be disadvantaged. Only when we have done that, and have further determined that an allegedly disadvantageous act or omission has the character required to disadvantage them as we have come to understand them, can we consider whether it in fact has done so.

It follows, in my view, that it is the *character* of disadvantage, and the character of sexual identity that it implies, with which feminism is primarily concerned. The question of whether the threshold of disadvantage has been crossed in the lives of women can arise only if the character of women's lives, and what may disadvantage them, is already agreed upon, which does not appear to be the case at present. To see why this is so, it is necessary to explore the distinction between the character of a disadvantage and the question of its threshold. That distinction is the second of the three elements in the relationship between disadvantage and what it means to be a woman, to which I referred above.

---

[12] This distinction is reflected in the ways in which we use the term "disadvantage" in ordinary speech. We typically distinguish between the disadvantage that a person experiences with respect to certain activities and the disadvantage that that person experiences in the project of his or her life. In the first case, the use of the term "disadvantage" corresponds to the question of the character of disadvantage, while in the second case the use of the term corresponds to the question of its threshold. In other words, the question of character distinguishes genuine and putative forms of disadvantage, while the question of threshold distinguishes morally significant and morally insignificant forms of disadvantage, disadvantage that has been found to be genuine in character.

B. The Character and Threshold of Disadvantage

i. CONTESTED CHARACTERISTICS. It may be helpful to begin with an illustration. If a society is charged with failing to provide some of its members with such basic goods as food and shelter, the question of whether that society disadvantages those people is simply one of whether it has failed to meet their need for food and shelter, a need that all human beings experience purely by reason of their existence as human beings, more or less without distinction, and more importantly, whose character we all understand and agree upon. It is only if their need has not been met that a denial of food and shelter will constitute a disadvantage to them. Actions are only disadvantageous to people if they deny what is necessary to their pursuit of a successful life. It is not a disadvantage to be denied what is surplus to one's requirements, whether those requirements be for food and shelter or for a sufficient range of valuable options from which to make a successful life.

What holds true for basic goods such as food and shelter, the need for which is universal and uniform, is also true for more specialized goods, such as participation in a culture. The need for these goods may be universal among human beings, but particular goods are valuable only in the hands of the particular human beings for whom they are appropriate.[13] Participation in a particular culture, or in the practice of a particular religion, or in a particular way of life, such as a life in the theatre or a life as a social or environmental activist, is valuable only in the hands of those who are or might be committed to those ways of life.[14] Yet, to take cultural participation as an example, as long as the requirements of participation in a particular culture are agreed upon and understood, a culture that I will for the sake of argument assume to be a worthy one (so that participation in its particular forms and practices is a genuine good), and more to the point for feminists, as long as the character of those who might wish to participate in that culture is *also agreed upon and understood* (so as to establish the appropriateness of the forms and practices of that culture to the project of those lives), the debate over whether a restriction on participation in that culture is a disadvantage to those people must be a debate as to whether their need for such participation is otherwise met. A restriction on cultural participation is a disadvantage to people only if their need for participation generally, and in that culture in particular, is not otherwise met.[15] It follows that whether a way of

---

[13] See below for a discussion of the distinction between goods that are both owed to all human beings and have uniform application to them, and goods that are owed to all human beings but have particular application to particular people.

[14] For the time being, I leave to one side the question of value, and note here only that many ways of life are in fact not valuable.

[15] The two problems referred to here – of understanding a culture and understanding the character of those who would participate in it – are interconnected, for to know what characteristics the forms and practices of a culture are potentially sensitive to is to know something about the kind of people who might successfully participate in those forms and practices. For feminists,

life and its needs is universal or is confined to certain people, as long as that way of life is properly understood, so that agreement exists as to its character and its claims, and as long as the need of certain people for participation in that way of life is also understood and agreed upon, the debate over any alleged disadvantage to that way of life is a debate over the threshold of disadvantage for the people who pursue or might pursue it, and whether a particular form of denial crosses that threshold.

The distinction here is not between uniform and specialized goods, therefore, or between biologically and culturally determined goods, but between goods whose appropriateness for certain human beings is *agreed upon* or *contested*. If it is the former, the question of disadvantage can be only a question of threshold; if it is the latter, the question of disadvantage must, at least in the first instance, be a question of character. If it could be said, therefore, that women were properly understood in our culture, so that agreement now existed as to their character and hence as to their needs and capacities, the debate would be about the threshold of disadvantage in their lives, and whether particular forms of denial cross that threshold. In that case women could be disadvantaged by the denial to them of certain options, acknowledged to be true to their character, only if their capacity to lead successful lives in terms of who they are were otherwise not met.

However, to return to the example of cultural participation, if the character of a particular culture and the need of certain people for participation in the forms and practices of that culture are not agreed upon and understood, the debate over whether a restriction on participation is a disadvantage must necessarily be a debate, first, over the character of the culture, and second and more importantly, over the character of the people who might wish to participate in it. It is impossible to debate the threshold of disadvantage in any person's life as long as the character of that life remains uncertain. We cannot begin to discuss whether certain people have been disadvantaged by lack of access to certain options in life as long as we are uncertain about what kind of people they are and what kind of options in life they might value. It follows that we cannot begin to discuss the threshold of disadvantage for women and whether that threshold has been crossed by certain forms of denial while the content of what it means to be a woman, and hence the character of what may disadvantage them, remains uncertain. Without some form of agreement as to that content, we cannot know whether what is denied are goods in life that women could possibly value.

ii. DISADVANTAGE AND THE CHARACTER OF WOMEN. It is the *character* of disadvantage that is critical here, therefore, because the question of the

---

however, the primary issue must be the character of what it means to be a woman, for it may be necessary to reform the forms and practices of the culture in order to respond to women's needs and capacities.

threshold of disadvantage is necessarily consequent on general agreement as to its character. In the case of women, no such general agreement as to character exists. Few contemporary feminists believe that the predicament women now find themselves in is simply a matter of a failure on the part of our society to address a condition that it correctly understands. On the contrary, most believe that our society gravely misunderstands what it means to be a woman, and in particular misunderstands the content of women's needs and capacities. It is because most feminists believe that women are so misunderstood in our society that they have committed themselves to the enterprise of convincing the world at large that women are both more and less like men than we have taken them to be. Properly understood, women neither exhibit the distinctive incapacities that we have attributed to them nor share without distinction the needs of men, as we have often assumed. In other words, most feminists agree upon the need to reject the prevailing picture of what it means to be a woman, and hence are implicitly agreed that the debate over the character of sexual identity must be the primary issue in the enterprise of enabling women to escape their present predicament.[16]

Unfortunately, feminists disagree among themselves as to what it means to be a woman, and hence what might be said to disadvantage women in a particular setting. For some feminists, the refusal to subscribe to any conception of what it genuinely means to be a woman is based on a belief that the redemption of women depends upon remaining agnostic about that issue. For others, such as those who debate whether there is any truth to the difference between men and women, there is simply profound disagreement over the content of what it means to be a woman. Some of the latter are uncertain as to the character of the misconception of which they believe our society is guilty; others are uncertain

---

[16] Feminists such as Catherine MacKinnon take a special view of this misunderstanding. They believe that our society correctly understands the content of women's needs and capacities as they now exist, for the simple reason that it has defined those needs and capacities to suit its own purposes, chief among them being that of subordinating women. They further believe, however, that this socially constructed content of gender, while true as a description of women's present predicament, is not true in any fundamental natural or biological sense, and thus can and must be changed if we are ever to end women's subordination. It is in this sense, I am suggesting, that feminists such as MacKinnon believe our society gravely misunderstands the content of women's character, although they would certainly regard the use of the word "misunderstands" as unnecessarily charitable and potentially misleading. In their view, our society has not so much misunderstood as obliterated and redefined the content of women's character, so that while the image of women it presents is in one sense a misconception, it is in another sense, the sense that defines women's present predicament, true. As I see it, this approach to disadvantage and to the social construction of gender ignores the fact that, like success, disadvantage in any person's life is a function of the terms of that life and what is true of them. It fails to distinguish between what is now true of women, whether socially constructed or not, and what is false, and to recognize that the genuine features of women's character, whether socially constructed or not, are open to manifold application, both valuable and nonvaluable, and so are open to valuable application, even if constructed for the purpose of a nonvaluable application, or as the consequence of a history of subordination.

as to the character of the conception that they believe should replace it. All acknowledge, however, that the debate over the content of sexual identity is at the heart of the debate over women's disadvantage, despite the fact that few are agreed about what it means to be a woman, and hence what can be said to disadvantage women.

This is not to suggest that it is necessary to agree on every detail of sexual identity.[17] On the contrary, such a level of agreement is neither to be expected nor desired. Where, however, critics of the prevailing picture of sexual identity disagree about whether women are or are not different from men in any relevant respect, it cannot be claimed that we understand women well enough to understand the disadvantage we believe they experience, and so cannot begin to consider the question of its threshold in their lives. That being the case, all those concerned with women's disadvantage are committed, at least in the first instance, to a debate over the true content of what it means to be a woman. Anyone who wishes to establish the existence of disadvantage in the lives of women, as all feminists hope to, must call upon a genuine conception of what it means to be a woman in order to do so, a conception whose content is implicit in the character of the disadvantage they seek to establish. If, as I take to be the case, the content of that conception cannot be taken for granted, it must be explained and defended.

The point should not be overstated. Although feminists disagree with one another about what it means to be a woman, they are entirely clear that it does not mean what it was once thought to mean. The long struggle for recognition of women's equality with men, for example, has been a struggle to overcome misconceptions of what it means to be a woman, which have portrayed women as lacking capacities they in fact possess. At the heart of every claim to equality, and correspondingly, of difference, lies such an assertion, without which the claim would not be intelligible as a claim about women's disadvantage and what is needed to remedy it.

To the extent that such claims are well founded, we already know what it means to be a woman. Conversely, when we notice that such claims do not appear to serve women well, what we are noticing is that the assumptions they embody about what it means to be a woman are not well founded. However, we need to be clearer and perhaps more careful than we have been about the assertions that underlie and sustain such claims. For while it is possible to overstate the present degree of ignorance about what it means to be a woman, it is also important to remember that many claims about women's disadvantage, most obviously that women must change in order to escape disadvantage, are predicated on the assumption that it is not necessary to know what women are in order to know that they are disadvantaged or what needs to be done about it. In my view that assumption is false.

---

[17] See the discussion of knowledge in the next chapter.

iii. WHAT WOMEN ARE AND ARE NOT. Some clarification is needed here as to what I mean by a genuine conception of what it means to be a woman, for to refer to it ambiguously, as I have done so far, is to risk claiming too much.[18] There are in fact two aspects to the conception: that which describes what women are and that which describes what women are not. It is not always necessary to know the former in order to know the latter, for in any context in which there are more than two possible descriptions of what women really are, it is possible to know that women are not what they have been taken to be without knowing which of the two or more possible descriptions of what they really are is the right one.

It follows that while it is necessary to establish what it means to be a woman in order to consider the question of the threshold of disadvantage in women's lives, it might be that all that needs to be established is that women are not what we have taken them to be. Lack of agreement as to what women are, therefore, would not in itself bar feminists from establishing the existence in our society of a misconception of what it means to be a woman, and in some circumstances the very existence of that misconception will be enough to establish that women are disadvantaged there.

The moral significance of any misconception about human beings is a product of its tendency to frustrate its subjects' capacity to lead successful lives.[19] It is this that makes a misconception a genuine disadvantage to those upon whom it is imposed. If a misconception is widespread and profound, so as to govern entirely the options and resources available to those whom it misconstrues, it will necessarily frustrate the capacity of those people to lead successful lives. In that case there is no need to inquire into the particular character of their lives and what might make them successful, because we know that whoever they are and whatever they might value does not include any part of the picture now held of them and the options and resources that have been assigned on the strength of it. If, however, a misconception about certain people is local and limited in scope, its tendency to frustrate its subjects' capacity to lead successful lives will depend upon the character of those lives and the impact of the misconception on that capacity.[20] To establish that, it is necessary to establish what those people are and not merely what they are not. In short, to establish the existence of genuine disadvantage in the lives of women it is in all cases necessary to establish the true meaning of sexual identity, and in many if not all cases that will require us to establish what women are and not merely what they are not.

This, however, is to risk claiming too little, for if we hope to move beyond a general condemnation of the conception of sexual identity that is held in this or

---

[18] I should stress that despite my singular description of it, what it means to be a woman is not singular but plural in form.

[19] For a discussion of the moral significance of a misconception, see the next chapter.

[20] I discuss below the particular character of the successful life to which all human beings are entitled.

any other society, as I take it we all hope to do, by specifying either the character of the wrong done to women or the steps needed to remedy that wrong, we must establish what women are, and not content ourselves with simply establishing what they are not. In other words, the necessary ambitions of feminism compel feminists to establish the positive content of what it means to be a woman if they are to understand and remedy the disadvantage now experienced by women, a content that is implicit in the character of the disadvantage they seek to identify.

C. Distinctive Forms of Disadvantage

i. UNIVERSAL GOODS AND PARTICULAR PEOPLE. This explanation discloses yet another element of ambiguity, however, one that masks the kind of disadvantage at issue here and the character of the way of life that the assertion of disadvantage implies. I have already argued that it is only in circumstances where the character of a way of life and hence the character of what may disadvantage it is already agreed upon that it is possible to shift the focus of the debate from the question of the character of disadvantage to that of its threshold, so as to ask whether any particular denial to those defined by that way of life is a denial of something critical to the success of their lives. As I have said, this makes agreement over the character of an allegedly disadvantaged way of life and of what may disadvantage it the primary issue in any consideration of disadvantage. That agreement, however, itself depends upon the resolution of another, prior issue.

Any assertion of disadvantage on the part of certain people raises two possible questions as to the character of those people, for there are two aspects to the character of disadvantage. There are aspects that reflect facts about all human beings, and so are disadvantages to anyone, and those that reflect particular facts about particular human beings, and are disadvantages to particular people only. It is my view that the values that render misconceptions about certain people morally illegitimate are those that call into issue particular facts about those particular people, whether the facts are about people's oneness with others or their difference from others. To see why this is so, it is necessary to explore the distinction between universal and particular forms of disadvantage. This is the third and last of the three elements in the relationship between disadvantage and what it means to be a woman, to which I referred above.

Some might be prepared to acknowledge that it is necessary to agree on the content of what it means to be a woman in order to understand and remedy the disadvantage that women are now alleged to experience while also believing that, with respect to the disadvantage women now suffer, that content is both universal and already agreed upon. They argue that women have been deprived of certain universal human goods, to which all human beings are entitled by virtue of their very status as human beings because they are crucial to a successful life, whether those goods are properly understood as access to an adequate range of valuable options in life, or as the resources necessary to pursue those options, or as the resources necessary to satisfy basic human needs, or as something of the kind. It follows that we know all we need to know about women in order to understand and criticize their present disadvantage. That being the case, the current debate over sexual disadvantage is quite properly understood as a debate over the threshold of disadvantage in the lives of women, not as a debate over the character of that disadvantage.[21]

In my view, however, this line of reasoning is misconceived. The facts that are implied by a charge of disadvantage founded on an alleged denial to women of the goods to which all human beings are entitled in order to lead successful lives are particular facts about what it means to be a woman, and not, other than at the level of the existence of the entitlement itself, universal facts about women as human beings. The universal entitlement takes particular shape for particular people, and it is in that shape, and only in that shape, that a particular person can claim the entitlement and be disadvantaged by its denial.

There are two reasons for this. First, the selective denial to certain people of goods to which all human beings are entitled would be simply arbitrary and without any pretence of explanation, let alone justification, if there were not some at least purportedly rational connection between the denial and the people who are said to suffer it. Universal human goods can be rationally denied to particular people only in instances where, first, the sensitivity to character of the goods is emphasized (a sensitivity that requires that the application of those goods be appropriate to the character of particular people), and, second, where the universal character of the human beings to whom they are owed is denied (at least with respect to the ground of entitlement to those goods).[22] It is then possible to argue that the universal good has no application to women in this form, so that what they are denied is not, for them, a denial of the universal good, despite the fact that it is, or would be, a denial of the good for others. If a society hopes to justify the denial to women of goods to which all human beings are nominally entitled, therefore, it must both interpret those goods in such a way as to explain their sensitivity to sexual difference and understand what it genuinely means to be a woman in such a way as to explain the particular character of the universal goods to which women, as particular human beings, are entitled, and how that differs from what they have been denied.

Second, and more important, even where no explanation or justification is offered for it, the apparent denial to women of these universal goods cannot be confirmed and so cannot be understood as a disadvantage to women without an

---

[21] Catharine MacKinnon might be classed as a critic of this kind, as might Iris Young, *Justice and the Politics of Difference* (Princeton, 1990), from the perspectives of equality and difference, respectively.

[22] Societies often refuse to justify such deprivations, or offer only empty justifications for them. Even so, it remains the case that it is impossible to understand such deprivations as disadvantages to women without an understanding of what it means to be a woman. See the next subsection.

understanding of what women are and what may cause them disadvantage. The application of these universal goods, and hence the fact of their extension or denial to particular human beings, is dependent upon an understanding of the particular human beings to whom they are owed. It follows that both the need of apologists to justify any apparent denial of universal human goods to women and the need of critics to establish the impact of that denial on women and so show it to be a genuine disadvantage to women require us to develop a genuine understanding of what it means to be a woman. Let me explain more fully.

Where a genuine understanding of what it means to be a woman shows that women do not in fact possess the qualities on which entitlement to the particular goods in question is based, women are not disadvantaged by being denied those goods, for one cannot be disadvantaged by the denial of what one does not need and cannot enjoy. No woman is disadvantaged by the denial to her of options that she cannot value and resources that she does not need. A society that tells its members that they cannot have what they do not need and cannot enjoy is not disadvantaging those members, but on the contrary may just be giving them good advice.[23]

Where, however, a genuine understanding of what it means to be a woman shows that women do indeed possess the qualities that entitle them to the goods in question, and so have been denied those goods as the result of a misconception (be it innocent or malign) of who they are and the qualities they possess, women have been disadvantaged as a consequence of their sex,[24] or at least as a consequence of what their sex has been taken to be. In showing that women are the same as men where they have been thought to be different, or are different from men where they have been thought to be the same, a genuine understanding of what it means to be a woman shows that women have been denied that to which they are entitled, and so have been disadvantaged as a result of our society's failure to understand them as they genuinely are.

It follows that sex-specific disadvantage may arise in either of two ways: first, where a false picture of women's difference from men denies women access to goods that men possess by denying the reality of sexual equality; second, where a false picture either of women's equality with men or of the nature of their difference from men denies women access to goods that they need or would enjoy as women, by denying the reality of sexual difference. The comparisons to men in each case are merely secondary and consequential. In both settings women's disadvantage is the product of a misconception of what it means to be a woman. It is this form of disadvantage alone that can be genuinely understood as sexual disadvantage.

---

[23] See the discussion of the meaning of disadvantage below.

[24] To be more precise, it shows that women may have been disadvantaged by denial of the good. Whether they have been in fact disadvantaged will turn on the question of the threshold of disadvantage.

ii. DENIALS OF HUMANITY. I have assumed up to this point that it is incumbent upon any society to justify the selective withholding from women of what is alleged to be an instance of a universal entitlement. As a matter of social practice this is clearly an overly benevolent assumption. I am well aware that many societies fail to recognize any such obligation and that a good number of them are actually prepared to flaunt their failure to do so, in an attempt to elevate the status of their dominant members and diminish the status of their subordinate members through an overtly arbitrary denial to the latter of goods that are owed to all human beings. Within such societies it is sometimes claimed, particularly with regard to racial minorities, that the victims of this arbitrary disadvantage are not full human beings and so are not entitled to universal human goods. At other times it is claimed that although such people are human beings they are nevertheless to be arbitrarily excluded from the range of social concern.[25]

These purported justifications are not, of course, justifications at all, but merely attempts to cloak brute authority with the appearance of justification and so make practices of persecution seem rational. Nevertheless, the fact that such social practices are without justification does not mean that when applied to women they are not properly understood as sex discrimination. Many of their victims might quite understandably contend that such practices constitute sex discrimination, despite the fact that sex is merely the locus of the disadvantage that they create and not, in rational rather than arbitrary terms, its ground. In my view, however, to the extent that such a contention claims to bypass the need for a particular understanding of what it means to be a woman, it is not supportable.[26]

---

[25] Many societies either deny or ignore the existence of the universal entitlement and so deny or ignore their obligations to those of their members who lack the options or the resources to make a successful life. This is generally the predicament of the poor and underprivileged. However, it is not the predicament of people who are discriminated against in those societies, who are selectively denied access to a universal entitlement the existence of which is acknowledged.

[26] Martha Nussbaum has drawn attention to the number of missing women in sexually discriminatory parts of the developing world: see *Sex and Social Justice* (New York, 1999). As I read Nussbaum, in certain societies that are poor and sexually discriminatory, women die earlier than they do in poor and nondiscriminatory societies, because customs and politics describe women as unfit to engage in the activities that would make them respected, valued, and so worthy of nourishment and medical treatment, activities that women are fully capable of engaging in, and which their survival depends upon. As an account of discrimination, this appears to match my own, for it identifies a misconception that gives rise to the disadvantage and ultimately death of women. Yet it is not clear to me that the wrong Nussbaum describes is one of sex discrimination. Discrimination as she describes it and as I understand it occurs when a discriminator treats a woman in ways that would be proper if she was as he takes her to be, but that are improper given the person she is. Yet the wrong Nussbaum describes is a wrong to any person, however understood, for those who are incapable of doing what women are thought to be incapable of doing in such discriminatory societies are as entitled to survival as anyone else. It does not take an accurate perception of women's capacities, and the respect that would give rise to, to know that women, as human beings, are entitled to food, shelter, and medical treatment.

What is more, if it is assumed that some are bound to starve to death, an egalitarian policy of nondiscrimination would simply ensure that as many men died as women, and that cannot be what Nussbaum has in mind. And if it is assumed that nobody should starve to death, as

As I have described them above, there are two kinds of universal human goods. The first of these are such basic human goods as adequate food and shelter, that is, adequate for survival, the need for which is not only universal but largely uniform in character. Clearly, it does not require a particular understanding of what it means to be a woman to know that women may be disadvantaged by the denial to them of goods such as these, for no one believes that women have distinctive requirements with regard to adequate food and shelter, which would make it necessary to understand the particular character of what it means to be a woman to know whether what is agreed to be an instance of those goods for men is also an instance of those goods for women.

Yet this is to claim too little, for in fact one can know that a good is universal only by knowing that the need for it is universal and uniform in character; and that is something one can know only by knowing people well enough to understand the character of their needs. Take the example of adequate food and shelter. This good may or may not be sex-specific, depending upon how it is described. As I have said, it seems implausible that men and women have distinctive requirements with regard to adequate food and shelter where adequate food and shelter is understood as bare sustenance. Beyond bare sustenance, however, it is possible that men and women have somewhat different dietary requirements. To take the most obvious example, pregnant women need to eat for two, in the colloquial phrase, so that an account of their needs must incorporate the needs of their foetus: much calcium, say, and little or no alcohol. There may be other differences in women's dietary requirements that have been suppressed in the conventional understanding of a proper diet. But we can know whether women's needs are universal or sex-specific, and to what extent, and so can know whether the goods that meet those needs are universal or sex-specific, only by knowing what women are (including here the fact that at any given moment many of them will be pregnant), so as to know whether they are the same as men or different.

On the other hand, the second kind of human good that might be thought of as universal is differentiated rather than uniform in character, so that its application to a particular person requires an understanding of that person and the appropriateness of any particular instance of the good to his or her life. Goods such as access to the ingredients of a successful life, be they opportunities or resources or the satisfaction of needs, are goods to which entitlement is universal but whose application depends upon the character of those to whom they are applied and what that character makes appropriate. Such goods may well be denied to women in particular, but one can know this, and know that that denial

Nussbaum plainly believes, it is that assumption we should act upon, for it is that which will save the lives of all those women who would otherwise go missing, not an egalitarian policy of nondiscrimination, which is indifferent to women's starvation, provided its burden is equally shared.

constitutes a disadvantage to women, only if one already knows what it means to be a woman. In short, one cannot even know that sex is the locus of disadvantage without understanding the meaning of sex and what may disadvantage it. The reason for this lies in the particular character of a successful life, the ingredients of which are owed to all human beings.

III. Sexual Disadvantage

The truth upon which entitlement to the requirements of a successful life is grounded is at once universal, governing that entitlement in the abstract, and particular, governing it at the level of its application. In the abstract, people may be disadvantaged by a denial to them of certain goods, such as resources or opportunities, to which all human beings are entitled. At that level any alleged disadvantage is a matter of being deprived of a universal entitlement, and it is quite correct to say, therefore, that the only truth such an allegation of disadvantage implies about those who are said to be disadvantaged is that they are human beings. At the level of application, however, which tells us what a universal entitlement means in certain hands, people may be disadvantaged by the denial to them only of the resources and opportunities to which they are particularly entitled, because universal entitlements are sensitive to the character of the people to whom they are addressed so as to be resources and opportunities for those people and not for some other. At that level, therefore, an assertion of disadvantage is an assertion about the particular character of those who are said to be disadvantaged. The truth that it implies is a particular truth about the character of the people in question. Indeed, it is only through an understanding of the particular character of those who are alleged to be disadvantaged, and the character of what may disadvantage them, that it is possible for us to know that the universal entitlement has been denied.

It follows that different people are entitled to goods of the same character as one another, be they opportunities or resources, only in the respects in which they are not truly different from one another. In all those respects in which they are indeed truly different from one another, people are entitled to different goods, which reflect who they genuinely are, so as to be genuinely valuable in their hands, be they the opportunities they can genuinely seek or the resources they can genuinely use. In short, at the level at which these universal moral entitlements are applied, an assertion of disadvantage is an assertion as to the character of those who are said to be disadvantaged, because what one is entitled to, and hence what one can be disadvantaged by the denial of, depends upon who one is.

It further follows, it will be clear, that a uniform conception of disadvantage, one that regards people as being necessarily disadvantaged by the denial to them of that to which others have access, implies a uniform conception of what it means for human beings to lead successful lives. A pluralistic conception of what it means to lead a successful life requires a pluralistic conception of disadvantage, one that regards people as being disadvantaged only by the denial to them of the opportunities and resources they need to make a success of their particular lives. These are issues that I explore more fully in the next chapter, where I address the meaning of disadvantage generally and in particular the implication of a pluralistic conception of what it means to lead a successful life, where there can be universal and uniform disadvantage only if and to the extent that people are not different in the facts of their lives to which universal entitlements relate.

At this point, I want to emphasize the conclusions that follow from the preceding examination of what I have taken to be the three elements in the relationship between disadvantage and what it means to be a woman. Any allegation of disadvantage that is founded on a denial to certain human beings of the ingredients of a successful life, as allegations of sexual disadvantage clearly are, depends for its intelligibility upon a genuine understanding of the particular character of the people who are alleged to be so disadvantaged. Where that character is in dispute, because the prevailing image of it has been subjected to fundamental challenge, as in the case of women, any allegation of disadvantage must be read initially as an allegation as to the proper understanding of the particular character of those who are said to be disadvantaged, the content of which is implicit in the character of the denials that are said to constitute a disadvantage to those people. It follows, as far as feminism is concerned, that the question of sexual disadvantage must first and foremost be a question of what it means to be a woman, and further, that any allegation as to the particular character of the disadvantage that women now experience must be read as an allegation as to the particular character of what it means to be a woman.

The significance of this conclusion is not merely to make the question of what it means to be a woman the first question in considering the disadvantage that women now experience, but to make it the crucial question. I have argued so far that we must agree on the content of what it means to be a woman in order even to contemplate the question of sexual disadvantage. If we find we cannot agree on that content, as I have also contended is the case at present, we discover that the disadvantage women now experience is in fact the product of a failure to understand what it means to be a woman. Since it is clear that as a society we do not deliver goods to people randomly, but rationally, on the basis of some conception of who those people are, our inability to reach agreement on the content of what it means to be a woman must be predicated on a basic disagreement with the prevailing conception of that content rather than on general ignorance about it, and so must be predicated on the belief that the conception of what it means to be a woman generally held in our society is profoundly mistaken and not simply underdetermined, for ignorance as to the true meaning of womanhood makes it necessary for a society to invoke an arbitrary, and therefore almost certainly false, conception of what it means in order to deliver goods to women. That being the case, the disadvantage that women now experience in our society can only be the product of our misconception of what it means to be a woman.

Without agreement as to the content of sexual identity there is no threshold of disadvantage for us to consider. If we reject the prevailing conception of what it means to be a woman, we necessarily reject the possibility that the opportunities and resources assigned to them on the basis of it are ones that women can value. If we mistake who women genuinely are, we cannot believe that we are now providing them, except by the purest chance, with the goods to which they are entitled. That being so, the question of sexual disadvantage must be a question of the inability of women to obtain goods that they can value as women, as a result of the failure of the societies that allegedly disadvantage them to understand who they are and what they can value.[27]

IV. Disadvantage, Limitation, and Inferiority

What does this leave of the view that women must change if they are to escape their present disadvantage? Any allegation of disadvantage is intelligible only in light of an understanding of what is said to be disadvantaged, the particular character of which is implicit in the particular character of the disadvantage that is alleged. The disadvantage that this approach alleges women now experience, namely, to be limited and ranked as inferior in their existence in comparison to men, is intelligible only on the basis that what it means to be a woman is not to be in any way limited or inferior in one's existence in comparison to men. Yet women cannot be thought to be in truth not in any way limited or inferior in their existence in comparison to men if they are thought to be in truth in any way different from men, that is to say, if there is thought to be any true meaning to sexual difference. Any picture of human difference is necessarily as limited as it is specific, and any forms of human difference that are commensurable, as some forms of sexual difference must be thought to be if men and women inhabit a world in common, will reveal superiority and inferiority in the dimensions and respects in which they are commensurable. These types of limitation and inferiority are inescapable features of what it means to lead different lives in and through a setting of common social practices. As I argue below, they are no more than another way of describing what it means for people to be different from

---

[27] In this respect, disadvantage faced by victims of sex discrimination differs from that faced by the poor. The poor do not have enough of what they need (a threshold issue); victims of sex discrimination have what might well be enough (if they needed it) of what they do not need (a character issue). The disadvantage of the poor proceeds from a failure to meet a recognized need; the disadvantage of women proceeds from a failure to meet a need that is not recognized. This is why it is perfectly possible to suffer from sex discrimination in circumstances of apparent privilege.

one another yet inhabit a world in common.[28] That being the case, they govern the lives of all human beings, and so are inherently incapable of serving to distinguish the disadvantaged from the advantaged. It follows that these types of limitation and inferiority cannot be understood as genuine disadvantages. Indeed, it is vital that they not be confused with genuine disadvantage, which may be confronted by human beings in attempting to make a success of the project of their lives, for to do so is to obscure altogether the distinctive and morally significant character of the experience of disadvantage as it is now suffered by women.

In other words, if the disadvantage that women now experience is the product of a misconception of the content rather than the existence of sexual difference, so that women are in truth not equal to but different from men in ways other than we have taken them to be, then to maintain that women are disadvantaged by any limitation or inferiority they may experience in any plane, whether it be as the result of a comparison with men in general or with some men only, or as the result of frustration in the achievement of goals that they have set themselves, is to say that what defines women as women means everything and nothing at once. It is to say that women are disadvantaged by their inability to be anything and everything that they are not. In effect this is to assert the truth of a deconstructed picture of sexual identity, which I have already argued is not only false but incompatible with the very existence of sex. It is to contemplate a world without the experience of limitation or inferiority, one that in any specific setting would yield the consequences that we now know as advantages without understanding them as advantages and so entailing the existence of disadvantages.

As I argue, that world is inconceivable. Indeed, the very quest for it derives from a confusion between disadvantage in terms of one's access to the ingredients of well-being and those forms of limitation and ranking of existence that produce advantages and disadvantages in particular settings but in doing so do not in themselves make a particular life advantaged or disadvantaged. To see why this is so it is necessary to explore the meaning of disadvantage further, so as to eliminate from the consideration of women's predicament those features of women's experience that cannot be regarded as genuine disadvantages, whatever their appearance.

---

[28] In the respects in which a difference is commensurable, there can be no equality, but only inferiority and superiority, for equality in those respects would preclude the existence of the difference. On the other hand, in the respects in which a difference exists without the parties to it being superior or inferior to one another, there can only be incommensurability, for the existence of difference in those respects precludes the existence of equality there.

7

The Role of Sexual Identity in a Successful Life

I. The Significance of Limitations and Inferiority

If there is any kind of difference between men and women that matters to us, as there must be if we are to subscribe to the very existence of the distinction in our culture, we need to know what that difference is and what it makes possible for women and what it makes impossible. Once we know what sexual identity genuinely means, we can begin to understand the disadvantage that is now illegitimately imposed upon women, denying them access to what is both possible for them as women and necessary to the success of their lives. As I have argued above and argue further below, it is only denial of access to such goods that can constitute genuine and hence illegitimate disadvantage, or what I from here on call *deep disadvantage*. Those limitations of experience and capacity that are simply part of the meaning of sexual difference, the product of what it means to belong to one sex rather than the other, may give rise to inferiority in certain settings, so as to be disadvantages to women in those settings, but they are not in themselves disadvantages to the project of a woman's life, despite the fact that they may appear to deny women access to many valuable forms of experience, including most obviously the experiences of men. They are no more than another way of describing the existence of sexual difference and the specificity of womanhood, this time in terms of what being a woman makes impossible rather than in terms of what it makes possible. It is the distinction between these limitations of experience and capacity – which constitute disadvantages in certain settings – and disadvantage in the project of one's life, what I have called deep disadvantage, that I want to explore in this section.

Women seeking to pursue successful lives as women do not suffer disadvantage in the deep sense, in the project of their lives, simply because they cannot pursue successful lives as men. There are only two kinds of disadvantage that women may suffer in the pursuit of the project of their lives. First, they may suffer if, although correctly understood as women, they are denied access to goods in life they can value as women, whether those goods are opportunities, resources, an adequate range of valuable options, the satisfaction of needs, or anything else in life that is sensitive to the condition of those to whom it is addressed, where access to those goods is essential to their capacity to lead successful lives. This is the kind of disadvantage often experienced by certain cultural minorities in Western societies, for whom recognition of and access to the acknowledged difference of their cultures is indeed an essential part of their capacity to lead successful lives, a recognition and access they are all too often denied by the majority or dominant culture. This is also, many would argue, the kind of disadvantage experienced by underprivileged members of the cultural majority, who are denied the opportunities and resources necessary to the pursuit of a successful life by a culture that is fully aware of who they are and what they require. It seems clear, however, that this is not the kind of disadvantage experienced by women as women,[1] who function within a culture that is largely ignorant of who they are and what they require, and who suffer therefore from a misconception of the very meaning of their existence as women. As I have argued, as far as women are concerned the question of disadvantage in their lives is a question of the character of disadvantage, not a question of its threshold.

Second, then, women may suffer disadvantage in the conduct of their lives, as indeed may cultural minorities, because they are forced to live in terms of a conception of themselves that is false and thus a bar to the success of their lives. So misunderstood, women are prevented from leading successful lives because a misconception of what it means to be a woman[2] either conceals their equality with men or misrepresents their difference from men, where recognition of one or the other of those facts is essential to their capacity to succeed in life.

---

[1] Obviously, many women are members of cultural minorities and many more are underprivileged members of the cultural majority. It follows that many women suffer disadvantage that is not based upon a misconception of sexual identity. To the extent that they do so, however, they suffer disadvantage in common with men and so do not suffer sex discrimination. Conversely, to the extent that women do suffer discrimination, they suffer sex-specific disadvantage, although sex-specific disadvantage may well and often does take race-specific and class-specific forms.

[2] In referring to what it means to be a woman, I refer to the content of women's qualities and capacities, which in some respects are no different from those of men, and in other respects distinguish women from men and so define them as women. In referring to women in this broad sense, I refer to the condition of certain people and not merely to those aspects of their character that distinguish them from men. Misconceptions of what it means to be a woman, understood in this sense, may take three forms: they may describe a sexual difference where none exists; they may describe a particular sexual difference where some other exists; or they may describe sexual equality where sexual difference exists. The possibility of this last form of misconception means that a society can misconceive what it means to be a woman in respects in which it has no conception of sexual difference, and so has no conception of what it means to be a woman in the narrow, definitional sense. It can also misconceive what it means to be a woman in respects in which there is no difference between the sexes to misconceive. Women can be party to such misconceptions, and so pass on to their daughters the disadvantage that they themselves have suffered, by passing on false assumptions about sexual identity that they have acquired from their parents, their peers, and all those from whom and in common with whom they inherit, succour, and bequeath the social practices that constitute their culture.

These kinds of disadvantage are morally significant because they deny women what all human beings are entitled to. By contrast, specific instances of limitation and inferiority, in and of themselves, lack moral significance, because they do not deny women anything to which any human being either is or could be entitled. The distinction between what is and what is not a morally significant disadvantage turns on what it is possible for a woman to be or to imagine being. As I have indicated, I am assuming that human beings are entitled to those goods that are essential to their capacity to make a success of the project of their lives, whether those goods are opportunities, resources, an adequate range of valuable options, the satisfaction of needs, or otherwise. It follows that human beings are disadvantaged in a morally significant sense by the denial or the misapplication to them of those goods.

Given that what it means to lead a successful life is different for different human beings, however, the character of the goods to which particular human beings are entitled reflects the character of those human beings and the lives they seek to lead, as does any disadvantage they may suffer as a result of being denied those goods. It follows that human beings are entitled to goods of the same character as one another only where the lives they seek to lead are of the same character as one another, or if of different character nevertheless require access to the same opportunities or resources. Correspondingly, human beings can be thought to be disadvantaged by the denial to them of goods of the same character as others are assigned only if the lives they seek to lead and the goods required to make a success of those lives are no different from the lives and related goods of those with whom they are compared.

When different people engage in the same activities, they do so in different ways, as part of the different projects of their different lives. The significance of those activities, and of success or failure in them, is a function of the role those activities play in the lives of the people who engage in them, which is in turn a function of the different character of their different lives. It follows, however, that the fact that a woman is superior to a man in a given realm of human endeavour, and so is by reason of her sex at an advantage there, can be significant to her only to the extent that success in that realm contributes to the success of the project of her life, as an individual and as a woman, a project that is as distinctive as she is. Conversely, the fact that a woman is inferior to a man in a given realm of human endeavour and so is by reason of her sex at a disadvantage there, be it by reason of naturally created or culturally created elements of that sex, is significant to her only to the extent that failure in that realm is capable of damaging her prospects of success in the project of her life, and so disadvantaging her as a person.

To reiterate, truly different people are not engaged in the same life projects as one another, despite the fact that they are necessarily often engaged in the same endeavours, the endeavours that define the world they have in common. Men and women share many activities, but in doing so they may well differ in their understanding of the significance of those activities. Indeed, they are bound to so differ if the difference between the sexes is of any significance with respect to those activities. In such a case not only may shared activities mean different things to men and women, but they may have a different import, so that what is central for one sex is peripheral for the other.

Whether disadvantage in any particular realm of human endeavour disadvantages a woman or a man in the project of her life or his depends on the role that success in that realm of endeavour plays in the success of that project. In other words, disadvantages in particular realms, and the lack of resources or opportunities that may produce them, are related only contingently to disadvantage in life. They become disadvantages in life when their character and scale is such as to give them a real impact on the success of the lives of those whom they affect. It follows that disadvantages that are not relevant to the project of a particular life, and those that while relevant to that project do not affect its success, cannot be regarded as disadvantages in the project of that life, although they might well be disadvantages in the project of some other life. That is why the distinction between what is and what is not a morally significant disadvantage turns on what it is possible for a woman to be or to imagine being.

An analogy would perhaps be helpful here. Maurice Greene is, as I write, the world's fastest runner. The fact that neither I nor any other human being can run as fast as he can may, at least when fully explained and described, tell us something significant about the practice of athletics, that is, about the nature of athletic endeavour and achievement. It tells us what most human beings can achieve within that practice (very little) and what a few can achieve (something remarkable). In doing so it describes both the meaning of achievement within that practice and to some extent the meaning of the practice itself, which is by its nature constituted in terms of competition and the superiority and inferiority that competition reveals. Athletics, we might say, is all about winning and losing.

To put the point in general terms, superiority and inferiority, or advantage and disadvantage, when conceived of in relation to a particular social practice that embodies an aspect of human endeavour, describe the meaning of achievement in that practice, and in doing so help to establish the meaning of the practice itself. In some cases, those in which competitive ranking is only a peripheral element, the different achievements of its participants may tell us little about the meaning of the practice itself. In other cases, such as athletics perhaps, they may tell us much of what we need to know about it. The fact that I and all other human beings are inferior to Maurice Greene as sprinters, and so would be at a disadvantage if forced to confront him in an athletics event, tells us something significant about sprinting in particular, about athletics in general, and very probably about the life of Maurice Greene, subject to what I say below.

However in itself that inferiority tells us nothing significant about my particular life or that of virtually every other human being who is less talented and less accomplished as a sprinter than Maurice Greene. It does not tell us that I, for example, am disadvantaged in the project of my life by my limitations as a sprinter, for that will depend upon the character of my particular life and the role, if any, that success or failure as a sprinter plays in it. As I have argued, different people engage in the same activities as one another in different ways, as part of the different projects of their different lives. It follows that inferiority in a particular activity is a disadvantage to a person in the project of his or her life only when its character and scale are such as to give it a real impact on the success of that project.

To know that my inferiority as a sprinter is a disadvantage to my life, we would need to know that I see myself as an athlete and a sprinter. Otherwise my inferiority in that respect would be as remote from my disadvantage in life as my inferiority as a Sumo wrestler or a mountain climber, a financier or an actor. None of these activities forms any part of the project of my life. I am unlikely to engage in them at all, and if I do, my success or failure will be unimportant to me. They may be endeavours to others, in the project of whose lives they play a constitutive role, but they would be no more than distractions to me, if that. If the idea that they could be regarded as disadvantages to my life seems ridiculous, as surely it does, it is because it seems so obvious that my inferiority with respect to them is a fact that is entirely remote from my life. That seems obvious, however, only because and to the extent that it seems obvious that these activities form no part of the project of my life.

Correspondingly, superiority as a sprinter is an advantage in Maurice Greene's life only to the extent that it contributes to the success of the project of his life. It is reasonable to assume from what we know of his life that the fact that he can run faster than his Olympic rivals is a critical element in its success. It may be equally reasonable to assume that the fact that his Olympic rivals run more slowly than he does is a critical element in the success of the project of their lives, for to reach the Olympics is normally to want to win. However, the fact that Maurice Greene can run faster than I and all those other human beings who are not his Olympic rivals is clearly not an advantage in his life. The advantage and disadvantage that count for him are those that have a bearing on his capacity to lead a successful life, which in professional rather than personal terms is a life as a world-class athlete and sprinter. That life is not made more successful by the fact that he can run faster than the person beside him on the street.

To put the point in general terms once again, when conceived of in relation to a particular life, advantage and disadvantage describe the meaning of achievement in the project of that life, and by extension, the meaning of that life itself. It follows that the fact of inferiority in a particular realm, whether as a sprinter or in any other respect, is not a disadvantage in the project of a particular life unless success in that respect is a necessary element in that particular life's success. To believe otherwise is to believe that at heart we all lead or seek to lead the same life, notwithstanding our different approaches to the pursuit of our different lives and the apparently different capacities and aspirations those approaches reveal.

To treat every inferiority that human beings may experience in various specific fields of endeavour as a disadvantage in the project of their lives is to assimilate the experience of different human beings. The ingredients of a successful life are in fact as varied as human beings and the values they draw upon. If and to the extent that women are genuinely different from men, therefore, the success of their lives and the ingredients required to sustain that success will be correspondingly different from the success of men's lives and its ingredients. That being the case, what makes a woman's life a failure is as distinctive as what makes it a success. Disadvantage and inferiority coincide only to the extent that lives do.

Let me elaborate. I have said that disadvantages in particular realms become deep disadvantages only when they have a real impact on the success of the lives of those whom they affect. It follows that disadvantages in particular realms are not deep disadvantages if they are either irrelevant or marginal to the project of a life. How then do disadvantages in particular realms come to have a real impact on a life, so as to become deep disadvantages? Let us suppose that women's difference from men is such that on average they are inferior to men in some particular form of human endeavour, such as sprinting. There are four possible ways in which that inferiority could be linked to women's disadvantage in the deep sense, all of which depend upon conclusions about the particular character of the respective life projects of women and men, and only one of which causes deep disadvantage to women.

I have already argued that the quality of a person's performance in a particular activity can be an advantage or a disadvantage to that person in the deep sense only if success in that activity is capable of contributing to the success of his or her life. It follows that ability in sprinting might matter to neither men nor women. It is sensible to pursue what one is or could be good at, but it is neither possible nor desirable to pursue all the things that one might be good at. Human beings have to choose between projects, for they have only one life to lead. If men neglect their ability as sprinters in favour of other activities in which they might flourish, and if women understandably avoid their disability as sprinters in favour of yet other activities in which they might flourish, their relative abilities as sprinters might not matter to either sex. If on the other hand some men pursue sprinting but no women do, men's ability as sprinters, and the opportunities and resources required to develop it, would be an advantage in the project of men's lives without being a disadvantage in the lives of women, for whom it would simply be irrelevant. In both these situations, then, women's inferiority as sprinters would find no place in the project of their lives, and so would be incapable of causing them deep disadvantage. Inferiorities that are irrelevant to the project of a life cannot disadvantage that life, although they might disadvantage some other life, elsewhere.

Different people, however, sometimes pursue similar or overlapping life projects. That being the case, both men and women might pursue life projects that included the practice of sprinting, although the significance of that practice for each sex would be as different as the difference between their life projects. This might mean that sprinting was only a marginal activity in the project of women's lives, something akin to what I have called a mere distraction. If that were so, however, women's inferiority with regard to it would again cause them no deep disadvantage.

It is often the case that people pursue, as part of the larger project of their lives, activities in which they are inferior to other people. They do this because they know that participation in such activities can contribute to the overall value of their lives, enlarging their meaning without diminishing their significance. Inferiority in those particular respects does not mean that the project of one person's life is inferior to another's, for it is nested within the much larger, more complex project of that life. That project is as different from other life projects as the person who seeks to pursue it, and consequently is as incommensurable with the projects of those other lives as that person is with the other human beings who pursue them. Disadvantage in a particular realm can cause no disadvantage to the project of a life as long as it remains marginal to it.

However, if sprinting formed part of the project of women's lives, it might be central, or at least pivotal to that project. If that were so, women's inferiority as sprinters might appear to disadvantage them in the project of their lives, even if men's superiority as sprinters did not correspondingly advantage them, as it would not if sprinting formed no part of the project of men's lives.[3] In fact, however, the disadvantage that women would experience in those circumstances would flow not from their inferiority as sprinters but from the decision to make that activity central to the project of their lives.[4] In other words, women would be so disadvantaged only if they were either so mistaken in their own judgment or so misled by the judgment of others as to focus the project of their lives on

---

[3] In reality, of course, women compete as sprinters against one another and not against men. This means that despite a common description, women's and men's sprinting are different activities. That being the case, women are not, at least in the context of professional athletics, inferior to men as sprinters and consequently are able to make sprinting a central element in the project of their lives without thereby disadvantaging themselves. Where sex-specific practices of this kind are unavailable, however, for whatever reason, as might be the case with sprinting itself if it were possible to pursue it seriously outside the context of athletics, women who make activities at which they are inferior to men central to the project of their lives may well disadvantage themselves.

[4] Some qualification is necessary here. This explanation is adequate for present purposes but needs to be refined if it is to be fully accurate, for not every disadvantage in a central aspect of the project of a woman's life is a disadvantage to that project itself. Whether or not it is so depends, for example, on the contribution made by ranking – or by a high ranking – in the activity to the value of the activity. While for many athletes winning is what athletics is all about, some are happy merely to place, or to be in the event at all. See the discussion of misconceptions and value, below.

an activity at which they were inferior. As I have argued, it is only sensible, and indeed in many respects only meaningful, to pursue what one is or might be successful at; that is, what might be fulfilling in the particular project of one's life. It follows that disadvantage in a given realm is a disadvantage in the project of one's life only if one is so mistaken or misled in the construction of that project as to call upon abilities that one does not possess, and thus to pursue ends that one cannot succeed at.

This is what I meant in alleging that in themselves limitation and inferiority lack moral significance because they do not deny women anything to which any human being either is or could be entitled. One cannot possibly be entitled to be what one cannot be, in this case adept at sprinting. One is not disadvantaged in the project of one's life by one's genuine limitations and inferiorities, for the project of one's life is something that can be imagined and pursued only in terms of qualities that one possesses and through which one might reasonably hope to flourish, or conversely, in avoidance of qualities that one does not possess and through which one could not expect to flourish.

On the other hand, however, one is certainly disadvantaged in the deep sense in committing one's life to a project in which one cannot hope to flourish, and limitations and inferiorities may constitute evidence that one has done exactly that. While the mere presence of inferiority in one's life is not in itself evidence of such a commitment, and so is not in itself evidence of deep disadvantage, the presence of inferiorities in aspects of one's life so central and definitive as to suggest that one is inferior as a person suggests that the project of that life may have been misconceived.[5]

It is with this in mind that I argued above that the distinction between what is and what is not a morally significant disadvantage turns on what it is possible for a woman to be or to imagine being. Those limitations and inferiorities that are part of the meaning of sexual difference become sexual disadvantage in the deep sense, the sense in which they are a disadvantage to the project of women's lives, only as the result of a mistake as to the meaning and implications of the character of sexual difference. If this kind of mistake is incorporated in the project of a woman's life to such a degree that it threatens the success of that project, it thereby disadvantages that project and that life.

It is vital to recognize, however, that this kind of mistake is not one committed primarily by women. Men and women are frequently mistaken in the project of their lives, but women are no more likely to be mistaken in that respect than men. Moreover, women are no more likely to be mistaken on the basis of sex than on any other basis. Indeed, women could be thought to be more often mistaken than men only if there was something in the difference between the sexes that made women particularly prone to that kind of error. Since that is

---

[5] For more detailed consideration of this point, see section II.B.iii, "The Implications of Inferiority", below.

clearly not the case, it cannot be that women are disadvantaged in their lives, in a way that makes them inferior to men, primarily as the result of misguided decisions on their part as to how to conduct the project of their lives. Rather, women are disadvantaged in this way because the decisions they make about the lives they hope to lead are reached within the context of the social forms in and through which their lives are necessarily conducted.

People do not invent or construct the worlds within which their lives find meaning and significance. On the contrary, they very gradually and inarticulately develop the project of their lives, by drawing on the resources of their own character, as individuals and in this case as women, and on the social practices of their culture, which make particular life projects both possible and meaningful by conferring relevance and hence practical significance on some portion of the manifold qualities, and their manifold implications, that genuinely distinguish human beings from one another. Different cultures, it need hardly be said, are characterized by their different social practices, which embody different conceptions of what it means to be a human being. It follows that people, in drawing on the practices of their particular culture in order to develop and pursue the project of their lives, as they must if that project is to be even intelligible to them, are compelled to participate in that culture's conception of what it means to be a human being. If that conception is in any way mistaken, and if such a mistake is endemic in the social practices of that culture, people will be compelled to participate in that mistake and suffer its consequences.

If the project of women's lives is now mistaken, that mistake, if not the product of what it means to be a woman, must be the product of the social practices that give relevance and significance to the qualities that distinguish the sexes, and in doing so determine what it is possible for a woman to be or to imagine being. Any misconception of the meaning and implications of sexual difference, if broadly embedded in the social practices in and through which the two sexes are compelled to conduct their lives, and in the options that those practices offer, will lead men and women to develop the projects of their separate lives in ways that are untrue to the difference between them, for the options we choose as individuals are dependent upon the options we have to choose among. If women commit the project of their lives to sprinting against men as well as women, an activity at which I am supposing they are inferior to men, it can be only because they have been impelled to do so by the social practices in and through which their lives have necessarily been developed, which express sexual equality and so lead women both to pursue sprinting, rather than something else at which they might flourish, and to pursue it on equal terms with men, thus forcing them to betray the difference of their sex twice over.

The pervasive inferiority of one sex to the other in a particular society, therefore, one that constitutes sexual disadvantage, is evidence of the existence of a widespread misconception of sexual identity there. The fact that the inferiority of one sex to the other in some respect has come to define the life projects of many, perhaps most, members of that sex, indicates that those projects are mistaken, for otherwise such inferiorities would be no more than incidents in an approach to life that was incommensurable with that of the other sex. Given that there is nothing in the difference between the sexes that would lead one sex or the other to be particularly prone to such an error, we can conclude that it has occurred only as the result of a misconception of sexual identity that has compelled women to define their lives in terms of goals that do not permit them to flourish. Sexual inferiorities, if and to the extent that they exist, do not deny women access to superior qualities, but rather indicate that women have been denied access to the value of their own qualities.

This is not, of course, the only way that human beings can be disadvantaged as the result of a misconception of their difference from other human beings. As I have argued, broadly held misconceptions of sexual identity may compel women to pursue critical dimensions of their lives in terms of sexual equality where sexual difference exists, or in terms of a supposed sexual difference where no such difference exists, or in terms of a supposed sexual difference where a sexual difference of a different character exists. Some such misconceptions may portray women as inferior to men. Others, however, may portray women as incommensurable with men, and so make their lives alien rather than inferior. Whether or not a broadly held misconception of sexual identity portrays women as inferior to men, therefore, it compels them to lead lives that disadvantage them, because the embodiment of a misconception of sexual identity in the social practices in and through which the project of their lives must be developed prevents women from pursuing lives they could truly value. It compels them to develop their lives on the basis of a false conception of the qualities they possess, so suppressing the existence of the genuine qualities on the basis of which they could develop and pursue valuable lives, or at least making it impossible to pursue life projects based upon those genuine qualities.[6]

I do not wish to dwell on these issues at any greater length at this stage, for they warrant more prolonged consideration than it is possible to give them here without obscuring the question of whether limitation and inferiority are in themselves properly disregarded in the search for the nature and origins of women's present predicament. What does need to be emphasized is that to say that the limits on human lives implicit in human difference, and the inferiority they may produce in a particular realm, do not in and of themselves constitute deep disadvantage, but rather are part and parcel of the specificity of existence

---

[6] As I noted above, people can also be disadvantaged by a society that offers no place for any of the projects that it acknowledges would make their life meaningful, or that simply fails to provide the opportunities or resources necessary to make a success of such projects. These disadvantages, however, do not involve a misconception of what it means to be a woman. For the reasons given above, I believe that women's present predicament is the product of a misconception of what it means to be a woman, one of the features of which is the apparent inferiority of women to men.

that any form of difference describes, is not to be complacent about women's suffering or conservative about what constitutes an appropriate response to that suffering.

On the contrary, it is no favour to women to pretend that these forms of limitation and inferiority are deep disadvantages to them, for to do so is in fact both misleading and itself disadvantageous to women. To impose a fictional existence upon women, one that denies the reality of their existence and pretends to transcend the limitations and consequent inferiorities that attend not only that form of existence but all other forms of human existence, is to impose upon women a renovated form of the very disadvantage from which they are now suffering. What is needed is an accurate diagnosis of their disadvantage, one that can distinguish it from the local disabilities that are often mistaken for it, the existence of which no more disadvantages women than it disadvantages men, and the removal of which, were it possible, would result only in the suppression of sexual difference and the reconstitution of that difference, with all its attendant and necessary limitations, in other planes and for other purposes.

In conclusion, the focus upon limitation and inferiority, and the consequent equation of local disadvantage with what I have called deep disadvantage, gives rise to a form of feminism that offers untenable accounts both of what it means to be a woman and how that experience is disadvantaged in our culture. What is needed instead is an understanding of what it means to be a woman that gives meaning and substance to women's history and prospects, and an understanding of the disadvantage that women now experience, as a consequence of our conception of them as women, that has moral significance.

II. The Significance of Misconceptions

Before turning to the question of the value of a woman's life and the ways in which it can be threatened by misconceptions of what it means to be a woman, it might be helpful to review briefly the different kinds of misconception that may arise, for they raise different issues of access to value. On the one hand, the failure to recognize women's equality with men raises questions of women's access to known values, in particular their access to those valuable activities now engaged in by men. On the other hand, the failure to recognize women's difference from men, or to recognize the true character of that difference, raises questions of women's access to values that only women are capable of realizing, and in particular their access to valuable activities that we as a society have neglected or remained largely ignorant of.

In circumstances of sexual equality, there is no difference between what advantages and disadvantages a man and what advantages and disadvantages a woman. If every human being is entitled to the goods that will enable him or her to make a success of his or her life, opportunities that he or she can truly enjoy and resources that he or she can truly use, in other words, to goods that are capable of mattering to him or her because they are sensitive to the particular character of his or her life, lack of difference between the sexes means that there is no difference in what men and women are entitled to, and so no difference in what is liable to cause them disadvantage.

If and to the extent that the sexes are equal to and so no different from one another, therefore, men and women will profit from the same opportunities and will depend upon the same resources, and consequently will be vulnerable to the same kinds of disadvantage. Conversely, if women are genuinely disadvantaged by a lack of those opportunities and resources whose lack would disadvantage a man, then the sexes are equal to and so no different from one another, at least as far as any of the purposes of the culture that is alleged to so disadvantage them are concerned. When we allege that women are disadvantaged by their lack of parity with men, we implicitly allege that women are no different from men.

If women are no different from men, however, then men are as vulnerable to what disadvantages women as women are themselves. It follows that where women are no different from men, the only way that women can be uniquely disadvantaged is through the promulgation of a misconception of their existence that presents them as different from men when in fact they are not. To put it more precisely, if men and women are equal to one another, then disadvantage can be confined to women and kept from men only by arbitrarily assigning significance to a difference that has none, either by inventing a sexual distinction where none exists, and so falsely extending the scope of sexual difference, or by giving weight to a sexual distinction that the practices of our culture have made irrelevant.

The fact that many and perhaps most allegations of sex discrimination[7] have tended to concentrate on what their adherents regard as the arbitrariness and irrelevance of sex distinctions, therefore, shows that the understanding of sexual identity on which those allegations are based is one of equality, namely, that women are no different from men as far as any of the purposes of our culture are concerned. Few would dispute that this understanding of sexual identity

---

[7] I have in mind here those allegations that have seen women's disadvantage in terms of their exclusion from domains of endeavour occupied by men, and that have sought to secure women's admission to those domains by demonstrating the irrelevance of sex and the qualities that define it to the capacity to flourish there. This position is often described as liberal feminism: see *Feminism Unmodified: Discourses on Life and Law* (Cambridge, Mass., 1987), at 117–18: "... I propose for your consideration two different strands of feminist theory. Most work on women in sport (most work on women in anything) comes from the first approach. In this approach the problem of the inequality of the sexes revolves around gender differentiation. The view is that there are real differences between the sexes, usually biological or natural. Upon these differences, society has created some inaccurate, irrational, and arbitrary distinctions: sex stereotypes or sex roles. To eliminate sex inequality, on this view, is to eliminate these wrong and irrational distinctions. . . . This is liberal feminism's diagnosis of the condition of women." Many who hold this position would not endorse the description of themselves as liberal feminists, however, and for that reason I have avoided the term, as unrepresentative of both liberals and feminists.

is correct in many, perhaps most, respects, the respects in which supposed differences between men and women have been shown to be spurious. Much of the history of feminism, as expressed in prominent strands of feminist argument and debate, in the achievements of women in domains once reserved for men, and in the criteria of legitimacy set by antidiscrimination law in its present form, has been dedicated to showing that the supposed incapacities of women simply have no foundation in fact.[8] To the extent that this brand of feminism has been vindicated, it is because men and women are genuinely equal as far as the forms and practices of our culture are concerned. The question remains, however, whether men and women are in this sense equal to one another in all respects, or whether there are certain genuine differences between men and women that remain relevant to our culture.

If men and women are not in this sense equal in terms of their ambitions and capacities, that is to say, if there is a real difference between the sexes that is relevant to our culture, then the success of a woman's life may well be dependent upon her access to her distinctive ambitions and capacities, to the qualities that distinguish her as a woman rather than to the qualities that she shares with men. If that is the case, then the project of her life will be based on sex-specific goals and so will need sex-specific opportunities and resources to sustain it, of a kind that are capable of mattering to her as a woman. Conversely, her life will be disadvantaged if she is denied access to those opportunities and resources because an entrenched misconception of what it means and does not mean to be a woman misrepresents what she is and what is capable of mattering to her.

A. Comprehensive Misconceptions

These are points I have defended above and there is no need to pursue them further here. However, they imply a further point I have yet to defend fully, namely, that the success of a woman's life depends not merely upon access to goods that are capable of mattering to her as a woman, in the sense of being consonant with her character and abilities, but upon access to goods that are genuinely valuable. Many goals in life that are consonant with a person's particular character and abilities are simply not worth pursuing. Some such goals are without value, while others have no place in the social practices of our culture and so cannot be rationally pursued by its members. As far as women are concerned, therefore, certain goals in life that are entirely consonant with their character and abilities as women, and so are apparently capable of mattering to

---

[8] This was particularly true of the modern feminist movement in its initial and in many ways most influential stages, which drew on models of race discrimination to entrench in the law, statutory and constitutional, the conclusion that it is equality that women lack and equality that they must be accorded if they are to escape their present predicament.

them as women, are in fact simply not worth pursuing, either because they are not valuable or because they are irrelevant, or both.

As I have emphasized, however, valuable goals are accessible only to those who possess the capacities and resources necessary to secure them and, more to the point, to those who know themselves and are known by others to possess such capacities. The enjoyment of any capacity, and by extension, access to the goals it makes possible, is dependent upon the knowledge that one possesses that capacity, a knowledge that is embodied in the prevailing conception, self-determined and socially determined, of who and what one is. It is not possible to pursue goals that oneself or others believe one lacks the capacity to enjoy, for the value of those goals, however genuine, would then be something that oneself or others believed one to be incapable of realizing. Goals that one believes oneself to be incapable of realizing cannot rationally form part of one's ambitions, while goals that others believe one to be incapable of realizing will either find no recognition in the social practices in and through which the project of one's life is necessarily pursued or be assumed to be accessible only to persons other than oneself.

Women may be disadvantaged in the development and pursuit of the project of their lives by the restriction of their lives to a range of goals that reflects a misconception of what it genuinely means to be a woman. But they may also be disadvantaged by the restriction of their lives to what they can be but cannot value, that is, by restriction to a range of goals that reflects an accurate but incomplete conception of what it means to be a woman, one that provides a diminished account of women's ambitions and capacities, and in so doing confines the project of women's lives to a range of goals that lacks genuine value. In either of these ways, disadvantage in principle can become disadvantage in practice.[9] In principle, a misconception of what it means to be a woman may disadvantage women by ascribing to them qualities they do not possess and failing to recognize in them qualities they do possess. In practice, however, a misconception will disadvantage women only if the qualities it misapprehends are those upon which the success of a woman's life depends, which they will be if the misconception is either *comprehensive* or *critical* in character.

If the prevailing understanding of what it means to be a woman is fundamentally misconceived, that is, if our misconception of sexual identity is *comprehensive* in character, then disadvantage will certainly result from it. In that case, whatever valuable goals women are thought to be capable of pursuing will be those they are in fact incapable of pursuing, goals that they can neither rationally endorse nor attain. However, a comprehensive misconception of this kind is not the only, or even the most plausible way in which women can be disadvantaged by a misconception of sex; for what we might otherwise

---

[9] A misconception of what it means to be a woman can also take the form of a misconception of the relevance of sexual differences to our culture. See the discussion of relevance below.

regard as relatively minor misconceptions are fully capable of disadvantaging women, and also constitute rather more plausible descriptions of women's present predicament than the possibility that we misunderstand sexual identity completely.

B. Critical Misconceptions

A relatively minor misconception of what it means to be a woman will disadvantage women if it recognizes in them only the qualities they possess that cannot be put to valuable use, or conversely, if it fails to recognize in them qualities that would otherwise be put to valuable use and upon which the success of their life depends. An understanding of what it means to be a woman that is largely accurate may nevertheless disadvantage women if it portrays them as lacking, altogether or in some key dimension, qualities they in fact possess that are necessary to the success of their lives. In short, the success of a woman's life may be as readily compromised by half-truths regarding her character as by comprehensive falsehoods. Both misconceptions render certain valuable goals inaccessible to a woman, goals upon which the success of her particular life depends.

It follows that there are three significant implications to the role played by value in the construction of a successful life, and it may be useful to outline them briefly before examining them in more detail.[10] The basic ingredients of a successful life are those qualities of a person's character that are capable of sustaining valuable activities, or more accurately, whatever selection of such qualities is necessary to ensure the success of his or her life. That being the case, the attempt to lead a successful life does not require a person, first, to alter the qualities of his or her character, or second, to correct all misconceptions of that character, or third, to avoid all experience of inferiority, even where that inferiority is central to the project of his or her life. This simply follows from the fact that, for any particular person, the ingredients of a successful life are as distinctive as the values that his or her character makes it possible to embrace, and so are a function of that character, not of some ideal to which each person and their character is expected to conform.

As I have said, we express different values in defining and pursuing the different projects of our different lives. This means it is possible for each of us to find within our own character, without any need for an alteration of that character,[11] the ambitions and capacities necessary to pursue valuable activities, and so make a success of the project of our particular life. The value of the activities that any one of us is capable of pursuing, on the basis of the character we have been given, is not inferior or superior to, but incommensurable with,

---

[10] See sections II.B.i–iii below.
[11] Apart from special cases of morally flawed character.

the value of the activities that are pursued by other, different human beings. Conversely, however, given that success in the project of one's life is dependent upon the pursuit of valuable activities rather than on full realization of the qualities of one's character, qualities that are not called into play by the pursuit of such activities are simply irrelevant to the success or failure of one's life, whether they are understood correctly or not.

i. LIMITING MISCONCEPTIONS.

a. Limited Value. Let me begin with the problem raised by those features of sexual identity that are said to be the product of the historic ill- treatment of women. It may be the case that certain misconceptions of what it means to be a woman, having been reiterated comprehensively and over an extended period of time, have now become true of women. Some contend, for example, that if it is true that women are more caring than men, it is only because providing care for others is part of the role that has historically been assigned to women. That role has been assigned to them because at least some of those cared for, namely, men, have wanted to be cared for by women and have possessed the ability to insist they be so cared for without any regard to whether a distinctive capacity for concern was part of women's character.[12] Many might argue that if this is indeed the historical record, not only with regard to concern but with regard to other qualities that distinguish the sexes, then the features of sexual identity it has given rise to ought not to be respected, because they carry with them the taint of their origins. Such features are inherently degrading, so that affirming them would only confirm women in their present predicament instead of releasing them from it. These are aspects of sexual identity that we should want to bring to an end, not endorse.

Nor are these features, which might be called tainted, the only features of sexual identity that are thought to be objectionable and so unworthy of affirmation. It may also be true, for example, that women's character genuinely, that is, without any original informing misconception, displays a number of features that constitute disabilities in a culture such as ours, which women would accordingly wish to see removed, not affirmed. With that possibility in mind, some[13] argue that if, for whatever reason, there is any aspect of women's

---

[12] Catharine MacKinnon in particular has argued this. See, for example, her discussion of the work of Carol Gilligan in *Feminism Unmodified, supra* n. 7.

[13] See, for example, Christine Littleton, "Reconstructing Sexual Equality", 75 *California Law Review* 1279 (1987), especially Part IV, "Making Difference Costless", at 1323ff. See also Deborah Rhode, *Justice and Gender* (Cambridge, Mass., 1989), at 312–13: "If women are to obtain adequate recognition of their distinctive experience, they must transcend its constraints. . . . The critical issue should not be difference, but the difference difference makes." I must stress that both Littleton and Rhode wish to change society, not the character of women. Nevertheless, Littleton's aim, for example, in her own words, "is to make gender differences, perceived or actual, costless relative to each other, so that anyone may follow a male, female, or androgynous lifestyle according to their natural inclination or choice without being punished for following

character, however genuine, that is capable of causing women disadvantage in a society such as ours, that aspect ought to be removed, whether through education or some other form of rehabilitation.

This desire to address and eliminate the disadvantageous features of women's character has a familiar ring to it, however, one that suggests that the proper answer to these issues lies in a proper understanding of the meaning of disadvantage. I have argued above that women are disadvantaged not only by the restriction of their lives to what they cannot be but by the restriction of their lives to what they can be but cannot value. The reason for this is that the authenticity of the characteristics on which a woman's life is based is a necessary but not a sufficient condition for the success of that life, which is also dependent upon the exercise of characteristics that are genuinely valuable. The corollary to this is that the inauthenticity of the characteristics on which a woman's life is based is a sufficient but not a necessary condition of what may disadvantage that life, for that life will also be disadvantaged if based on authentic but nonvaluable characteristics.[14]

It does not follow, however, that the authentic presence of nonvaluable characteristics in a woman's character causes her disadvantage. On the contrary, women are no more disadvantaged by the presence in their character of qualities that they cannot value than they are disadvantaged by the absence from their character of valuable qualities that others possess, provided, that is, that the project of their lives is not improperly restricted to the exercise of such qualities. Disadvantage in the project of one's life is not the product of the qualities that do or do not form part of one's character. It is the product of the fact that that project has been either so mistaken or so misguided as to be based on the wrong qualities, namely, those in terms of which one cannot flourish, whether they are qualities one does not possess or qualities one cannot value.

---

a female lifestyle or rewarded for following a male one": *id.* at 1297. That is to say, Littleton seeks to eliminate the disadvantages that now follow from the interaction of certain features of women's character with the features of our culture. It is merely a sense of fairness and shared responsibility, coupled with the assumption that it is easier to change society than to change the character of women, that leads her to call for the restructuring of society rather than of the character of women, not a recognition and acceptance of sexual differences that would impose limits upon women, or serve as the occasion for their disadvantage within those limits. As I have argued above, however, there is less difference between the two positions than might at first appear, as Littleton herself implicitly acknowledges, *id.* at 1309–10: "I believe that both the meaning of sex and the meaning of equality are socially constructed, and that they can be socially reconstructed from the ashes left by feminist critique." And later, in discussing the relationship between her position and that of Catharine MacKinnon, *id.* at 1333–34: "The social construction of 'woman' . . . can be disrupted either by revaluing what women have been perceived to be, or by reassigning the attributes that comprise the social sexes, or both."

[14] I am assuming that what is at issue is nonvaluable characteristics, and the misconceptions that lead women to live in terms of such characteristics. In fact, I suspect that what is at issue is the misconceptions that lead women to apply potentially valuable characteristics, such as the capacity for concern, to nonvaluable ends. Yet the same arguments would apply, mutatis mutandis.

To put it more succinctly, a proper understanding of disadvantage, one that takes into account the constitutive role played in the success of a woman's life by those qualities of her character that she can genuinely value, yields a proper understanding of the relationship between the qualities that describe a woman and the circumstances in which she may be disadvantaged. According to that understanding, disadvantage is not the product of the qualities that genuinely describe a woman, but of a misconception of those qualities, whether it be a misconception of their *character* or a misconception of their *scope*.

As one might expect, then, there is an element of truth in the contention that women may be disadvantaged by certain features of their sex, for women's lives may well be focused upon non-valuable features of their character as women, as well as upon false, or supposed, features of that character. It follows that I spoke too quickly, but not inaccurately, in saying that women's present predicament is the product of a misconception of sexual identity, for there are a number of different ways in which such a misconception can arise, and a mistake as to the *character* of what it means to be a woman is only one of them. A misconception of the meaning of sexual identity can also arise as the result of a mistake as to the *scope* of what it means to be a woman. The influence of this mistake will compel a woman to overlook the aspects of what it genuinely means to be a woman that she can value in favour of aspects that she cannot value.

Women are not disadvantaged, therefore, by the mere presence in their character of qualities that cannot be put to the service of valuable goals in our culture. Rather, women are advantaged and disadvantaged in the development and pursuit of the project of their lives, which is formed in terms of who they are and what they can value and is, as a result, as distinctive as they are, or more accurately, as distinctive as what they are capable of valuing. It follows that the existence of disadvantage in the lives of women can no more be inferred from the presence in their character of qualities that serve no valuable goals in our culture than it can be inferred from the presence in their character of qualities that may, for certain purposes at least, show them to be inferior to men.

Conversely, and as I have already indicated, women *will* be disadvantaged if the resources of character on which the project of their lives draws are restricted to dimensions of their character that have no valuable application in our culture. I have argued that this will occur if a misconception of what it means to be a woman is critical to the success of a woman's life in that it denies her access to qualities she must exercise if she is to succeed. This means, however, that the prevailing understanding of what it means to be a woman must be not only true but comprehensive enough to embrace a range of qualities that are capable of being applied to the pursuit of valuable goals in our culture, goals that will permit women to pursue a genuinely successful life. We need not know the whole truth of what it means to be a woman, but we must know enough of it to know what in it can constitute the basis for a valuable and thus a potentially successful life.

What is needed to end the disadvantage that women now experience, therefore, is not to change what it means to be a woman but to perceive that meaning correctly. Then we must see that women are enabled to devote the projects of their lives, as indeed is only rational, to whatever aspects of that meaning are capable of serving valuable goals in our culture and so are capable of forming the basis of a successful life. The problem women now face is not that they possess the wrong qualities on which to base a successful life, conceived without reference to who they are, but that they lack access to the right qualities, namely, those aspects of their character capable of being brought to bear on the pursuit of valuable goals in a life conceived and pursued in terms of who they are and what they can be.

What matters, and hence what we need to seek and affirm, is not a primordial picture of sexual identity, unaffected and so untainted by the actions of the human beings who have responded to it over the course of history and before, which would tell us only what men and women once were and might have remained but in fact did not. Rather, what matters is a picture of what men and women have now become, for good reason or bad, as a result of the impact on the content of sexual identity of influences sufficiently powerful and prolonged that their effects have acquired the force, if not the status, of natural facts. What men and women now are is what they have been given from which to build the project of their lives, and that and only that is what they may be disadvantaged in terms of. All those who contribute to the ongoing debate over the status of women in our culture, by their words or their actions, in support of the claims of feminists or in opposition to them, whether in the end proved right or proved wrong, contribute to the determination of that picture.

In fact, what is much more likely, as MacKinnon's example of concern suggests, is that women have been encouraged to focus their lives not on nonvaluable characteristics but on the nonvaluable application of potentially valuable characteristics. Here the answer is even clearer. Women need to discover whether it is true, for example, that they have a special capacity for concern. If they do, they need to appreciate the full implications of concern, and the many valuable applications to which it may be put. Finally, they need to ensure that their lives, if committed to concern at all, are committed to such valuable applications, rather than the many nonvaluable applications to which they have been historically confined.

b. Limited Relevance. This cannot be the whole story of the disadvantage now experienced by women, however. The character of what it means to be a woman, and the valuable activities that that character makes it possible, and even necessary, to pursue merely establishes the kinds of life that it is rational for women to pursue in some imaginable culture. It does not establish which of those kinds of life it is rational for particular women to pursue, women who inhabit particular cultures and so must pursue the projects of their lives in and through the forms and practices of those cultures. In other words, many activities that are both valuable and consonant with what it means to be a woman simply have no place in a culture such as ours.

That being the case, a conception of what it means to be a woman that is indisputably true and comprehensive enough to permit women access to genuinely valuable activities may nevertheless disadvantage women if the activities it permits access to are ones that have no place in the forms and practices of our culture. It is quite possible that some portion of what it means to be a woman is capable of being applied to the pursuit of valuable activities that have no place in contemporary culture, or in some particular contemporary culture. That being so, a society that confines its understanding of women to that irrelevant aspect of their character thereby prevents women from making a success of their lives. The valuable activities it regards them as capable of undertaking have insufficient relevance to its culture; while the valuable activities that are relevant to its culture are activities it regards them as incapable of undertaking. In other words, a society may fail to see the relevance of certain human qualities that it knows women to possess, or may fail to see that women possess certain human qualities that it knows to be relevant, and so may fail to see that sexual difference matters in that culture in ways other than it is taken to.

Some cultures, for example, although modern in themselves, view women in highly traditional terms, which might once have described a valuable way of life, but no longer do so, for the conditions that made that way of life possible no longer exist. Such women need to be understood in more contemporary terms if they are to flourish in contemporary society. The same is true, in reverse, of the place of certain modern, Westernized women in traditional cultures. If such women are viewed exclusively in modern, Western terms, which we may suppose also describe a valuable way of life, they will be denied access to crucial dimensions of the traditional culture in which they find themselves. Such women need to be understood in more traditional terms, that is, in ways that are compatible with traditional life, if they are to flourish in that traditional setting. Their modernity might be recognized as a contemporary variation on a traditional theme, so that their commitment to modernity is recognized as compatible with the capacity to engage in a traditional way of life.

Three clarifications are necessary here. First, this problem of relevance is not, as it might appear to be, one of a fixed understanding of what it means to be a woman, which sees women as they always have been, untouched by their history. That would be a false understanding of what it means to be a woman, for women are what they have become as a result of their history, for good reason or bad. Rather, as was the case with valuable activities, the problem is one of an accurate but incomplete understanding of what it means to be a woman, one that disadvantages women if the picture it presents of them lacks valuable application in our culture. This is what I have called a misconception of scope. Such a misconception may exclude women from valuable activities altogether, but it may also exclude them only from those valuable activities that are relevant to our culture, with just as damaging consequences.

Second, I should emphasize that to say that the project of a woman's life must be relevant to the culture in which she finds herself is not to be pessimistic or unimaginative about the range of activities that being a woman makes it possible to pursue in any particular culture. On the contrary, I take it for granted that women are capable of pursuing a wide range of valuable activities in every culture, as the evidence of their lives regularly gives proof. Nevertheless, it is essential to recognize that particular women can pursue the projects of their lives only through the forms and practices of the particular culture they happen to inhabit, a culture they at once draw on as a framework for those projects, and constantly redefine by the manner in which those projects are carried out.

The obligation to pursue activities that are relevant to our culture is in no way an obligation to conform to our culture's misconception of what it means to be a woman. Rather, it is no more than an acknowledgment that what it means to be a woman is relevant to a particular culture if and when it has a role to play in that culture, not some other. It is critical, therefore, to distinguish this sense of the relevance of sexual identity, which addresses the truth of what it means to be a woman, from the sense in which sexual identity is often thought to be relevant, which addresses our present conception, or misconception, of what it means to be a woman. In both cases it is the relevance of sexual identity that is assessed, but in each case something different is meant by sexual identity.

In the former case, it is the true meaning of sexual identity that is compared with the forms and practices of a particular culture, in order to assess the rationality of the pursuit in and through those forms and practices of certain valuable activities that are acknowledged to be consonant with the character of women. That assessment poses a challenge to the prevailing conception of sexual identity. In the latter case, however, it is the prevailing conception of sexual identity that is related to the forms and practices of the culture that subscribes to it, in order to assess the justifications that are offered for practices that prefer one sex to the other there. That assessment all too often collapses into a description of the very misconception of sexual identity that women are disadvantaged by; at best it reveals inconsistency in the application of that misconception.[15] The former approach expects us to accept the truth of what people are, as we must; the latter approach expects us to accept the truth of certain people's judgments of what people are, as we have no reason to do unless those judgments are actually shown to be correct.

As a third and final clarification, I must also emphasize that an assessment of the relevance to a particular culture of activities that are acknowledged to be both valuable and consonant with the character of women does nothing to preclude, as again it might appear to, the pursuit of ways of life that are at odds

---

[15] As Catharine MacKinnon emphasizes.

with the mainstream of that culture. Suppose, for example, that the success of some women's lives is dependent upon access to an aboriginal culture, either because they need access to the distinctive activities that it offers or because they need access to its distinctive setting for activities that might also be pursued in nonaboriginal settings. If that aboriginal culture is independent of any other culture, so as to function as a separate society, then the question of relevance must be directed to the forms and practices of that separate society. If the aboriginal culture is interdependent with another culture, its host, for example, so as to be part of a multicultural society, then the question of relevance must be directed to the forms and practices of that multicultural society. In neither case are aboriginal activities or an aboriginal setting liable to be regarded as irrelevant because they are marginal.

What matters, then, is the ability to draw upon the forms and practices of one's society in imagining and pursuing the project of a life and in carrying out that project successfully, an ability that depends upon a genuine understanding of what each person is and what she or he might value in that society. People have every reason to expect that the society of which they are members will understand them accurately and completely enough to permit them access to all those valuable activities that may be rationally pursued within its forms and practices, and no reason to expect more. If we are to end women's disadvantage, we need to discover not only what it means to be a woman, but the relevance of that way of life to our culture.

ii. NONLIMITING MISCONCEPTIONS. The corollary to this conclusion, and what I call the second implication of the role played by value in the construction of a successful life, is that a misconception of what it means to be a woman does not disadvantage women unless it touches those aspects of their character they must call upon in order to lead successful lives. As I have argued, it is neither possible nor desirable to pursue all the valuable implications of what one is, that is, to pursue all the valuable goals that one is capable of pursuing. Accordingly we do not need a complete, or fully accurate, understanding of sexual identity in order to prevent women's disadvantage, provided our understanding is both accurate as far as it goes and comprehensive enough to embrace qualities that can be applied to the pursuit of a range of valuable goals in our culture, a range that permits women to lead successful lives.[16] In other words, while the disadvantage that women now suffer is the product of a misconception of what it means to be a woman, it does not follow that all such misconceptions disadvantage women. On the contrary, many such misconceptions, annoying though they may be, simply have no bearing upon the success of a woman's life.

---

[16] See the discussion of knowledge in section III below.

As I have argued, misconceptions are disadvantaging if they are either comprehensive in their character or critical to the success of the project of a life. A comprehensive misconception of what it means to be a woman disadvantages a woman because it denies her access to all goals that are consonant with her character, and so denies her access to all goals that she is capable of valuing. Even an apparently minor misconception of sexual identity will disadvantage a woman, however, if it denies her access to goals that are critical to the success of her life. If, for example, women are understood to be different from men in some limited degree when in fact they are not, and if the success of at least some women's lives is dependent upon access to the very qualities that women are mistakenly thought to lack, then women will be disadvantaged by the prevailing misconception of them, despite its limited degree. Conversely, if women are understood to be the same as men in certain limited respects, when in fact they differ from men in just those respects, and if the success of at least some women's lives depends upon access to their difference in those respects, then women will be disadvantaged by the prevailing misconception of them, despite its limited degree.

It does not follow from any of this, indeed, is flatly contradicted by it, that a misconception of what it means to be a woman, or to be any person, in itself constitutes a disadvantage to that person. On the contrary, it is very often a matter of indifference that other people make mistakes about who and what one is. The true significance of a misconception, in terms of its capacity to cause disadvantage, depends upon who those other people are, the contexts in which their judgments are made, and the significance of the goals, access to which those judgments affect, in the project of one's life. It follows that the invocation of false generalizations or stereotypes, about women or about any other class of person, is not in itself a disadvantage to the people thus falsely described, whether those stereotypes are entirely false, that is, untrue of any member of the class described, or false as applied, that is, untrue of the individual in respect of whom they are invoked.

To repeat a point made earlier, men think many foolish things about women, but they do not always harm women in doing so. Some misconceptions of women are simply trivial, so that their perpetuation is an annoyance rather than an injury. If men think that all women love clothes, or conversation, or admiring babies, they are mistaken, but the mistake has no bearing on any woman's life, special cases aside. Other misconceptions have real potential to damage women but may fail to do so in a particular case, because they happen to be irrelevant to the lives of those against whom they are directed. If a man thinks that women are unqualified for scientific positions, he is mistaken in a way that has real potential to damage women, but his mistake will be irrelevant as long as it has no bearing on the success of any woman's life, which is just as long as he has no influence over access to scientific positions.

For the most part the attitude to such misconceptions is and must be "so be it." It is only when such misconceptions have a critical impact on the success of some woman's life, as they will if they form a basis for denying her access to opportunities and resources that she would otherwise value and on which the success of her life is dependent, that they are disadvantaging and wrongful. This is not to say, of course, that false generalizations and stereotypes are unobjectionable. On the contrary, it is almost always desirable to know the truth about other human beings. Nevertheless, however undesirable they may be on other grounds, false generalizations and stereotypes do not, without more, disadvantage the project of a life.

iii. THE IMPLICATIONS OF INFERIORITY. This brings me to the third implication of the role played by value in the construction of a successful life. The explanation I have just given of the relationship between a misconception of what it means to be a woman and the disadvantage women experience in the projects of their lives makes clear that it is necessary to qualify my earlier remarks concerning the significance of sexual inferiority. I argued above that inferiority to men in central aspects of a woman's life reveals the existence of a misconception of what it means to be a woman, a misconception that is the source of women's present disadvantage. It is clear from the discussion of value, however, that this is too quick a conclusion. Whether inferiority in a given respect disadvantages a woman's life depends upon the particular terms of the project of that life, considered as a whole, and the differences, if any, between those terms and the terms of the life of the person who is superior in that respect. The terms of a woman's life, and those terms alone, will determine whether inferiority with respect to a given activity disadvantages her life.

I have argued that to regard one person as inferior to another is to misconceive the character of the person so regarded as inferior, and perhaps to misconceive the character of both people, for different people are not comprehensively superior and inferior to one another, but incommensurable. Such a misconception of inferiority, being comprehensive in character, necessarily causes disadvantage to the people it affects. However, the fact that we regard one person as inferior to another with respect to certain activities does not mean that we regard that person as inferior to his or her more able peer as a human being, even when the activities in question are central to the project of that person's life. The fact that we regard Gentileschi as an inferior artist to Caravaggio, if indeed we do, does not mean that we regard Gentileschi as inferior to Caravaggio as a human being, despite the fact that artistic success was central to the life of each.

The true connection between a person's inferiority with respect to certain activities and disadvantage in the project of his or her life depends, first, upon the impact of inferiority upon the value of engaging in the activities in question, and second, upon the impact of any inability to realize the value of those activities upon the overall success or failure of that person's life. In short, whether inferiority disadvantages a life depends upon the terms of that life. This is because the different projects of different human lives constitute complex packages of commitments and activities, so that the impact of inferiority in any particular activity on the overall success or failure of the project of a particular life can be assessed only in terms of an understanding of the various components of that project and the weight given to each by the person who has designed and sought to realize it.

The fact that one person is inferior to another with respect to activities that constitute a central, or definitive, feature of the project of his or her life may show that that project has failed to exploit the full dimensions of the character of the person who pursues those activities with only limited success, and thus may show that the project is based on a misconception of his or her character. But it does not, without more, show that the project is without value, and thus that the misconception on which it is based has caused disadvantage to the person in question. On the contrary, life being what it is, most people sooner or later discover that they have committed their lives to activities in terms of which they can be ranked as inferior to other people. It does not follow either that the projects of their lives are without value or that the people who pursue those activities with only modest success are inferior as people to their more successful peers.

To put the point in terms of the relationship between women and men and the hierarchies it may produce, there is an important difference between activities in respect of which women are inferior to men and activities that are without value. Activities that are without value are not worth pursuing, by women or by men. Activities in respect of which women are inferior to men, however, are often valuable and so worth pursuing by whomever has the capacity to pursue them, be they women or men. It is only in special circumstances that inferiority with regard to an activity, even an activity central to the project of a life, will make that project a failure, or make it intelligible to regard as inferior the person who pursues that project, thereby disadvantaging him or her.

To be precise, inferiority with respect to an activity diminishes the value of that activity, suggests that pursuit of it has been a mistake, and invites the conclusion that one sex is inferior to the other only in cases, first, where ranking is central to the value of an activity, as may be true of athletics, for example; second, where an inferior ranking erases the value of that activity, as may sometimes be but is not always the case in athletics; and third, where one sex has devoted itself to some such activity, in relation to which not only is ranking central but that sex is ranked as inferior. Even then it would be possible to know that the sex in question was disadvantaged by pursuit of that activity only on the basis of a full understanding of the approach to the projects of their lives taken by those members of that sex who pursue the activity. If we learn thereby that the inferiority-producing activity plays a critical role in the success of those lives, we learn that the inability to find value in that activity is a disadvantage to those lives. Only in that way can inferiority be linked to disadvantage. It is simply not possible to infer disadvantage from the bare fact of inferiority in certain activities, even when those activities are central to the project of a life.

Inferiority in a certain activity leads to disadvantage in life only where it reveals either that the project of a life is not consonant with the character of the person who seeks to pursue it or that the project lacks true value. When it does either of these things, it reveals that the person in question has been disadvantaged by a misconception of his or her character. It does not follow as a corollary, however, that where there is no inferiority in any activity there is no disadvantage. On the contrary, just as inferiority does not always produce disadvantage, so disadvantage does not always produce inferiority. In fact, given that disadvantage in the project of a life, properly understood, can be conceived only in terms of that particular project and the qualities of character upon which it draws, little can be learned about the disadvantage that may be experienced in the conduct of any life from a comparison between that life and other lives, such as that which reveals its inferiority in a particular respect.

More profoundly, then, what consideration of the role played by value in the construction of a successful life confirms is that, contrary to what is generally assumed, not a great deal can be learned about the lives of women and the existence of disadvantage there through comparison with the lives of men. Disadvantage in the project of a life is revealed not through comparison to another life and what makes that life successful, but through comparison between the project of the life in question as it ought to be and as it is in fact. Success and disadvantage in the project of a life are related to what one is and ought to be, not to someone else and what he or she is and ought to be. It follows that women's disadvantage is intelligible only in terms of what it means to be a woman and the lives that that meaning makes possible. Women's disadvantage can never be fully perceived or explained by comparing the lives of women as they are now lived with the lives of men as they are now lived. On the contrary, it can be understood only by understanding women.

iv. DEVALUATION. One final point needs to be addressed and clarified. It might be argued that the preceding discussion of the role played by value in the construction of a successful life raises the possibility that women's present disadvantage stems not from a misconception of what it means to be a woman but from an undervaluing of what is correctly conceived. Some might argue that the existence of what are sometimes called female ghettos, that is, areas of employment dominated by women and characterized by low wages and poor working conditions, is evidence not of the existence of a misconception of what it means to be a woman but of our society's refusal to recognize the true value of activities that women engage in, either exclusively or predominantly, through the exercise of their distinctive capacities.

In fact, however, the undervaluing of activities that are predominantly engaged in by women can occur only through a misconception of what it means to be a woman, for only a misconception can explain the fact that women are more often undervalued than men. The only reason that undervaluing appears not to involve a misconception is that it involves a misconception not of the character but of the scope of what it means to be a woman, one that presents a true but incomplete picture of sexual identity, and in so doing fails to recognize in women those qualities that permit them to pursue genuinely valuable and distinctive activities. In short, the existence of female ghettos in our society tends to confirm rather than contradict the view that women are disadvantaged by a misconception of what it means to be a woman.

This can be made clear through an examination of the several different ways in which it is possible to think that an undervaluing of activities predominantly engaged in by women could take place without involving a misconception of what it means to be a woman. As I see it, there are three ways to interpret our present tendency to undervalue what women do, one of which is in fact not a case of undervaluing at all, while the others involve misconceptions of what it means to be a woman. First, it might be that we as a society are aware of the true value of activities predominantly engaged in by women, but refuse to acknowledge that value. We might simply be hypocrites. More plausibly, and in the same vein, we (or the men among us) might see women as members of an alien culture, whose distinctive values we felt no obligation to recognize. In that case, however, we would not undervalue what women do but rather would refuse to give it its due. While this involves no misconception of what it means to be a woman, it is not an accurate description of our society's treatment of women. As the allegation of undervaluing assumes, our society believes that the activities that take place in ill-rewarded, female-dominated ghettos are not alien but of little value. In short, the issue is not whether we undervalue women, but whether the undervaluing that we are guilty of involves a misconception of what it means to be a woman.

Second, it might be that we as a society are simply mistaken about the value of certain activities engaged in largely by women. In that case, however, our tendency to err more often with regard to women than with regard to men, so as to establish female rather than sex-neutral ghettos, can be explained only in terms of a misconception of what it means to be a woman. More specifically, it can be explained only in terms of a misconception of the scope of what it means to be a woman, which disproportionately excludes women from participation in activities that we value and directs them toward activities that we do not value. The proper response to such a misconception is to understand women as well as we understand men, so as to reveal their like capacity to engage in activities whose value we recognize. Of course, this would do nothing to end the presence of economic ghettos in our society, but it would end their discriminatory character.

Finally, it might be that we as a society are guilty of a false inference, namely, that if an activity is dominated by women, it must for that reason be of little or no value. Such an inference openly depends upon the misconception that women are not capable of engaging in genuinely valuable activities, a misconception that relies, directly or indirectly, on a misconception of the *scope* of what it means to be a woman. It remains the case that the undervaluing of activities dominated by women, and the disadvantage it may produce, is the product of a misconception of what it means to be a woman, not the product of an undervaluing of what is correctly conceived.

III. Ascertaining Misconceptions

A. *The Scope of Inquiry*

The above examination of the role played by sexual identity in the construction of a successful life suggests that if women are to be ensured access to a successful life, there are three things that we as a society need to know about them, the same things that we need to know about any person in order to ensure his or her access to a successful life. First, we need to know what it actually means to be a woman, for success in life depends upon the ability to pursue goals that are consonant with one's character, which in turn depends upon the availability of such goals in our culture and the recognition of one's capacity to pursue them. Second, we need to know what aspects of what it means to be a woman are essential to the pursuit of valuable activities in our particular culture, for the success of one's life further depends upon the ability to pursue goals that are both valuable and relevant to the culture in which one finds oneself. This in turn depends upon the presence of genuinely valuable goals in our culture and upon recognition of one's capacity to pursue them.

Third and critically, however, we need to know to what extent the success of a woman's life depends upon access to particular valuable activities, and thus upon acknowledgment that women possess the qualities of character that make pursuit of those activities possible. To put it in familiar terms, we need to know to what extent the success of a woman's life depends upon access to sex-neutral activities and thus upon acknowledgment that women possess the same qualities of character as men – that is, upon an acknowledgment of sexual equality – and to what extent it depends upon access to distinctively female activities and thus upon acknowledgment that women alone possess the qualities of character that make pursuit of those activities possible – that is, upon an acknowledgment of sexual difference.

The good at issue here, which a society owes each of its members, is the good of a successful life, not the impossible good of a culture whose forms and practices are fully consonant with the different characters of its different members and all the different values those members are capable of embracing and pursuing. A society's obligation is to ensure the availability of whatever valuable goals, consonant with a woman's character, are essential to the success of a woman's life. It has no obligation to ensure the availability of valuable goals, consonant with a woman's character, that are superfluous to the success of a woman's life. A society that attempts to ensure the availability of all valuable goals not only attempts the impossible, but is in danger of overlooking the very issue that would inspire such an attempt, namely, the need to end the disadvantage now experienced by women by assuring them the ingredients of a successful life.

What is needed is an understanding of what it means to be a woman that is sufficiently comprehensive to enable women to lead successful lives. There is no need for, and indeed no possibility of, an understanding that is fully comprehensive, for some things that womanhood makes possible are irrelevant to our particular culture, while others are incompatible within the setting of any one culture. Nor is there any need for an understanding that is explicit or integrated, for our knowledge of what it means to be a woman, like any other aspect of our knowledge of ourselves, cannot and need not be any more accurate, precise, explicit, or integrated than is necessary to clarify the existence and character of the capacities that are critical to the success of a woman's life and to correct disabling misconceptions of those capacities. It follows that women can and must pursue the projects of their lives within a culture whose forms and practices reflect a limited understanding of their character. It is possible, for example, that within some culture we can imagine women might be able to construct successful lives entirely on the basis of their equality with men, that is, entirely on the basis of qualities that they share with men, without reference to sexual difference. Conversely, it is possible that within some culture we can imagine women might be able to construct successful lives entirely on the basis of their difference from men, without reference to their equality with men. More plausibly, perhaps, it is likely that in our culture, women's ability to construct successful lives depends upon their access both to certain aspects of their equality with men and to certain aspects of their difference from men. We can know if that is so, however, only if we know what it means to be a woman, what valuable activities that makes possible, and what valuable activities that makes necessary.

B. Internalized Misconceptions

Can it really be maintained, however, that the true character of what it means to be a woman is always what matters? What status have those psychological truths that embrace a misconception of what it means to be a woman? Suppose that women believed themselves to be incapable of doing something that they were in fact, at least apart from that belief, capable of doing. In that case women would be disabled by a truth about themselves that embodied a falsehood about themselves. There are normally several dimensions to any human capacity or incapacity, psychological as well as physical or intellectual, dimensions that are connected without necessarily being congruent. As a result a person may well lack a capacity in one dimension that he or she possesses in another, so as to be psychologically incapable, for example, of doing what he or she is otherwise capable of doing. Given that participation in an activity normally requires more than one dimension of capacity, any dimension of incapacity is enough to prevent a person from taking part in most activities.

It follows that a woman may well be capable of taking part in an activity in one dimension yet incapable of doing so in another, and so may be on balance incapable. In particular, if a woman believes she is incapable of taking part in an activity that she is, apart from that belief, in fact capable of taking part in, then she cannot take part in that activity, for belief is an essential component of the capacity to take part. I have argued that such a misconception of a woman's capacities is itself the product not of what it means to be a woman but of the social order within which women pursue the project of their lives and that order's conception of what it means to be a woman, which shapes what is possible for women to be or imagine being. That is not enough, however.

What I have not yet considered and what needs to be clarified is the possibility that the social order has generated a comprehensive or critical misconception of what it means to be a woman that has been internalized in women's psychology, so as to become true of women in that dimension while remaining false of them in other dimensions. If that is the case, women may now be incapacitated, and so potentially disadvantaged, by the character of what it means to be a woman. The remedy for women's present disadvantage would then be to change, not affirm, that character. In my view, however, while some women may be disabled in this sense, most women are not. Moreover, if some women are indeed disabled by a psychological incapacity, our response must be to continue to seek the character of what it means to be a woman, and the valuable activities that that makes possible and necessary.

There are two ways in which belief in incapacity might be understood. The first is that women's belief in their incapacity is sufficiently shallow as to remain a misconception, in which case the proper response is to seek to dispel it. Misconceptions of one's character by definition form part of that character and for that reason are difficult both to perceive and to remove. However, it does not follow from the fact that they are internalized in one's psychology that they are impossible to perceive or remove. On the contrary, as long as a misconception of what it means to be a woman is not shared by all women or all men, there is reason to believe that it can be both addressed and removed.

If a woman believes she is incapacitated in some respect by the fact that she is a woman, with the result that she is incapacitated in that respect, the fact that other women do not share her belief, and so do not exhibit incapacity in that respect, must make clear to her that her belief is a misconception of her sex.

Of course, the knowledge that other women believe will not necessarily enable such a woman to believe, for self-doubt is often profound. That being the case, it is possible that some, perhaps all, women possess a belief in women's lack of capacity, either generally or in some particular respect, that is too profound to be considered a misconception. By lack of capacity generally I mean lack of capacity for any valuable activity, and by lack of capacity in a particular respect, I mean lack of capacity for some particular valuable activity. In my view, a profound belief in women's lack of capacity generally is not only a true incapacity but also a psychological aberration, false of most women, true of a few, that we are bound to remedy as best we can in those who suffer it. Profound belief in women's lack of a particular capacity, on the other hand, is a true incapacity we are bound to respect.

It might be argued that at least some women have a profound belief in women's lack of capacity generally. That belief is false to the extent that it takes that incapacity to be a necessary consequence of being a woman, yet is true to the extent that it takes that incapacity to be a possible consequence of being a woman, one that applies to those who hold it. If some women indeed believe this then it follows that they are incapable of leading successful lives, for as I have said, the capacity to lead a successful life is dependent upon the belief that one possesses that capacity.

In my view, however, very few women believe profoundly in their lack of capacity generally. Most believe they are capable of certain valuable activities but incapable of others, a belief that is frequently based on a misconception of what it means to be a woman and so is properly responded to by an assertion of what this genuinely means. If some women do indeed have a profound, patho-logical belief in their lack of capacity generally, it must be the task not merely of feminists but of all those concerned for the fate of those women as human beings to seek to enlighten them. This must be done with full understanding of and compassion for their predicament, including the possibility that they may not be able to escape it, by representing in words and in actions what it actually means to be a woman and the valuable activities that makes possible. Again, it is respect for the true character of sexual difference that matters here; this time it is the truth that being a woman need not lead to incapacity.

On the other hand, it may well be the case that some or many women have a profound belief in their incapacity in certain particular respects, respects in which they would be capable of pursuing valuable activities but for belief in their lack of capacity. In that case, however, it is an inescapable fact that those women lack capacity in those respects and must develop the project of their lives in terms of other capacities, at least until they discover or develop those capacities they believe they lack, as human beings constantly discover and develop their capacities in response to changing circumstances. As long as an incapacity is genuine, it does not much matter what its source is, for one can pursue the project of one's life only in terms of what one is capable of doing.

More important, one has no reason to reject one's present capacities and what they make possible as long as some portion of one's capacities is capable of sustaining valuable activities that are relevant to our culture, and so is capable of serving as the foundation for a successful life.

C. Rival Concerns

This is not to say that there are no reasons to try to change what one is, difficult as that change may be. The reasons, however, lie not in the attempt to make a success of one's life but in the desire to pursue goals outside oneself, an ideal, for example. Pursuit of goals such as these is, of course, one way of making a life go well, and to that extent must draw on all the considerations outlined above. That is to say, such goals must be both valuable and consonant with one's character. Nevertheless, there may be reasons to try to change one's character in ways that do not make one's own life go better but rather, without making it go worse, better serve ideals to which one has committed oneself. There may even be reasons to try to change one's character in ways that make one's life go worse but that better serve ideals to which one has committed oneself. Those reasons, however, cannot include the need to redress the wrong of sex discrimination, which has to do with the inability to pursue a successful life, not, except constitutively, with the inability to pursue goals outside oneself.

Nor is this to say that there are no reasons, other than the success of a woman's life, to call attention to the distinctive qualities of her sex and the distinctively valuable activities those qualities make possible. On the contrary, it may be that women are capable of pursuing successful lives on the basis of their equality with men, that is, without referring to their distinctive capacities and the activities those capacities make possible, but that as a culture we would be diminished by their doing so. Just as we would be diminished by a world without art even if all those who would otherwise be artists were capable of pursuing successful lives without it, we might be diminished by a world without the presence of those goods that only women can bring to it, even if women were capable of pursuing successful lives without them. This gives us reason to notice rather than to change sexual difference, but again it is not a reason that has anything to do with the need to redress the wrong of sex discrimination, which as I have said has to do with the inability to pursue a successful life.

Nor is this to say, finally, that there are no reasons to pursue myths about ourselves, including myths about sex, rather than truths. On the contrary, it is clearly the case that certain myths about ourselves are valuable and so are capable of mattering to us in the same way as does any cultural artefact. In other words, the creation, preservation, and communication of a myth or set of myths about ourselves is one way of making our lives go well. That being the case, however, the practice of myth making must draw upon all the considerations outlined above. That is, if myth making is to form part of the project of a successful life, it must be both valuable and consonant with one's character. While the truth about ourselves is not all we value, for we value goals and not, except instrumentally, the capacity to pursue them, the truth about ourselves is the only basis upon which a particular goal can become an aspect of making our life go well.

As part of the project of a successful life, therefore, myths about ourselves have something of a paradoxical character, for their value depends upon their capacity to take the form of truths about ourselves, yet at the same time they should never be mistaken for such truths, for only on the basis of truths about ourselves are we capable of valuing myths at all. Of course, there may be reasons to pursue myths as goals in a way that is indifferent to the success of the project of one's life. Some take religious faith to be such a reason. As I have noted, however, such reasons cannot include the need to redress the wrong of sex discrimination, which has to do with pursuit of a successful life, not, except constitutively, with pursuit of goals outside oneself.

D. Sources of Knowledge

Where, then, are we to look for the answer to the question of what it genuinely means to be a woman, and in so doing, how are we to distinguish truth from misconception? As I have argued, there is no reason to look for a precise answer, for it is enough that the answer we arrive at be sufficiently accurate and comprehensive to enable women to lead successful lives. Moreover, there is no reason to expect a stable answer, for what it means to be a woman and the valuable activities that makes possible is something that, like the universe, is constantly if very slowly expanding, although only a small portion of that meaning is accessible within any given culture. In the end, perhaps the most that can be said is that collectively, as men and women, we come to know our sex as we come to know the other dimensions of ourselves, roughly, tentatively, always subject to correction, yet well enough to be able to make sense of the project of our individual lives, as distinct from the lives of others.

In other words, the answer to the question of what it means to be a woman, or correlatively to be a man, is something we discover through the conduct of our lives. More particularly, it is something we discover through actions that test the prevailing conception of our character and the activities that conception allows us to pursue, and through subsequent reflection on the success or failure of those actions. This is very familiar territory, of course, for feminism has always dedicated much of its effort to questioning and exploring accepted understandings of sexual identity in an explicit search for a genuine understanding of what it means to be a woman, what that meaning makes possible, and what it makes necessary. As I have said, all those who contribute to the ongoing debate over the status of women in our culture, by their words or their actions, in support of the claims of feminists or in opposition to them, whether in the end proved right or wrong, contribute to the determination of those issues.

Feminists such as Catharine MacKinnon depart from this approach, of course, in that they explore what it means to be a woman in our culture only in order to expose the institutionalization, in the forms and practices of the culture, of sexual hierarchy. More specifically, MacKinnon's enquiry into the meaning of sexual identity takes as its premise the belief that women are, as a matter of natural fact, no different from men. Her inquiry is thus designed to expose the ways in which sexual difference as we know it is generated by a social order in which women are constructed so as to be both different from and inferior to men. As far as the question of what it means to be a woman is concerned, what is striking about MacKinnon's account is the belief that certain features of womanhood in our culture, including the capacity for concern identified by Carol Gilligan, are true of women yet ought to be denied because they have been improperly acquired, as the result of a practice of subordination.[17] The real issue, however, is not why or how something has come to be true of women, but whether it is indeed true. If and to the extent that feminists such as MacKinnon agree that differences exist between men and women, the real question is whether in so doing they are agreeing on the existence of a misconception or on the existence of the truth.

E. Responsibility for Change

Who, then, are we to charge with the responsibility of establishing a new understanding of what it means to be a woman? How are we to remove misconceptions, once we have recognized them? These are issues it is not possible to enter into fully here, but to which the short answer is that a misconception can be removed only by those who hold it, and need be removed only by those whose holding of it disadvantages a woman's life. It follows that all those who contribute to the content of our culture, by their words and their actions, and the convictions that those express, and whose understanding of what it means to be a woman thus establishes the framework through which a woman's life is necessarily lived, are authors of the present conception of what it means to be a woman, and must bear the responsibility for changing that conception, insofar as it causes disadvantage to women. This includes not only the state, public organizations, private organizations, and individuals, but more profoundly, any

---

[17] *Feminism Unmodified, supra* n. 7, at 39. I must emphasize that I am assuming for the moment that qualities such as those identified by Gilligan are true of women. In that case, to deny sexual difference is to promote a misconception of what it means to be a woman. However, it is possible that MacKinnon believes that the apparent differences between men and women produced by subordination are not true. In that case, to deny sexual difference is to promote the truth of what it means to be a woman. In fact, I do not find it possible either to read MacKinnon this way or to believe that the differences to which she draws attention are entirely false.

and all forms of human activity, such as the arts, sports, and social life, that express attitudes to what it means and does not mean to be a woman in the very way that they are imagined and pursued.

Change needs to be thought of, then, in terms not only of institutions, or even of individuals, but also of attitudes that are embodied in our beliefs and our actions. This is all the more important if and to the extent that women need access to the fact of their difference from men rather than to the fact of their equality with men in order to lead successful lives. While equality can be legislated by institutions, as indeed can differences where institutions have a role to play in sustaining the goals that those differences affect, such as childbearing, many forms of difference form part of our conception of what it means to be a woman only because they are expressed by each of us in the conduct of our lives, and so can be changed only if each of us changes the conduct of his or her life and the attitudes that conduct expresses. It is for this reason that feminist argument and debate have always had, and must continue to have, as important a place in changing women's prospects of a successful life as legislation and judicial decision.

8

Equality, Difference, and the Law

I. The Importance of Being Understood

What women are entitled to, and what a misconception of their character may deny them, is the opportunity to make a success of the projects of their lives. That opportunity is not one that is owed to women in particular, as a special entitlement born of their special condition, but one that is owed to all human beings yet finds its particular meaning in its application to particular human beings, in this case, women. The particular character of what women are owed is simply a consequence of the fact that human beings can develop and pursue the projects of their lives only on the basis of the particular qualities of character, distinctive and nondistinctive, that they happen to possess, and more important, that not only they but the societies in and through which those projects are pursued understand them to possess.

It follows that if a society misunderstands what it means to be a woman, either comprehensively or in some respect that is critical to the success of the project of a woman's life, as I have contended we now misunderstand women, it thereby denies them the opportunity to which they are entitled as human beings. No society is obliged to understand its members perfectly, of course, but every society is obliged to understand its members sufficiently well to ensure that they are not denied the fundamental ingredients of a successful life, and so is obliged to understand them in terms that are not false, or irrelevant to its forms and practices, or incapable of valuable application. To put the point from the opposite perspective, the reason that the character of what it means to be a woman, and the accuracy and completeness of our understanding of that character, is of central importance to the success of a woman's life is that the understanding that any society owes to its members, if it is to give them a genuine opportunity to make a success of their lives, is necessarily as specific, particular, and distinctive as the people to whom it applies, and the particular projects of their particular lives.

Some maintain, however, that what people are entitled to in life is not the opportunity to make a success of the particular projects of their particular lives, and hence to the opportunities and resources appropriate to those projects, but to equal opportunities, or equal resources, or some other form of equality.[1] The argument that I have offered clearly denies this. As I see it, there are three ways to understand claims to equality of this kind, depending upon whether what is to be made equal is the character of the good owed, the value of that good, or the possession of the entitlement to the good. In every case the argument for equality of the good is sensible only when understood in such a way as to take account of the role played by a particular conception of what it means to be a woman in a woman's construction of a successful life. As I have just noted, such claims to equality are sometimes couched in terms of opportunities and sometimes in terms of resources or some other good. In what follows I address the argument for equal opportunities, in the belief that the conclusions I reach about equal opportunities will apply, with necessary modifications, to any claim to equality that is not based on the fact of equality.

First, the claim that all human beings are entitled to equal opportunities might be understood as a claim that all human beings are entitled to the same opportunities as one another. For reasons given above, however, what human beings are in fact entitled to are those opportunities that are necessary to sustain and, more important, make a success of the different projects of their different lives, projects that are pursued through the medium of common social practices, yet remain as distinctive as the people who define and pursue them, the people for whom they are desirable and accessible. It follows that to accord people the same opportunities as one another is to accord them what they are entitled to only when they are similar enough that the success of their lives is dependent upon access to the same opportunities as one another.

---

[1] I have in mind here all those who believe that what human beings are entitled to in life is equality with their fellow human beings, be that equality of opportunity, resources, welfare, or some other dimension of equality. Those who hold beliefs of this kind are committed to the position that the differences between human beings should not be permitted to undermine their equality, or more precisely, to the position that we must not allow the differences between human beings to be exploited in such a way as to suppress or betray the more fundamental and morally significant fact of their equality. In the familiar phrase, all people are not created equal, but they must be treated as such.

The alternative view is that people must be treated as the people they are, whether they have been made so by nature or society. On that view, people are not, strictly speaking, created equal and should not be treated as equals. Rather, the infinitely complex pattern of human similarities and differences reveals that people have been created, by nature and by society, in such a way as to make them incommensurable as people, albeit commensurable with respect to many if not most of the activities they undertake, so that people must be treated not with reference to the lives of others, as an entitlement to equality would require, but with reference to their own lives, their own capacities and aspirations, good and bad, a reference that can be undertaken only on the basis of a proper understanding of particular people. It follows that on this view, equality of treatment, or opportunities, or resources, is contingent upon a coincidence of character and of goals in the lives of apparently different people. All people are created different and must be treated in a manner that acknowledges that difference and its significance in what it means for them to lead successful lives.

Second, the claim that all human beings are entitled to equal opportunities might be understood as a claim that all human beings are entitled to opportunities of the same value as one another. Once again, however, what human beings are in fact entitled to is not opportunities of the same value but opportunities of a value that is as distinctive or nondistinctive as the projects of their particular lives. In other words, we can know that the apparently different opportunities assigned to different human beings should be of the same value only if and when we know that the different lives to which those opportunities are assigned are directed to the same ends. We can know that apparently different lives are directed to the same ends only if we genuinely understand, in the sense that I have outlined, the character of those lives and the activities that that character makes it both possible and necessary to pursue. To maintain that different human beings are entitled to opportunities of equal value is thus to assume what must be established, namely, a genuine understanding of the particular character of those apparently different human beings.

Of course, some believe that all human lives are directed to the pursuit of the same value, such as, perhaps, a uniform conception of happiness.[2] On that view, it is unnecessary to know the character of particular human beings, for the differences that distinguish human beings, including that of gender, are no more than arbitrary incidents in the human condition that affect the form but not the substance of human life. Just as one's race has no impact upon one's need for sustenance or one's capacity for suffering, so other forms of human difference have no impact upon one's desire for happiness, or upon the character of the happiness that one desires. This is a view that I do not share, as I have already made clear. On the contrary, it is my contention that the values toward which genuinely different human lives are directed are ultimately incommensurable. I return in a moment to a brief review of that contention and its implications.

Finally, however, the claim that all human beings are entitled to equal opportunities might be understood as a claim that all human beings are equally entitled to the opportunity to make a success of the projects of their lives. That claim is true enough but sensible only when understood in such a way as to take account of the role played by a particular conception of what it means to be a human being in the construction of a successful life. To assert without going further that human beings are equally entitled to the opportunity to make a success of the projects of their lives is to overlook the role played in the application of that entitlement, quite correctly said to be enjoyed by all human beings, by particular conceptions of what it means to be a human being and to pursue a successful life.

---

[2] These include, for example, those who are committed to securing the greatest happiness of the greatest number, who believe both that all human lives are directed to the pursuit of happiness and that the apparently different forms of happiness pursued by different people are in the end commensurable, and so can be assessed in the same coin.

In other words, any commitment to equality is contingent upon the fact of equality and upon the need for access to that fact in order to lead a successful life. As far as the welfare of human beings is concerned, equality is not a principle in its own right but a fact about human beings that is made salient by the application of the principle that every human being is entitled to the ingredients of a successful life, that is, to the opportunities and resources that are necessary to make a success of his or her particular life. If and to the extent that human beings are equal to and so no different from one another, and furthermore require access to their equality in these respects in order to make a success of their lives, then that equality must be reflected and embodied in the prevailing conception of who and what they are and in the opportunities and resources that are assigned on the basis of it, although it is not equality that we respond to in so acting, but the separate characters of the people in question and the separate content of what those characters make both possible and necessary for those defined by them. In other words, even the fact of equality forms no part of the premise for our conduct here, but is simply a feature of our conclusion that is as coincidental as the similarity of apparently different lives.

Conversely, however, if and to the extent that human beings differ from one another, and furthermore require access to their difference in order to make a success of their lives, then that difference must be reflected and embodied in the prevailing conception of who and what they are and in the opportunities and resources assigned on the basis of it. In short, a society's obligation to recognize the equality and difference of its members is dependent upon the truth of that equality or difference and on its members' need for access to that truth in order to lead successful lives.

This is not to suggest that our society's pursuit of sexual equality has been entirely misguided, for there is every evidence that men and women are in fact no different from one another in many respects in which they have long been thought to be different from one another, respects in which a demonstration of women's equality with men, and hence a demonstration of their capacity to engage in certain activities on a like basis with men, has been critical to the success of women's lives. Rather, it is simply to contend that this is not the whole story of what it means for women to lead successful lives; to think that it is the whole story is to misunderstand gravely the character of a successful life and the disadvantage that is experienced by those who are denied it. The reason that it has been taken to be the whole story, it seems to me, lies in a faulty but widely, although not always consistently, held understanding of the character of a successful life, which has only recently begun to be displaced by an acknowledgment of value pluralism.[3]

---

[3] Even a value monist must recognize that each person has a different way of arriving at the good of a successful life, however arbitrary and without ultimate value that difference is, and so must understand what it means to be a woman in order to ensure that women's lives are successful.

It is simply a fact about the intellectual and social history of Western culture, albeit a very significant fact, that we have tended to take a monistic, one-dimensional, although evolving view of the character of a successful life, and so have denied the enjoyment of such a life to all those for whom a life of that character was inaccessible, either because they were genuinely different from the norm and dependent upon access to that difference for the success of their lives or because they were falsely perceived to be so. To flourish in such a culture, people have been forced to demonstrate their capacity to conform to the prevailing view of what constitutes a successful life, by demonstrating their possession of the qualities necessary to sustain a life of the kind that is recognized as successful there. The result has been to make salient the many false assumptions of human difference that exist in our culture and to highlight the disadvantage that they have generated for many people, including women. To remedy that disadvantage, a broadly based and very successful enterprise of exposing the falsity or irrelevance of a great many of the accepted differences between men and women has been undertaken, largely if not entirely at the instigation of women. In the long run, however, the success of that strategy in remedying sexual and other forms of disadvantage depends upon the extent to which women and other disadvantaged groups either do not differ from other human beings in any way that is relevant to our culture or do not need access to their difference in order to lead successful lives.

If, on the contrary, women are different from men in ways that matter to the success of their lives, or to put it from the opposite perspective, if what it means to lead a successful life is in fact plural rather than one-dimensional in character, and if in addition the difference between women and men is one facet of a plural understanding of the meaning of a successful life, then a successful life is denied to all those women for whom such a life, if it is of the same character as a successful life for men, is inaccessible because they are genuinely different in character from men and require access to their difference to make a success of their lives. If this is so, if what it means to lead a successful life is plural in character and if sexual difference is one facet of that plural character, then the result is to make salient the many misconceptions of sexual identity that exist in our culture, misconceptions that either assimilate the condition of women to that of men or misrepresent the character of sexual difference, and to highlight the disadvantage that those misconceptions have generated for women. To remedy that disadvantage, it is necessary to expose the falsity of certain of women's supposed equalities to men as well as certain of their supposed differences from men, so as to establish the true content of what it means to be a woman in all its dimensions, different and equal.

My argument is not dependent upon acceptance of the truth of value pluralism, therefore, although I myself accept it and have elaborated my argument in terms of it.

In the context of a plural understanding of value, therefore, sexual equality continues to have importance as a fact that is made salient by the application of the principle that all human beings are entitled to the ingredients of a successful life, that is, to whatever opportunities and resources are needed for them to make a success of their particular lives, which are in many respects no different from one another, contrary to what we have often assumed, and thus whose equality needs to be affirmed. But in the context of a plural understanding of value, the fact of sexual difference is as likely to be important to the success of a life as the fact of sexual equality – more likely perhaps, given its relative neglect.

In conclusion, the equality of men and women is a condition that we are obliged to recognize and respond to as a consequence of the application of a particular moral principle to particular facts, namely, as the consequence of the application of the principle that all human beings are entitled to the ingredients of a successful life to the fact that in certain respects men and women subscribe to the same conception of a successful life and have the same capacity to sustain it. Similarly, however, the difference between men and women is made significant by the same principle, that all human beings are entitled to the ingredients of a successful life, applied to a different set of facts, namely, that in certain respects at least men and women subscribe to different conceptions of a successful life, simply because their different capacities make different goals both possible and necessary for them. It follows that there is no real inconsistency involved in the claim that what is rhetorically called sexual equality, by which is meant the ending of the disadvantage now experienced by women, at once requires that women be treated as equal to men and that they be treated as different from men, not so that we as a society may ensure the relative advantage of women, but so that we may ensure all women the opportunity to lead successful lives. As far as the capacity of human beings to make a success of the project of their lives is concerned, this is the importance of being equal, and also of being different, for it is the importance of being understood.[4]

II. Where Difference Matters

Where a culture takes a one-dimensional view of the character of a successful life, difference from the norm necessarily becomes a source of exclusion and oppression. In such a culture, the demonstration of one's capacity to conform to the prevailing conception of what constitutes a successful life, through en-dorsement of that conception and proof of one's possession of the qualities necessary to sustain it, is the only way to make a success of one's life, while

---

[4] As I have noted, this imposes a condition not only upon any doctrine of equality but also upon any description of the goods to which all human beings are entitled, whether those goods are understood as opportunities, as resources, as an adequate range of valuable options, as the sat-isfaction of needs, or as anything else that is sensitive to the condition of those to whom it is addressed: see Chapter 4, at note 11.

acknowledgment of one's difference, through endorsement of a rival conception of a successful life or through recognition that one's qualities are other than those that serve the prevailing conception, is tantamount to acknowledgment of one's inability to make a success of one's life. In such circumstances, difference is to be avoided as much as equality is to be sought, for where access to a successful life is dependent upon showing that one has the same qualities as the paradigmatically successful person, and so is equal to that person in all the significant respects that govern success in life, showing one's difference is inevitably a source of disadvantage.

For that reason, and as I have noted, the misconceptions that feminism has worked to remove have for the most part been those that have concealed the fact of women's equality with men, misconceptions that have falsely portrayed women as different from men in ways that have prevented women from making a success of their lives.[5] Once it was thought that women should be wives and mothers because they lacked the capacity to make a success of the kind of tasks that men perform in the job market and of the lives in which such tasks play a defining role. Feminists have shown that women are as capable as men of participating in the job market and as interested in doing so, and conversely, that women are often denied successful lives by their inability to participate in the job market on the same basis as men. More broadly, where once it was thought that women were unfit for a wide range of tasks, because they were passive, or vulnerable, or irrational, or incompetent, feminists have shown that women are as enterprising, as hardy, as rational, and as competent as men, and that for many women success in life depends upon recognition of this. The list of such misconceptions of what it means to be a woman, and of their correction through proof of women's equality with men, is long and likely to get longer, for in many respects, those that we have yet to acknowledge as well as those that we have already recognized, there is simply no difference between men and women. We share ambitions, we share capacities, and we share certain conceptions of what constitutes a successful life, the kind of life that men now lead and that a comprehensive misconception of what it means to be a woman has until recently denied to women.

Ironically, however, endorsement of the very conception of a successful life that men subscribe to, either that now dominant in our culture or some replacement for it, and proof of women's capacity to conform to that conception, where comprehensively engaged in by women as the exclusive strategy of feminism, necessarily reduces the number of conceptions of a successful life available in our culture. It makes capacity to conform to the surviving, sex-neutral conception of a successful life critical to the success of any life in that culture, be it a woman's or a man's. As I have said, for some women, and perhaps for a great many, who share men's conception of what constitutes a

---

[5] See Chapter 7, at notes 7 and 8 and the accompanying text.

successful life and who possess the capacity to conform to it, this reduction in options is no disadvantage. On the contrary, proof that they are as capable as men of conforming to the dominant conception of a successful life is essential to ending their disadvantage. For such women, recognition of their equality with men is the key to a successful life, for the simple reason that a successful life for them is no different from a successful life for men.

For other women, however, the reduction in the number of conceptions of a successful life that would follow from the endorsement of the same conception that men subscribe to, and more profoundly, that would follow from the conception of sexual identity that would explain and justify that reduction, would actually confirm if not compound the disadvantage they now experience as women. When and if a culture overlooks the existence of genuine differences between men and women, which are not only relevant to that culture but critical to the success of at least some women's lives, it necessarily disadvantages women. Insistence upon the equality of women's experience with that of men is justified in many respects, as I have said, but not in all respects, or for all women. In short, and as a genuinely pluralistic society should acknowledge, the recognition of sexual difference and its reflection in our social forms and practices is almost certainly necessary to the success of some women's lives.

If that is true of at least some women in some respects, then equality in those respects is to be avoided as much as difference is to be sought, for where access to a successful life depends upon recognition of capacities that are sex-specific, insistence upon equality will produce rather than remove sexual disadvantage. The list of sex-specific differences in capacity, and of the misconceptions that conceal them, be they conceptions of equality or conceptions of difference that mistake its character, is likely to be as long as the list of unrecognized sexual equalities, for in many respects, those we have yet to acknowledge as well as those we have already recognized, there are significant differences between men and women, which make the fact of their sex matter to women. It is neither my place nor my purpose to attempt to draw up a list of the real and relevant differences between men and women. I have no special insight into such matters and it would be presumptuous of me to dwell on them. Nevertheless, I propose to examine briefly two popular and recurring candidates for any such list, one biologically created and the other culturally created, in order to suggest some of the practical implications of my argument.

To start with a biologically created difference: the capacity to bear children is, first, unique to women; second, valuable; third, relevant to this and indeed any other culture; and, finally, critical to the success of many women's lives. It is valuable not simply because it ensures the survival of the human race, although it does that, but because the act of bearing children and the acts of fostering that go with it, only some of which can be shared by men, is in itself a valuable activity, one that expresses valuable feelings and sustains valuable relationships. It is critical to the success of some women's lives, not because a capacity demands that we act upon it, so that women should bear children simply because they can, but because for some women acting upon that capacity is a critical element in the success of their lives. Yet the capacity to bear children is a capacity that we may mistake and so fail to recognize in the forms and practices of our culture, not because we doubt that it is a genuine aspect of what it means to be a woman, but because we see only its necessity and neglect its value, or more accurately, because we see its value only in terms of the contribution that it makes to our survival and so neglect other aspects of its value, those that I have just referred to, and because we assume further, perhaps correctly, that enough women will bear children to ensure the survival of the species whether or not we take any steps to accommodate childbearing in the forms and practices of our culture.

As far as childbearing is concerned, then, we may mistake what it means to be a woman in two ways. On the one hand, we may hold a conception of women as equal to and so no different from men in that we take the success of their lives to be entirely dependent upon careers in the job market and not upon childbearing, and so may overlook their difference in this respect and the role it plays in the success of some women's lives. On the other hand, we may hold a conception of women as people for whom success in life is entirely dependent upon motherhood, a role whose value we take to lie in the contribution it makes to human survival, in which we see women as largely self-sufficient and in which we assume that poverty and limitation of horizons are not disabilities. That conception recognizes sexual difference but mistakes its character. In my view, we subscribe to both misconceptions and see individual women as properly conforming to one or the other, so that we regard women who try to combine parenting and career as misguidedly attempting to live up to both when they should choose one or the other.

In fact, contrary to the first conception, childbearing is critical to the success of some women's lives; and contrary to the second conception, the women for whom that is true need many forms of support if childbearing is to do for them what it should, ranging from maternity leave and maternity allowances, to prenatal services, and access to midwives and other professional childbearing and maternal support systems. More important, the bearing and subsequent rearing of children is not today, if it ever was, the whole story of a successful life, so that women need to be able to integrate parenting with participation in the job market. What is needed, then, is a conception of women as people for whom success in life will typically demand the integration of family and career rather than a choice between the two, and so will demand access to resources such as daycare, part-time work, flexible hours, work from home, interrupted or abbreviated careers, and so on. In some respects, those in which parenting can be performed by either sex, that conception will be as true of men as it is of women, and so will be a conception of sexual equality. This will be equality on a new footing, however, defined by the common needs of women and men, not by the lives of men. In other respects, those in which biology or culture make the capacity or the inclination to perform certain functions either exclusive to women or more prevalent among them, that conception will be true of women only. This will be difference on a new footing, not the footing defined by the prevailing conception of motherhood. The establishment of these conceptions of sexual identity, and the corresponding elimination of our present misconceptions, will not matter to all women, of course, but will certainly matter to a great many of them, as many as bear children, which is likely to be most women, for if the human race is to survive, women must bear, on average, two children each.

However, the capacity to bear children is as likely to contribute to the failure of a woman's life as to its success. Unwanted pregnancies disable women's lives, whether they are dedicated to careers in the job market, and so do not involve plans for childbearing at all, or are dedicated, at least in part, to rearing existing children and so to integrating parenting with a career. In other words, some women never need to bear children; others need to bear children at a time of their choosing or no more than the children they already have; all are at risk of unwanted pregnancies, therefore, which may have a critical impact on the success of their lives. Women need to be able to protect themselves against such pregnancies, by whatever means are appropriate to the risk at stake, including contraception, sterilization, and abortion.

To turn to the question of culturally created differences, it is often alleged that women are unusually concerned for others, unusually sensitive to the nuances of human relationships, and unusually skilled at communication, whether because of their long history of bearing primary responsibility for the raising of children or for some other reason. It is not suggested that these capacities are unique to women, but it is suggested that they are more prevalent among women. These are clearly valuable capacities, relevant to this and any other culture, and critical to the success of many women's lives. Yet, as in the case of the capacity to bear children, they are capacities that we may mistake, first, by assuming that they have the same incidence in women as in men, and second, by assuming that they have the same character in women as they do in men.

Such misconceptions may cause women disadvantage. If the capacity for concern is particularly prevalent among women, and if women's ambitions are consistent with their capacity in this respect, as they may be, then we should expect women to predominate, and not merely to be equal participants, in fields of human endeavour in which capacity for concern is at a premium. In other words, women's equal presence in such fields, and the conception of sexual identity that would sustain it, may be as discriminatory towards women as their minority presence in those fields in which their ambitions and capacities are no different from those of men. This is a possibility that we need to take into account in the design of any programme of affirmative action that sets targets for the presence of women in fields in which they are now a minority, and in the evaluation of any charge of indirect discrimination against men in fields in which women are now a majority.[6]

We also need to take into account the possibility that the character of women's concern is not the same as that of men's, so that women care about different things and in different ways than men, as well as the possibility that women's concern is different from men's in ways other than we have taken it to be, so that it is not confined to rearing children or to nursing, to take but two examples. If we have mistaken the character of women's concern, in ways that are critical to the success of at least some women's lives, then again our conception of what it means to be a woman will need to be amended if women are to lead successful lives. At the same time, we need to recognize that many women display the same kind of concern as men, so that the success of their lives depends upon not being stereotyped by a conception of sexual identity that takes all women to be distinctively concerned and committed to lives that reflect that fact.

In conclusion, and as I have already said, it is in settings like these, where sensitivity to the existence and character of sexual difference plays a critical role in the success of women's lives, that we need to understand sexual difference and incorporate it in the practices of our culture. This is where difference matters.

III. Discrimination and the Law

This study is an inquiry into the meaning of sex discrimination as a species of wrongdoing that impairs the ability of women to lead successful lives, through the propagation of a false image of their character and qualities. It is not an inquiry into the meaning of sex discrimination as a *legal* wrong. Such an inquiry would tell us something, perhaps a great deal, about the shape of the law in this respect. It would tell us what the law defines as sex discrimination, but it would not tell us anything about the law's justification, or the law's ability to address the problem actually confronted by women. If for these reasons antidiscrimination law cannot serve as the starting point for an inquiry into the meaning of sex discrimination, it is nevertheless bound to be the principal focus of any conclusions to that inquiry, for one of our main reasons for wanting to know what sex discrimination means is that we want to know what should be done about it, through the law or otherwise, and correspondingly want to know whether what we now do about it is adequate or even justifiable. While I cannot say a great deal about the extent to which existing laws on sex discrimination

---

[6] It is also true that men have a greater capacity for certain activities, such as weightlifting, than women. However, men's and women's distinctive capacities do not logically compel one another. It does not follow from the fact that women have a heightened capacity for communication that they have a diminished capacity for mathematics, as is sometimes assumed, for the two capacities are not correlative. It is entirely possible that women are as good at engineering as men and better at English. What women cannot be, at least in the same context, is both more concerned and no more concerned than men.

are justified, for to do so would be well beyond the scope of a work whose focus is primarily on determining what sex discrimination means and what makes it wrong, it is only right that I at least suggest what I take to be the implications of the ideas advanced here for the status of the present law against sex discrimination.

The three principal devices currently employed by the law in order to remedy sex discrimination, in somewhat different form in different jurisdictions, namely, the prohibitions against direct and indirect discrimination, and the sanctioning of affirmative action policies, are typically explained in terms of equality.[7] It is said that women and men should not be distinguished from one another, because they should be treated as one another's equals: hence the prohibition on direct discrimination. It is said that women and men should not be asked to meet requirements whose burden falls disproportionately and so unequally upon one sex: hence the prohibition on indirect discrimination. It is said that government should seek to ensure that the presence of women in any particular arena is equal to the presence of men in that arena (although not vice versa): hence the sanctioning of affirmative action policies.

The justification of these provisions in terms of equality gives rise to certain concerns that I am not able to examine here, despite their importance, for they have no bearing on the question of the meaning of sex discrimination. For example, if the various legal strategies designed to combat sex discrimination are explained and justified in terms of a supposed principle of equality, then it is an obvious question why that principle attaches itself only to sex, race, age, ethnicity, religion, and the other distinctions addressed by antidiscrimination law, and not to the innumerable further distinctions that are employed to prefer some and denigrate others. If inequality is inherently objectionable, why do we treat it as objectionable only when it affects certain people in certain dimensions of their existence? Why is it that the inequalities created by a job description become objectionable only when they affect women or men, for example, whether directly or indirectly, and not otherwise? The inequality in question is no greater, is no more unequal, because it happens to resonate with sexual identity rather than with some other aspect of the human condition.

That being the case, there must be some further significance to sexual identity, and to the other identities protected by antidiscrimination legislation, that warrants their special protection. The answer sometimes given is that the prohibited distinctions are irrelevant, while the permitted distinctions are not. Yet this claims both too much and too little, for in fact the prohibited distinctions are

---

[7] These provisions are given somewhat different names in different jurisdictions. Direct discrimination is also known as intentional discrimination; indirect discrimination is also known as disparate impact or adverse effect discrimination; affirmative action (to the extent that it is permitted by the law) is also known as employment equity.

often relevant while the permitted distinctions are often not relevant.[8] Lacking a good answer to questions such as these, the law finds itself in the position of conferring its protection upon what appears to be an élite of the disadvantaged, and so to be in the position of unequally benefiting an arbitrarily determined selection of the unequally treated.[9]

These are difficult questions that I cannot and need not address in this study. My concern here is with the present condition of women and with the ability or inability of equality to remedy that condition. There may be reasons to doubt the value of equality that are unrelated to the condition of women, but the reason that matters here is that equality does not and cannot explain the meaning of sex discrimination, for the reasons given above. Nevertheless, even if lack of equality is not a good explanation of sex discrimination, as I have contended, equality may nevertheless be a good *strategy* for the ending of that discrimination in certain circumstances, provided that the means is not mistaken for the end. Is this true of present antidiscrimination legislation? Is its egalitarian character justifiable in strategic terms, as a device for ending the wrong of sex discrimination, a wrong that is properly understood in nonegalitarian terms? Is its egalitarianism no more than a means to some sounder end? Or is its egalitarianism its true end?

Laws against direct discrimination, which prohibit any reference to sex, are sometimes restricted to certain settings, such as the provision of employment, services, or accommodation, and are sometimes unrestricted, as when they take the form of a constitutional provision, for example. Where they are restricted to certain settings they can be justified by the contention that there is in fact no difference between the sexes that has any relevance in those settings. In other words, they can be justified by the contention that women and men are in fact equal in those settings. This contention would not by any means be easy to establish. It is far from clear that women and men do not differ in any way that is relevant to the provision of services, for example. Nor is it clear that they do not differ in any way that is relevant to employment or accommodation, for there may be good reason to choose women to provide accommodation and services to other women, as in a battered women's refuge, or a rape crisis centre, or any

---

[8] In the case of indirect discrimination, where a distinction is regarded as discriminatory not because it refers to women and men but because it has an adverse impact on one sex or the other, it is clear that we are concerned with irrelevant criteria because they adversely affect women or men, not with women and men because they are adversely affected by irrelevant criteria. We do not prohibit the irrational consideration of certain personal qualities in a job description, for example, unless the quality in question is more common in one sex than the other. Our objection is not to irrational criteria, therefore, but to criteria that favour one sex over the other.

[9] This is not a difficulty in the account I have offered, which claims that there is a prevailing misconception of what it means to be a woman; that this misconception prevents the success of many women's lives; and that any misconception that has such a consequence must be remedied. However, only certain misconceptions, including those about women and others now addressed by antidiscrimination law, actually have that consequence.

other setting where questions of sexual solidarity are an issue. And where laws against direct discrimination are unrestricted, as in the constitutional setting, the contention that the difference between the sexes is irrelevant seems altogether impossible to establish, for it amounts to a contention that there is in fact no meaningful difference of any kind between the sexes, which is plainly untrue.[10]

Laws against direct discrimination can also be justified by the contention that the prevailing conception of sexual identity is so tainted that it is best to abandon it and focus instead on its underlying elements, namely, the qualities and characteristics that genuinely distinguish women and men. It will be clear from all I have said that I share the view that the present conception of what it means to be a woman is deeply tainted, to a degree that damages women's prospects of leading a successful life. Yet the question remains whether that conception should be reformed or whether it should be abandoned in favour of its underlying elements, so that we no longer conduct ourselves as women or men but as human beings, and so think of the capacity to bear children as we think of the capacity to write novels, not as a capacity of women but as a capacity of human beings generally. In my view the answer to that question depends upon two further issues. First, is sexual identity more than the sum of its parts; that is, is there anything more to being a woman than possessing the qualities that distinguish women from men, as there would be if there was a synthesis among the qualities that comprise sexual difference in which the meaning of each was enhanced by its relation to the others? Second, does any woman need access to her identity as a woman in this sense in order to lead a successful life? If the answer to both of these questions is yes, then sexual identity must be reformed, not abandoned. If and only if the answer to either is no, is abandonment of sexual identity a valid strategy.

Laws against indirect discrimination, which prohibit any requirement or condition whose burden falls disproportionately on one sex or the other, are, it seems to me, justifiable only in terms of an egalitarian end, and so must stand or fall on the legitimacy of such ends. They do nothing to redress misconceptions of what it means to be a woman. On the contrary, their application is restricted to settings where there is no direct reference to sex (and hence no reference to any conception of what it means to be a woman), and where the indirect reference that they seek to address is established by proof of a real connection between the impugned requirement and what it genuinely means to be a woman. Distinctions are prohibited, therefore, not because they are false but because they are true. Any recognition of the difference between the sexes in the values

---

[10] Constitutional laws typically contain a saving provision, implicit or explicit, which allows sex discrimination to be justified in certain circumstances. However, such a provision applies only where there has been a prior finding of sex discrimination, and it is that finding that I am questioning. In other words, the saving provision cannot be used as a means of preserving relevant distinctions between the sexes, for on this account of discrimination it applies only where the distinction has already been determined to be discriminatory and so irrelevant.

and practices of our culture is prohibited, in whatever settings the law applies to, be those settings restricted (as in the case of ordinary legislation) or unrestricted (as in the case of constitutional law).[11] Yet to prohibit the recognition of sexual difference in this way is to promote a misconception of what it means to be a woman or a man, a misconception that presents women and men as no different from one another in any way that matters, in other words, in any way that is relevant to value, a conclusion as to sexual identity that is, as I have already observed, highly implausible.[12] That misconception is promoted by ensuring that as far as possible the values and practices of our culture contain nothing that is responsive to the distinctive qualities of women or men. That is bound to damage a woman's prospects of leading a successful life if, as is often the case, she depends upon the recognition of her distinctive qualities in order to flourish.

On the other hand, and perhaps surprisingly, laws permitting or requiring affirmative action, which seek to ensure the presence of women in certain fields of endeavour, a presence that is generally but not always in proportion to their presence in the population at large, can in a good many cases be justified without relying upon an egalitarian end. The reason is that affirmative action can be a highly effective means of demolishing misconceptions of what it means to be a woman, because it insists that all preconceptions of what it means to be a woman or a man be set aside, and that women be introduced into certain fields of endeavour at least in part because they are women. In these fields of endeavour their presence can serve as a role model for the aspirations of other women, who genuinely possess the qualities necessary to that field of endeavour but who would not have known that, or knowing that would not have pursued their knowledge, in the absence of the role model. Affirmative action

---

[11] Indirect discrimination can be defended by showing that the requirement or condition constitutes a bona fide occupational requirement. However, recent trends in antidiscrimination law make clear, first, that the defence exists only where it can be shown that the requirement or condition is reasonably necessary, meaning that it could not be abandoned without undue hardship, and second, that the defence is simply a defence to what has already been established to be a case of discrimination, rather than a rebuttal of that case. In short, it is discriminatory to impose a requirement or condition that has an adverse impact upon either sex. Whoever imposes such a requirement must bear its cost if he or she can do so without undue hardship. Otherwise, the cost of discrimination must be borne by its victim. See, for example, *British Columbia (Public Service Employee Relations Commission) v. BCGEU*, [1999] 3 S.C.R. 3, especially at 21 ("the standard itself is discriminatory precisely because it treats some individuals differently from others, on the basis of a prohibited ground") and at 35–38 (on undue hardship).

It is not the labelling of the adverse effect as discriminatory that is significant here. What matters is that the justification of an adverse effect is dependent upon the absence of any reasonable alternative to that effect. The consequence is that all values that reflect sex are to be eliminated, if at all possible. This is as true of the moderate interpretations of laws against indirect discrimination as it is of their newer, more radical counterparts. Laws against indirect discrimination may not eliminate sexual difference, therefore, but they make it irrelevant, by ensuring that our values and practices do not register that difference, if at all possible.

[12] If there were no real differences between the sexes, no adverse impact could be found.

programmes are objectionable, therefore, only where they disregard women's true qualities (as is rarely, if ever, the case), or where the goal or target that they set for themselves is fundamentally egalitarian, so that they commit themselves to ensuring the equal representation of women in certain fields of endeavour, and to that end, to the removal of any requirements or conditions that would have an unequal effect upon the presence of women there.

It is often contended that affirmative action programmes are objectionable because they constitute direct discrimination, in that they distinguish the sexes in order to favour one over the other. It is for that reason that affirmative action programmes are known in Britain as reverse discrimination. Yet if direct discrimination is not objectionable in itself, as I have suggested is the case, then affirmative action programmes for women cannot be faulted just because they directly discriminate against men. Rather, they are to be faulted only when their favouritism is directed to egalitarian ends, or to some other misconception of what it means to be a woman or a man, and that favouritism deprives some person, woman or man, of the ability to lead a successful life.

It is as often contended that affirmative action programmes are objectionable because they deny people, in this case men, the opportunity to be evaluated on merit alone, since they insist that sex be taken into account in settings where, but for that insistence, sex would not be regarded as part of merit. Yet if the consideration of irrelevant criteria is not objectionable in itself, as the law against indirect discrimination assumes, and as must be the case where that consideration deprives no person of the ability to lead a successful life, then affirmative action programmes cannot be faulted just because they invoke an irrelevant criterion, if that is what they do. That being the case, affirmative action programmes are valid where they seek to introduce women into valuable environments that women have previously played little or no part in; where the reason for doing so is that women are not only capable of contributing to such environments but would be deprived of a successful life if they could not do so; and where the goal of the programme is not the equal representation of women in the environment in question, but a degree of representation that is sufficient to inspire other women to seek entry to that environment, women who not only have the ability to flourish there but need access to it in order to lead a successful life.

This sketch of the status of the current law against discrimination may seem jaded. However, the fact that a law is ultimately misguided, or even causes harm to some people, does not mean that it does no good. Women and men are indistinguishable in many respects, and to the extent that they are, laws that insist that they not be distinguished may serve women well. In particular, they will serve women well wherever it has been pretended, to women's cost, that women and men are different when they are not. The difficulty arises, therefore, when women differ from men, need access to that difference in order to lead successful lives, and find access barred by laws that insist that they not be distinguished from men, directly or indirectly. In other words, antidiscrimination laws do women harm whenever they deny recognition to the distinctive qualities and characteristics that at least some women need access to in order to lead successful lives.

A final point. As I have already suggested, one of the attractions of egalitarian legislation is that it is straightforward to draft and to enforce. The same cannot be said of the recognition of women's difference, to the extent that it is necessary. That being the case, if we as a society need to respond to a wide range of women's qualities in order to ensure that no woman is deprived of the ability to lead a successful life just because she is a woman, qualities that distinguish women from men as well as those that do not, it may be that we must act in ways that the law is incapable of giving effect to. Yet this is no cause for concern. The law is only rarely in the vanguard of social change and when it is, it never acts alone. More often and more typically, law crystallizes certain aspects of a change that society has already committed itself to, wittingly or unwittingly. By and large, laws against sex discrimination exist in societies that have otherwise committed themselves to ending such discrimination, and so serve as the product and expression of that commitment. When I say that it is necessary to understand women well enough to ensure that they are not denied the ability to lead a successful life, therefore, I have in mind an understanding that will in all probability be only partially embodied in law. Ultimately, it is up to each of us, in the conduct of our own lives, to acquire the knowledge and concern for others that will enable us to avoid discrimination. The law may help us to meet this responsibility, but it cannot discharge it for us.

Index